Oxoniensis ecclesiæ Ch[risti]
facies aquilona[ris]

Ric: Rawlinson delin:
D. King sculp.

THE KING'S CATHEDRAL

The ancient heart of Christ Church, Oxford

THE KING'S CATHEDRAL

The ancient heart of Christ Church, Oxford

Judith Curthoys

Epilogue by the Very Reverend Professor Martyn Percy

P
PROFILE BOOKS

First published in Great Britain in 2019 by
Profile Books Ltd
29 Cloth Fair
London EC1A 7JQ
www.profilebooks.com

1 3 5 7 9 10 8 6 4 2

Copyright © Christ Church, Oxford 2019

The moral right of the author has been asserted.

All rights reserved. Without limiting the rights under copyright reserved above, no part of this publication may be reproduced, stored or introduced into a retrieval system, or transmitted, in any form or by any means (electronic, mechanical, photocopying, recording or otherwise), without the prior written permission of both the copyright owner and the publisher of this book.

All reasonable efforts have been made to obtain copyright permissions where required. Any omissions and errors of attribution are unintentional and will, if notified in writing to the publisher, be corrected in future printings.

A CIP catalogue record for this book is available from the British Library.

ISBN: 978 1 78816 248 7

Text design by Sue Lamble
Typeset in Photina by MacGuru Ltd

Printed and bound in Great Britain by TJ International, Padstow

Contents

List of illustrations	vii
Introduction and acknowledgements	xiii

Part I   The priory 1

1	St Frideswide and the beginnings of the priory	3
2	Patronage and pilgrimage: the twelfth century	16
3	Crown and convent: the thirteenth century	32
4	'Misrule and adversities': the fourteenth century	42
5	Finance and finality: the fifteenth and early sixteenth centuries	55

Interlude: From priory to cathedral 63

Part II   The cathedral 77

6	Trouble and turmoil: the later Tudors	79
7	Revolution and restoration: the seventeenth century	100
8	Torpidity and tranquillity: the eighteenth century	129
9	Reform and renewal: the nineteenth century	140
10	Openness and outreach: modern times	174

Epilogue: Christ Church and the future ministry of English cathedrals   195

Appendix 1: Priors of St Frideswide's   201

Appendix 2: Bishops of Oxford and Deans of Christ Church	202
Appendix 3: Organists at Christ Church	207
Conventions and monetary values	209
Notes	210
Bibliography	239
Index	247

Illustrations

Except where otherwise indicated, all illustrations are from the Christ Church Archive and are reproduced by permission of the Governing Body of Christ Church. Abbreviated sources refer to entries in the bibliography on pages 238–44.

Endpapers

Front: Christ Church, from William Dugdale's *Monasticon Anglicanum*, first published in 1655. (CCL SE.3.11)
Back: Ground-plan of the cathedral, from Browne Willis's *A Survey of the Cathedrals of Lincoln, Ely, Oxford, and Peterborough*, 1730. (CCL WT.4.1)

Colour plates *(between pages 112 and 113)*

All photographs by Ralph Williamson except where credited otherwise.

Details from Edward Burne-Jones's St Frideswide window in the Latin Chapel.
Burne-Jones's window at the east end of the Latin Chapel.
The Romanesque Chapter House doorway.
The interior of the cathedral, looking west.
Map of estates situated in the parishes of St Thomas and Binsey belonging to William Tuckwell. (Photograph by Alina Nachescu)
Fragments of the shrine platform, from the second translation of the saint in 1289.

The Lady Chapel, an example of Early English Gothic.

The central boss of the Chapter House ceiling. (Photograph by Cambridge Jones)

The tomb of Lady Montacute. (Photograph by Dave Stumpp)

J. Bennett's map of Christ Church Meadow in 1799. (CCA Maps Ch Ch M5) (Photograph by Alina Nachescu)

The Becket window in the Lucy Chapel, containing the oldest glass in the cathedral.

The St Catherine window in the Latin Chapel.

The fifteenth-century Perpendicular 'watching loft'. (Photograph by Eleanor Sanger)

The choir roof, showing the lierne ribs terminating in pierced pendants.

The tomb of Bishop Robert King, first bishop of Oxford. (Photograph by Eleanor Sanger)

A late eighteenth- or early nineteenth-century watercolour of the north transept. (CCA Prints Cathedral 6) (Photograph by Alina Nachescu)

Items of the silver-gilt chapel set given to Christ Church by John Fell after the Restoration.

The St Michael window, inserted in the north transept in 1875.

Picture by Robert Buss showing the chancel before Billing and then Scott started work. (CCA Prints Cathedral 3) (Photograph by Alina Nachescu)

Window designed by Burne-Jones in the Lady Chapel.

The Virtues window in the south nave aisle, also by Burne-Jones.

The wheel window, by George Gilbert Scott.

Black and white illustrations

All photographs by Alina Nachescu except where credited otherwise.

The statue of St Frideswide on the west face of the cathedral's north transept. (Ingram, 1837)	3
A conjectural drawing of the priory site in the time of Frideswide. (Jim Godfrey)	8

Illustrations

The foundation charter of King Aethelred. (CCA D&C vi.c.1, 7)	11
The late twelfth-century seal of the priory. (Heslop, in Blair (1990), 271–4)	15
The grant of the Fair to the priory in 1122. (D&C vi.c.1, 16)	18
Oseney Abbey in ruins, engraved in 1820 by Thomas Dale.	19
Grave slab in Purbeck marble, possibly marking the grave of St Frideswide. (Blair (1990), fig. 105; drawing by Sarah Blair)	22
Details of some of the Romanesque capitals in the cathedral. (Britton, 1821)	25
The Norman doorway to the Chapter House. (Britton, 1821)	27
Plants carved on the shrine of St Frideswide. (Photograph by Ralph Williamson)	37
Tomb of Alexander of Sutton. (Photograph by Eleanor Sanger)	40
Plans showing the development of the north-east chapels in the priory around Frideswide's shrine. (Blair (1990), Fig. 100)	41
The Lady Chapel, watching loft and Montacute and Sutton tombs. (Britton, 1821)	52
The tomb of James Zouch, in the north transept. (Photograph by Dave Stumpp)	57
The first page of a valuation of the monastic institutions that were dissolved to fund Cardinal College. (CCA DP iv.b.1)	61
A conjectural drawing of the priory immediately before its dissolution. (Jim Godfrey)	64
A page from Robert Amadas's account of work done for Cardinal Wolsey. (CCA DP iv.b.2)	66
A page from the accounts dealing with the interim period between the creation of the diocese and the foundation of Christ Church. (CCA iii.b.99)	72
A copy of the oath to the House, probably dating to the end of the reign of Elizabeth, between 1595 and 1603. (CCA D&C i.b.2, 299)	74
A portrait of Peter Vermigli, a radical appointment in 1548. (Christ Church Picture Gallery; after Hans Asper)	82

A page from Canon Calfhill's account of the exhumation of the
   bones of Catherine Dammartin. (CCL WR.8.21, 196)   87
A page from a Tudor part book, showing the treble part of John
   Taverner's *Gaude plurimum*. (CCL Mus 979, no. 48)   93
A list dated 1 October 1550 from the first Chapter Book, showing
   the first members of Christ Church to be paid from the
   endowment. (CCA D&C i.b.1)   95
A detail of an engraving of Christ Church by David Loggan, from the
   1670s.   98
The doorcase of the seventeenth-century Cuddesdon Palace.
   (Photograph by Eleanor Sanger)   106
Screens inserted by Brian Duppa underneath the arches between the
   transepts and the chapels. (East–west section from Britton, 1821) 107
The box stalls. (Winkles, 1851)   108
A late eighteenth-century image of the nave looking east.
   (Agefotostock)   110
The cathedral register of baptisms, marriages and burials.
   (D&C ix.b.1, 43)   113
The oak pulpit, by William Bennett.   114
The Directory for Public Worship. (CCL WS.4.16)   116
Chapter decree of 2 June 1651, ordering the removal of the stained-
   and painted-glass windows from the cathedral. (D&C i.b.3, 40)   117
The Commonwealth Dean, John Owen.   120
The memorial to Dean Henry Aldrich.   131
Engraving of Charles Wesley, by W. H. Gibbs.   133
Two plates from Browne Willis's account of the cathedral from 1730.
   (CCL WT.4.1)   136
Estimate by Henry Keene for the conversion of the north cloister walk
   into a muniment room. (CCA MS Estates 143, 30)   138
Bust of Edward Bouverie Pusey in the Chapel of Remembrance.
   (Photograph by Ralph Williamson)   143
A sketch by Henry Liddell of his predecessor as dean, Thomas
   Gaisford.   144

Illustrations

Drawing of a chamber between the pillars of the east tower arch uncovered by John Billing in 1856. (CCA D&C vii.c.1)	150
Elevations of the cathedral showing George Gilbert Scott's designs. (CCA Maps ChCh 119/31–34)	154–5
Scott's rough sketch for the east end of the cathedral. (CCA DP vii.a.8)	158
A letter from Scott to Dean Liddell. (CCA DP vii.c.1 fol. 67)	162
Drawing by F. P. Barraud (1824–1900) of the nave and chancel about ten years after Scott's restoration.	163
Thomas Banks Strong, Dean 1901–20.	175
An example of the service sheets issued from 1883 until the 1960s, showing a typical week during the First World War. (CCA D&C xii.c.30)	176
The thirteenth-century grave slab of Ela Longspée, Countess of Warwick. (Photograph by Dave Stumpp)	180
Verger William Francis and his memorial plaque. (Photograph by Dave Stumpp)	182
The form of service prepared for the Sunday after the end of the Second World War.	189

Introduction and acknowledgements

My knowledge of Christ Church was, until recently, almost exclusively of the foundation of Cardinal College and the joint establishment of the cathedral and college that is Christ Church. When the Dean asked me to lay aside, temporarily, the history of Christ Church's estates and to concentrate instead on a history of the priory and cathedral from its beginnings in the pre-diocesan eighth century through to modern times, I realised that I was going to have to learn a lot in a hurry.

Little has been written about the priory of St Frideswide, largely because very little is known. We have gained information from archaeological and architectural investigations, but the written texts are limited. The legend of Frideswide is here treated at its fullest, with the earliest texts filled out with later accretions. I hope that I differentiate between the two sufficiently to satisfy the purist, but to be too confined by the 'truth' would spoil a good story! The later additions, though few, are enticing.

Writing on the cathedral, post-1542, turned out to be a struggle too. It should have been the easiest part; after all, I have already written a history of the college, and there should have been much more material to draw on than there had been for the medieval history. But it proved otherwise. The college has always, at least until very recently, been the dominant partner in this extraordinary dual foundation of college and cathedral. Through much of our history the cathedral barely appears in the records except as college chapel, and even then often with entries concerned only with the attendance of the students at chapel or with the purchase of candles and cushions. In the eighteenth century the cathedral was virtually moribund, and it was not until the later part of the nineteenth century, when the two strong characters of Dean Henry Liddell and Bishop Samuel Wilberforce worked together, that the cathedral really began to open up as a diocesan church. Still, however limited the sources, I hope I have managed to give a sense of Christ Church as cathedral rather than as chapel, but it has been essential to show how parts of the history of the institution, while primarily connected with the academic establishment, have had an impact on the history of the cathedral. I apologise if there is an element of repetition.

There is also the difficulty that Christ Church is a peculiar and does not fall under the same jurisdiction as 'ordinary' cathedrals. Time and again throughout the text that follows, Christ Church is seen to be different, unique, an oddity or an anomaly. Consequently, it is hard to compare and contrast Christ Church's history with and against the events and decisions that affected nearly all other cathedrals. Nevertheless, these are part of the story, and I have tried to look at the broader picture beyond Oxford too.

This is not an architectural history of the priory and cathedral, although, of course, its building features heavily. Stephen Warner wrote, in 1924, a detailed account of the periods of the cathedral fabric, and my own history of the buildings of Christ Church includes the cathedral, cloister and Chapter House.[1] It does not need to be done again. References to architectural styles have, as far as possible, been restricted to notes and captions. There are only so many 'Early English', 'Decorated' or 'Perpendicular' tags that one can read without glazing over. Neither is the book a history of the diocese. I have tried to draw in the characters of some of the bishops, but few had any real impact on the cathedral until the arrival of Wilberforce. Their absence from the history underlines just how far the cathedral was principally a college chapel until the later nineteenth century.

There are many people – friends and colleagues – who deserve heartfelt gratitude for their continuing support as I work my way through the Christ Church 'saga'. Above all, thanks must go to Dean Percy and to the cathedral registrar, John Briggs, for their encouragement and generosity. The Dean has been good enough to pen the afterword. I hope the book even begins to be worthy of their kindness.

Without the enthusiasm and knowledge of Jim Godfrey, verger and communicator *extraordinaire* of the cathedral's history and treasures, no word could have been typed. He has diligently read each chapter and made comments that are always helpful and insightful. His reference notes, used by the cathedral stewards and guides, are invaluable. The Dean's Verger (until August 2018), Matthew Power, has always been generous with his encyclopaedic understanding of the complicated history of the cathedral windows. Any mistakes, and I am certain there are some, are mine.

Nor could I have made a start were it not for the wonderfully compact, thorough and tremendously interesting *History of England's Cathedrals*, by Nicholas Orme. This was published in 2017, and never was a book more timely. I have learned so much and have been saved from error after error. The Library at Christ Church, whose staff have, as always, been a tremendous support, purchased this slim volume for me in January 2018, and it has been my boon companion ever since.

In acknowledging the librarians, particular thanks must be given to Alina Nachescu, who took the photographs of all documents, maps and books with alacrity and great professionalism. Dave Stumpp has taken pictures 'in the field', and Ralph Williamson, lately chaplain of Christ Church, has allowed me to choose freely from the pictures that he captured during his time here. Eleanor Sanger, the College Communication Officer, has also supplied a few, as has Don Somner. I am very grateful to all.

For their knowledge of the archaeological and architectural aspects of the cathedral, I am indebted as always to Jon Down (House Surveyor), Graham Keevill (Consultant Archaeologist), Jane Kennedy (Architect to the Foundation), Julian Munby, Paul Barnwell, Geoffrey Tyack, Peter Howell, Michael Hall and Dan Miles. John Blair and Richard Halsey have been generous with their thoughts and with permission to use illustrations and diagrams from their published work on the priory.[2] Abbot Geoffrey Scott of Douai Abbey, Professor Peter Davidson of Campion Hall, Dr Roger Bowers of Jesus College, Cambridge, and Dr Andrew Foster of the University of Kent have also been kind in sharing their thoughts on odd obscure points.

As ever, my colleague archivists in Oxford have been supportive, whether in their patient answers to sometimes very silly questions or in offering to do my shopping and supply wine when deadlines have loomed.

Their ongoing friendship is valued and much appreciated. I am also relieved to have the input of the executive committee of the Cathedrals' Archives, Libraries and Collections Association (CALCA). Little do they realise how much I absorb of the life of 'ordinary' cathedrals, if any can be called such, from our discussions at meetings and our conferences. It is easy to forget, with all the peculiarities of Christ Church, that it is but one of the nation's cathedrals, whose clergy and staff do tremendous work in the maintenance of our glorious buildings and treasures as well as caring for the people of our dioceses in all manner of ways.

Last, but most certainly not least, thanks are due to the wonderful people at Profile Books, including Matthew Taylor, who copy-edits with an eagle eye, but particularly to Paul Forty who is forever calm, encouraging, wise and extraordinarily kind.

Christ Church
July 2019

Part I
THE PRIORY

1

St Frideswide and the beginnings of the priory

The beginnings of Christ Church Cathedral date back to the eighth century and the foundation of a small convent by a local noblewoman, Frideswide. The life of Frideswide, or Frithuswith, is shrouded in legend. That she actually existed is no longer really in doubt; her cult was active well before the Norman Conquest, and a charter was issued to the priory by Aethelred II in 1004, but her real life has been coloured and blurred by time.[1]

The statue of St Frideswide, dating from the mid-fourteenth century, on the west face of the cathedral's north transept.

The earliest surviving text of the legend is by William of Malmesbury, who included it in his *De gestis pontificum anglorum*. Its date can be firmly fixed between 1122 and 1125, and it is probably a summary of a now lost, longer version. The first of the two principal versions of the tale (Life A) dates from the same time, or very soon after, and was written before 1130.[2] It is anonymous, but may have been written by a later canon of the Priory. Life B was probably written by Robert of Cricklade, the prior of St Frideswide's from 1139 to 1175.[3] It is considerably longer than Life A, although the two tell much the same story. The two Lives, with William of Malmesbury's account, are the only sources for the legend, and are definitely not to be regarded as histories. Any material that has been added and embroidered over later years cannot be taken very seriously. There are, however, just a few nuggets of each tale that should be considered to contain elements of truth.

The stories, with the later accretions, tell that, at the end of the seventh century, a local ruler called Didan and his wife, Safrida, had a daughter called Frideswide. She was taught by Algiva, or Aelfgifu, the abbess of Winchester and, so legend has it, by St Cecilia and St Catherine. Frideswide was famed for her intelligence and her sweet nature. On the death of Safrida, Didan built a church in honour of his wife, dedicated to the Holy Trinity, the Immaculate Virgin Mary and All Saints. Frideswide asked her father to give her the church and to allow her to become a nun. Twelve virgins of noble birth would be her companions. Didan duly did so, and the church was supplemented with a cloister, refectory and dormitory, and 'religious men' were appointed to serve them. The land surrounding the priory site was also given as its endowment, along with the manor of Thornbury and other property. That this happened in the later years of the seventh century seems to be confirmed by the discovery of the burial of a woman of that date in the cathedral cemetery, a little to the east of the early priory church.[4]

When Didan died, Frideswide lost the protection of her father, and she was soon to be wooed by Algar, Prince of Leicester. The prioress refused his proposals, so he, feeling snubbed by the rejection, sent some of his men to take Frideswide by force. As the men were climbing the walls of the priory, Frideswide woke up just in time, and the intruders were miraculously struck blind, apparently causing uproar in the town as they rushed about in panic. The next day, terrified and begging for forgiveness, the men returned to the priory. Their contrition must have seemed genuine, for Frideswide restored their sight and sent them back to Algar. The prince was incandescent over the treatment of his men – his own behaviour appears not to have troubled him at all – and he swore to take Frideswide himself. In another miracle, an angel appeared to Frideswide in a dream, forewarning her of Algar's approach. She, with two ladies, slipped away to the river and found a boat with a mysterious figure in white waiting to take them safely upstream.

The ladies reached Bampton and took refuge in a small hut or byre, which was rapidly covered with ivy and other greenery, hiding them most effectively. Their pursuer entered Oxford and immediately suffered the same fate as his envoys. He remained blind for the rest of his life.[5] Frideswide stayed away from the city for several years – presumably making the barn a trifle more comfortable – and soon became renowned for her healing powers.

After a time Frideswide's fears began to subside, and she moved closer to Oxford, founding a small oratory on the land her father had given her at Binsey, and caused a healing spring to burst out of the ground.[6] Towards the end of her life, so the legend tells, Frideswide returned home to Oxford – leaving Binsey as a subordinate oratory and retreat from the mother house – performing miracles of healing. Frideswide settled down to run her priory until, on 12 October 727, an angel appeared to her announcing that she would receive her heavenly rewards the following Sunday. On the Saturday she asked for her grave to be prepared, so that no one would have to work on the Lord's Day. At the time of her death a bright heavenly light was said to issue from her house and a sweet smell pervaded the whole of Oxford for three hours. Frideswide was buried in her church of St Mary's, close to the tombs of her parents, on the south side.[7]

The surviving versions of Frideswide's life are, of course, hagiographical and designed to enhance the miraculous and the saintly, but there are elements of the story that have a ring of truth.[8] The place-names and personal names are appropriate Anglo-Norman versions of Anglo-Saxon words, and the topography in Life B makes sense. The foundation of Frideswide's priory at this time fits perfectly with the growth in the number of monastic establishments in the late eighth century in Wessex and Mercia, often founded by aristocratic or 'royal' ladies, with male priests and servants in subordinate roles.[9]

Didan's kingdom, to which Algar may have succeeded, fits tidily into an area bounded by the Thames, the Cotswolds and the Chilterns, an area for which no identity is otherwise known. This may have been centred on Eynsham, with important churches at Bampton and in Oxford.[10] The Lives state that Frideswide's priory was given property in Oxford, up to a third of the town, the manor of Thornbury and other estates. The earliest record of the actual land is the 1004 foundation charter by Aethelred (of which more below). It included manors at Cowley, Cutteslowe and Whitehill in Oxfordshire, and Upper Winchendon in Buckinghamshire. The priory also appears to have had parochial jurisdiction over most of the churches in Oxford and over the royal manor of Headington.[11]

Binsey, with its enclosure known as Thornbury, was recognised as an ancient monastic retreat at least as early as the twelfth century. The enclosure earthwork may have been constructed much earlier than Frideswide,

---

The French cult of St Frideswide

In Bomy, in the Pas-de-Calais, the cult of Ste Fréwisse has been observed for many years. In a remarkable parallel to the Oxford legend, there is a hermitage site, a miraculous spring and a feast day of 19 October.

Evidence for the cult and its traditions derives largely from three books of the seventeenth and eighteenth centuries in which the Frideswide story is picked up lock, stock and barrel, and her exile in Bampton moved instead to Bomy. However nonsensical this may be, there is evidence – archaeological, documentary and traditional – that the cult was not a late adoption. The likeliest time for the export of Frideswide to France is the tenth or eleventh century, when there were links between English and Flemish churches, particularly St Bertin's monastery at St Omer.

Blair (1987), 119–27

perhaps dating from the Iron Age, or it may have been created specifically by Frideswide and her entourage for their seclusion. There would have been little more than a few wattle-and-daub thatched huts with a simple single-celled wooden church. Its purpose as a place of seclusion close to the mother house, but sufficiently isolated to allow for meditation and calm, fits well with evidence from other places from the seventh and eighth centuries.[12]

* * * * *

Nothing survives of the earliest days of St Frideswide's priory except for the few burials dating back to the seventh and eighth centuries.[13] The church is, in all likelihood, beneath the existing cathedral, and the description of the convent in Life A, with its dormitory, refectory and cloister, reflects the appearance of a monastery at the time the Life was penned – the early twelfth century – rather than one of the eighth.[14]

To get any idea of the appearance, we have to rely on archaeological and literary evidence. Early monastic sites all seem to have been enclosed by fences or walls, or by natural features in the landscape.[15] St Frideswide's was built on a gravel promontory (much more obvious than it is today) above the Cherwell and one of the innumerable streams of the River Thames and the marshy land of the meadows. At the beginning of the eighth century the bank of the Thames stream was recut and lined with stakes, perhaps to improve the defence and seclusion of the monastery or to provide for a mill stream or make a shallow stream deeper for navigation. On the north and west, the early precinct may have been bounded by a ditch – with a wall or fence – running north to south to the west of St Ebbe's Church.[16]

Apart from the defensive position and boundaries, it may have been difficult to tell at first glance an eighth-century monastic settlement from a secular village, except that the concentration of buildings, which would have all been of timber, tended to be tighter.[17] Even the churches were simple, with the earliest only single- or maybe two-celled structures. At the end of the seventh century some were adding one or more small porticuses or porches, perhaps to house notable burials or altars. By the beginning of the eighth century, when Frideswide was founding her priory, it was

A conjectural drawing of the priory site in the time of Frideswide.

becoming increasingly common to enlarge at least the principal church with these additional 'rooms' and porches, some of which had separate entrances to that of the nave, possibly to allow the general public to have access to important relics.[18] Could this be the reason why Frideswide was buried on the south side of her church?

In the late nineteenth century an investigation was carried out to try to determine the reason for the small, infilled arches evident on the outside walls of the north choir aisle and the Lady Chapel.[19] Were these entrances to porticuses? Excavation revealed what was interpreted as the remains of three stone apses: two small ones, which appeared to relate directly to the arches, with a larger and longer apse between in an eastern, basilica style. Arthur Evans, discoverer of Knossos and then Keeper of the Ashmolean Museum, while visiting the site, found the remains of a third arch in just the right position, which had been invisible at first glance as the bonding stones were concealed behind a square rainwater down-pipe. While apses are relatively common features of early churches, with some dating back to the ninth century, it is now accepted that these features at Oxford do not date back to the eighth century.[20]

Archaeological as well as written evidence suggests that there may have been multiple churches on these early monastic or 'minster' sites. And it is possible that there was more than one church within the bounds of the community of St Frideswide's. Life A tells us that the church built by Didan for his daughter had three dedications – to the Holy Trinity, the Virgin Mary and All Saints. But Frideswide asked specifically to be buried in St Mary's Church, and a writ of Henry I refers to the church of the Holy Trinity. Documentary and topographical evidence from sites such as Canterbury, Glastonbury, Wells and Jarrow shows a linear east–west arrangement of churches or chapels. If this was the case at St Frideswide's, then the line of churches may be perpetuated in the present cathedral, and St Aldate's and St Ebbe's parish churches.[21]

Life A also tells of Didan providing 'religious' men to serve the women, and St Frideswide's may have been a double house of monks and nuns. This was not uncommon: at Barking, the complex was divided into two by a wall, and the men and women were even buried separately. Other places were less strict.[22] Excavations at St Frideswide's have revealed cemeteries on the south side and to the west of the cathedral which could indicate two burial sites, but without any knowledge of the position of the priory church it is still all to be discovered.[23]

Again the layout of the domestic buildings is unknown. Excavations at other sites from the period and documentary accounts suggest divisions between the sick and the fit, between the novitiates and the professed nuns, and between the nuns and guests or business contacts. But there would have been a series of probably timber buildings, with each function separated by low walls or fences.[24] Although this double house did not survive for long after the death of the founder, and became a purely male province of secular canons, the buildings probably changed very little.

* * * * *

St Frideswide's Priory may have been on a defensive site on its promontory, but it was also close to a major crossing point on the Upper Thames. Archaeological evidence indicates that there may originally, as far back as

Roman times, have been two fords: one at the end of St Aldate's and one slightly further to the east, following the line of the present Parks Road and Catte and Oriel streets. This second, easterly, ford was revealed during the building of Meadow Buildings in 1863. But this crossing was abandoned as the other was improved at some point from the mid-eighth century to the mid-ninth, possibly by Offa.[25] As to whether the works to improve the ford were carried out by the priory or by the king, more later; either way, in the earliest days of the priory, if its boundary really did stretch to the west of St Ebbe's Street, then the main north–south route, with all the commercial and political travellers who used it, ran straight through the centre of the precinct.[26]

Many minster sites attracted settlements around them, and it seems likely that St Frideswide's was no exception. The excavations to discover the improvements to the ford revealed pottery, shoes and other domestic items from the ninth century, but Oxford does not appear in any records until the end of that century or the beginning of the tenth, and it was not until around 900 or a little later that the town was laid out to a formal plan. It is one of the towns included in Alfred the Great's *Burghal Hidage*, part of his defensive system against the Vikings, but it is the only one, apart from London, that stands on the north bank of the Thames, and its construction and defence may, like that of London, have been entrusted to the Mercians, under first Aethelred and then Aethelflaed, Alfred's daughter and Aethelred's wife.[27]

In the accounts of the life of the saint, Didan endowed his daughter's nunnery with property and land for its income. It is not until the charter of 1004 that we have any certainty about the priory's property, which included three manors in Oxfordshire, each of three hides, in Cowley, Cutteslowe and Whitehill, and the ten-hide manor of Winchendon in Buckinghamshire, all of which are described in the charter in old English, for a wider understanding.[28] There were also tenements in the town immediately surrounding the priory: according to Life A, one third of Oxford.[29] How the estates were managed is unrecorded, but it is to be expected that much of the property was leased out to tenants.[30] None was too far away, so a canon may have been given charge of land or tenant management. Minsters such as

St Frideswide and the beginnings of the priory

The foundation charter of King Aethelred from 1004, as it is written into the fifteenth-century cartulary of St Frideswide's Priory, recording the burning of the priory church with the Danes locked within.

St Frideswide's were becoming increasingly part of secular life in the ninth century.

While Oxford had been developing around the priory, things had changed within the enclosure. At some point, probably not long after Frideswide's death in 727, the nunnery, run by its 'she-monasticks', as the seventeenth-century Oxford antiquarian Anthony Wood rather ungraciously called them, was left with just its male priests. The records are silent on why and when this happened. Wood reckoned that the nuns were so distraught at the death of their superior that they took themselves to their homes and were eventually married into respectable Saxon families.[31] In fact, nothing is recorded of the priory until the turn of the eleventh century, when the political upheavals in the nation struck close to home.

* * * * *

During the last decade of the tenth century, during the reign of Aethelred II (the Unready), Viking raids on the country were almost continuous. In 991 a Viking fleet arrived off Kent and Essex, and the consequent Battle of Maldon was a disaster for the English. Defeat must have knocked Aethelred, his policies (adopted in opposition to those of his advisers and his mother) and the nation sideways. To the king, divine disfavour was obvious.[32] In the following years Aethelred realised that he had been foolish to ignore his counsellors and showed his remorse by restoring lands and privileges to churches previously despoiled, such as Abingdon and Rochester, or founding new houses, as a form of penance and to restore divine favour.

Aethelred also tried more practical solutions to the Viking problem. After the Battle of Maldon, the Norsemen decided to consolidate their position by further incursions on the Kent, Essex and south coasts in 994. In an attempt to secure a permanent peace, the English promised winter supplies and a tribute of £16,000 on the condition that the raids ceased. The treaty that followed effectively brought some of the Viking force into service for Aethelred. These mercenaries were to cause problems.

For a few short years the country was at peace. But 997 saw fresh attacks, with the aggressors probably including some of those mercenaries who had reneged on their deal, this time in Wales, Devon, Dorset and the Isle of Wight, to be followed in the next two years by further hostile activity in Kent. The English battled hard, perhaps even partly successfully, for no new pay-offs were made and the Viking force retired for a short while to Normandy, which can have done little for England's relationship with its neighbours. But not for long; in 1001 they were back, ravaging the south coast, and another huge payment of £24,000 was made early in 1002. It seems to have had little effect, as Aethelred issued a decree, to take effect on 13 November, ordering that all Danish men in England were to be slain. There is debate over the targets of this decree: they were unlikely to have been the long-settled Danish communities in the east of England, who were soon to fight ferociously against their former kinsmen. It is more likely that the targets were the recent arrivals, perhaps the mercenaries who had proved so fickle. Whatever and whoever, massacre or execution, the St Brice's Day carnage was an act of desperation.[33]

In Oxford, the Danish community – possibly including Gunhilde, the alleged sister of the Danish lord, Swein, and her family – fled their executioners, taking sanctuary in the priory church, supposedly breaking down doors and forcing locks to get in.[34] The hostile locals, fired up and taking revenge for decades of uncertainty on the mercenaries who had turned back to fight with their countrymen, tried to force the Danes back out. When they found this was impossible, they set fire to the building, apparently destroying it and everyone and everything within it.[35] Aelthered's policy failed, however, as attacks and incursions began again when Swein invaded in 1003, to be

Aethelred's charter of 1004 describes the St Brice's Day massacre:

Since a decree was sent out by me with the counsel of my leading men and magnates, to the effect that all the Danes who had sprung up in this island, sprouting like cockle in the wheat, were to be destroyed by a most just extermination, and this decree was to be put into effect even as far as death, those Danes who dwelt in the afore-mentioned town [Oxford], striving to escape death, entered this sanctuary of Christ [St Frideswide's], having broken the doors and bolts, and resolved to make a refuge and defence for themselves therein against the people of the town and the suburbs; but when all the people in pursuit strove, forced by necessity, to drive them out, and could not, they set fire to the planks and burnt, as it seems, this church with its ornaments and its books.

CCA D&C vi.c.1, 7 and 8; Wigram (1895), 2–6

forced back only briefly in 1005, when a great famine struck the British Isles and much of Europe. Divine displeasure showed itself in both war and starvation. Aethelred tried again, with a reorganisation at court and with another new monastic foundation – this time at Eynsham, an abbey and Saxon estate that had close ties with St Frideswide's Priory.[36] But things did not improve for Aethelred, and, in spite of efforts to reform and rearm, the Vikings returned time and time again, with increasingly large forces. In 1009–10 Oxford was sacked in a campaign that covered much of southeast England. The mint ceased turning out the coin of the realm soon after, and only three years after that Swein descended on the town again, which submitted before it was laid waste once more.[37]

* * * * *

As with much of the previous three centuries, very little is known of the priory after the massacre of 1002. The account of the events of St Brice's Day in Oxford appears in Aethelred's 1004 charter commissioning the rebuilding of the priory church and renewing its title deeds.[38] It smacks of self-justification.

The church was reconstructed, probably in stone, in such a way that the relics of St Frideswide were then at the centre of the building rather than on the south side, but it seems doubtful that any of the surviving masonry dates from the post-massacre rebuilding, as was suggested in the late nineteenth century.[39] By the Conquest, and certainly by the early twelfth century, the priory church was said to be in a ruinous state.[40] The canons were ousted, apparently for being lax in their duties. This was, perhaps, a late response to the monastic reforms of the mid- to late tenth century or, more likely, as part of Cnut's patronage of the church. Whichever it was, the priory came under the control of Abingdon Abbey.

The period of the management by Abingdon is unknown but is likely to have been short and possibly during the reign of Cnut (1016–35). Cnut was a patron of churches and monastic foundations throughout the country, repairing and re-endowing those that had suffered at the hands of the Vikings and buying support from the archbishops he had inherited from

The late twelfth-century seal of the priory, showing St Frideswide enthroned and holding an open book, perhaps to represent her religious calling and learning. In her other hand is a flower, a common feature of women's seals. The seal matrix must have been made soon after the translation of 1180.

Aethelred while ensuring that regions that had been loyal to the English Crown were brought firmly into line.[41] Locally, towards the end of his reign, around 1030, Abingdon was treated generously by Cnut with material gifts and land grants; St Frideswide's may well have benefited from this generosity.[42] But Abingdon lost control over St Frideswide's before the Conquest, possibly in 1049, when Edward the Confessor may have restored the priory as a house of secular canons again, under royal control. It remained as such into the twelfth century, and may have been counted among the royal free chapels.[43]

2

Patronage and pilgrimage: the twelfth century

Little changed at the priory with the Norman Conquest.[1] The church was still run by secular priests, not bound by the rules of monastic orders. The Domesday Book reveals that land holdings had not increased at all since 1004, and eight of the fifteen houses in Oxford were 'waste', either untenanted and therefore bringing in no income or in a state of disrepair. St Frideswide's was relatively insignificant, and not rich, in 1086.[2]

But in the early twelfth century, probably in 1122, the monastery passed into the hands of Roger, bishop of Salisbury and chief minister to Henry I, who installed regular Augustinian canons from London, with Guimond, the king's chaplain, at their head. Guimond evidently thought that he deserved his position. Legend has it that he was frustrated as he saw less intelligent men than himself being granted benefices and even bishoprics, so, when reading a lesson before the king one Rogation Day, he pretended to be almost illiterate. The king knew Guimond well, and was confused by his chaplain's behaviour. When the king asked him why he was acting in this manner, Guimond burst out that from now on he would only serve Christ, who knew how to reward his servants with both temporal and eternal gifts.[3]

The king took the hint and, by his confirmation charter of 1122, Henry formally founded the monastery and gave churches as an endowment, including a new chapel of the Holy Trinity at the east gate to the town, and country churches at Headington, Marston, Elsfield and Binsey.[4] Substantial

> ### Priors of the twelfth century
>
> Guimond 1122 Philip 1175
> Robert of Cricklade 1139 Simon c.1195
>
> Knowles et al. (2001), 180, 284

privileges were given too, including an exemption from the payment of customs due to the bishop and archdeacon; priory tenants were to owe no suit to any secular court in Oxford; and the liberty to alter the lane outside the priory gates was a benefit that the canons were soon to take up.

But possibly the most lucrative gift was the right to preside over the annual fair that began on the feast day of the translation of St Benedict (11 July).[5] During the five days of the fair, which seems to have been primarily for cloth in the early days, the priory held sway over everything that happened in town. This was not popular and was the cause of much unrest between town and priory. During the twelfth century there was a long-running dispute over the positions of the stalls at the fair with, apparently, the priory reserving all the best sites for itself.[6] It was evidently very profitable, and Bishop Roger, possibly secular minister first and ecclesiastic second, could not resist; he seized the right to the fair for himself.[7] Roger hung on to it, in spite of confirmations to the priory by Pope Honorius in the late 1120s and by Henry I again in 1133. Eventually, although it is not known what forced Roger's hand or pricked his conscience – possibly his approaching death – not only the profits from the fair but also land, in Binsey and at Walton, and various churches, were returned.

And, at last, the priory was beginning to expand its property. The advowsons of seven town churches had been obtained, including St Mildred's, All Saints, St Michael at the Northgate and St Peter in the Bailey, along with the right to place canons to serve those churches.[8] Benefactions continued to come in too. Some were valuable additions to the priory's portfolio, including Richard FitzOger's gift of a mill – with the miller and

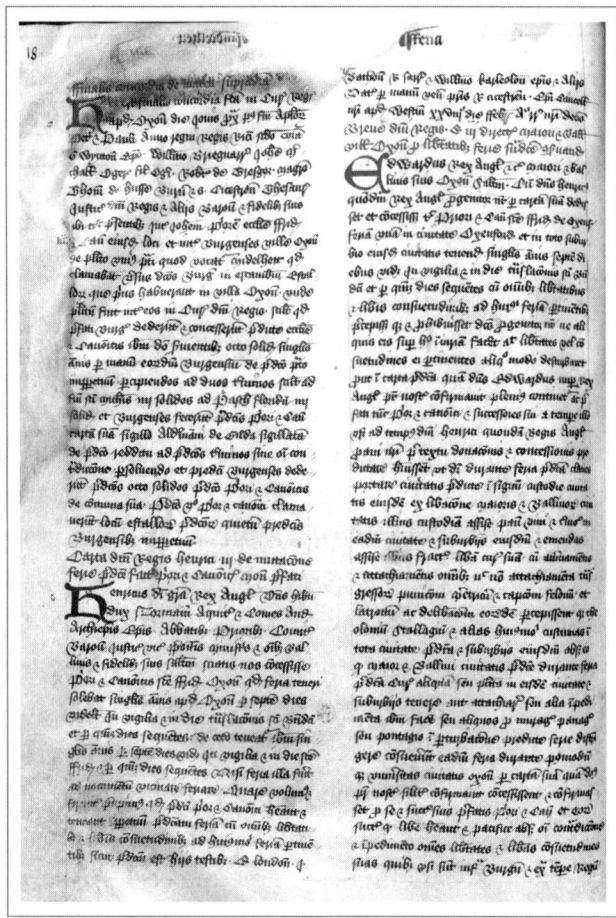

The grant of Henry I of the Fair to the priory in 1122.

his family – at Houghton. Others were more practical, such as the 18d. per annum to provide firewood for the priory infirmary.

Occasionally, St Frideswide's ran up against the increasingly important Oseney Abbey. The Augustinian priory had been founded by Robert d'Oilly in 1129, just a few years after the refoundation of St Frideswide's. Its initial endowment, at least of Oxford property, was quite small, but d'Oilly presented his priory with churches across the county and beyond and with the valuable collegiate chapel of St George's within Oxford castle. Riches attract riches, and Oseney had soon acquired property across the country, and even

Oseney Abbey in ruins, engraved in 1820 by Thomas Dale. The priory and the abbey were frequently at loggerheads throughout the medieval period. The abbey became the diocese's first cathedral in 1542, but only until 1546, when Christ Church was founded by Henry VIII. Much of the abbey's stone, lead and furnishings – including the bells – was taken for the building and maintenance of Christ Church.

into Ireland. In the mid-twelfth century St Frideswide's and Oseney came head to head over the ownership of at least two properties. Around 1138 the burgesses of Oxford had given to St Frideswide's the island of Medley, near Binsey, in exchange for stalls in the market, but the town's merchants, just nine years later, gave the same property to Oseney. It took the best part of fifty years to sort out and was probably more of a battle between powers in the town, rather than between the two religious institutions, but the success of Oseney's claim underlined its pre-eminence.[9] Another dispute running at the same time was over the ownership of the church of St Mary Magdalen. St Frideswide's claimed it, but Oseney disputed the claim, and between 1145 and 1200 appeals went backwards and forwards to the pope, with the pontiff coming down on the side of Oseney every time. During the course of the dispute Pope Adrian IV raised Oseney to the rank of abbey, confirming its supremacy in Oxford.[10]

But Adrian was not always against St Frideswide's. He confirmed the charters of Henry I and imposed a bull, probably at the request of the canons, that prevented the bishop of Lincoln from holding any synods or ordinations in the priory church or any dependent chapels without consent, so that the canons' peace and quiet could be preserved.[11]

* * * * *

It was Prior Robert of Cricklade, Guimond's successor, who wrote the B version of the life of Frideswide, probably as a deliberate attempt to promote the cult of the saint and to bring more pilgrims to her shrine. It was already popular – Archbishop Thomas Becket was said to send the sick there for healing – but, as far as we know, there was no shrine above ground to focus veneration.[12] The rebuilding of the church after 1004 is said to have ensured that the grave was central, but there were real fears that Frideswide's bones had been stolen by the monks of Abingdon during the short period of that abbey's control. In order to establish the priory as an important place of pilgrimage, it was essential to demonstrate that the relics were safe and to place them in a visible reliquary.[13] Robert understood the importance of shrines: he is said to have experienced healing himself at the shrine of Thomas Becket in about 1174. So he initiated a search.[14] After three days of fasting, the canons began to search secretly at night. As they dug, they came across an empty coffin and were about to give up in despair when someone suggested that it had been common practice to place an empty coffin over the bodies of saints in order to deter thieves. Needless to say, underneath, the canons found a skeleton. Their torches were miraculously blown out and then re-ignited. The grave of the saint had undoubtedly been found.[15]

> ## Robert of Cricklade
>
> Robert was born in Cricklade in Wiltshire. He entered the monastic life as a canon at Cirencester Abbey before coming to St Frideswide's as its prior in 1139. The presence in Oxford of Robert – perhaps the best-known and the most scholarly of the priors – along with that of other known teachers may have been an attraction for young men wanting to learn. But it was a while yet before the university, or even its early schools, was to make an appearance.
>
> Some of Robert of Cricklade's writings survive, including an account of the life and miracles of Thomas Becket. The original Latin version is lost, but the text was translated into Old Norse and was incorporated into a late thirteenth-century Icelandic saga.
>
> Robert was also a traveller. He was in Rome twice, in 1141 and 1158, travelling via Sicily and Paris. He also went to Scotland in 1160 and was given by King Malcolm – perhaps not entirely legally – an estate at Piddington, near Bicester, for the maintenance of five canons.
>
> *ODNB*; Warner (1924), 195; Wigram (1896), 92; *VCH Oxon*, ii (1907), 98

But, although much of the work to develop the importance of Frideswide, and to discover the bones, had been done by him, it was not Robert who saw the translation to a new shrine but his successor, Philip, who took over control of the priory around 1179.

After the death of Thomas Becket there was a huge increase in hagiographical writing, and Frideswide was not forgotten. Prior Robert had written his Life, and Prior Philip penned an account of Frideswide's miracles.[16] Local traditions, such as the miraculous well at Binsey, were being adopted by the church, and the importance of local topographic features was emphasised. St Frideswide was, and would remain, Oxford's saint.[17]

The translation of the saint took place on 12 February 1180.[18] A royal council had been convened at Woodstock, and Philip took full advantage of the gathering of dignitaries.[19] He must have hoped for a royal attendee, but this was not to be. Even so, the service was conducted by the archbishop of

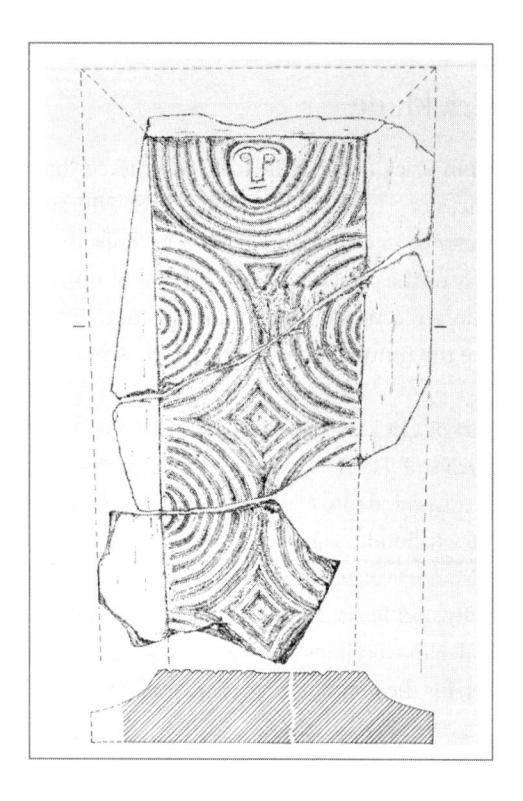

This drawing from 1990 shows a grave slab which was found during the restoration work in the 1870s. The slab, in Purbeck marble, probably dates from the early twelfth century, or even the late eleventh. It may just be the marker for the grave of St Frideswide, given by the priory's patron, Roger of Salisbury, whose diocese included the Purbeck quarries.

Canterbury, Richard of Dover, and watched by the bishops of Winchester, Ely, Norwich and St David's. The papal legate to Scotland, Alexius, was there too.[20] The rediscovered grave was opened, and the archbishop placed the bones into a new reliquary. The heavenly scent that had accompanied the death of Frideswide was said to be evident again. No sooner had the shrine been consecrated than the canons made the place ready to receive the sick in their numbers, and for extended periods; at least one of the women who came to the shrine stayed in the church for three weeks.[21] There were probably two focuses of veneration: the new shrine and the old grave. The feretory, or relic casket, which was probably portable, would have been the liturgical focus for veneration and ceremony, while the grave, marked by the tombstone provided by Bishop Roger, was a place for vigil and contemplation.[22] Miracles were said to be even more abundant, and the pilgrims coming to visit served to increase the commercialisation of Oxford.[23]

Philip's record of the miracles performed at the shrine of Frideswide show that it was largely a local cult, although with the continued patronage of Archbishop Richard it looked as though it might have become more widely known for a short while.[24] Many of the healed had suffered for a long time, and some had consulted doctors in vain before turning to the saint for relief. Anthony Wood wrote that the shrine was popular with rich and poor, noble and common, clergy and gentry alike.[25] Frideswide was particularly popular with women, often for psychological problems associated with puberty, sex and marriage, rather than difficulties in conceiving or with childbirth. Beatrix, for example, had sex once and immediately developed a headache which lasted for two years; and Helen, the mistress of a priest, suffered pain and insomnia after the priest had rejected her for no longer being attractive. Emelina had tried to commit suicide, was rescued and returned home, but she was suddenly dumb. Her mother brought her to the shrine for healing, less in love than in desperation and impatience (presumably there was no way the poor girl could be married off while she was ill), and Emelina was healed after some days. It seems that the canons cared more for the teenager than her mother had done, and she remained as a servant in the priory, where she would have been displayed as a shining example of the healing powers of the saint.[26]

> Perhaps the most famous female visitor to the shrine was Catherine of Aragon. While the court was *en route* between Abingdon and Woodstock in April 1518, the queen, already pregnant, stayed with the Warden of Merton College, Richard Rawlyns, who had conducted the funeral service for the first of her three baby sons. She took time to pray to Frideswide for the miracle of a male heir. This time there was no miracle, and a still-born daughter was delivered in November.
>
> Highfield, in Blair (1990), 274–5

Prior Philip himself received healing, spiritual as well as physical. His account of his night of pain, prostrate before the relics, speaks of doubt and fear, but also of a great delight – after his healing was assured – that he could now relate much more closely to all those who came in faith.[27]

* * * * *

By the end of the twelfth century the University was beginning to emerge. Why it did so is hard to pin down, but Henry II's ban in 1167 on scholars leaving for the university in Paris must have been one driver. There were schools in the 1140s and 1150s, but for a short period significant teachers made their way to the flourishing schools in Northampton rather than to Oxford. Both Oxford and Northampton were used by Henry II as royal administrative centres; both had mints, both had royal residences and both were archdeaconries in the enormous diocese of Lincoln. However, during the Anarchy (the civil wars of Stephen and Matilda, from 1135 to 1153) Oxford began to be recognised as strategically important, and, following on from its military significance, ecclesiastical courts were increasingly held in the town. Gerald of Wales recorded in his autobiography that he had brought his lecture series to Oxford in 1187 or 1188 because that was where he considered the best clerical minds to be.[28] Judges and their retinues needed somewhere that was easy to get to and that could provide appropriate lodgings. Oxford was geographically better placed than Northampton, and it had two litigious religious houses in St Frideswide's and Oseney, providing considerable work for lawyers. Those lawyers attracted students who came to watch and learn legal practice. Even foreign scholars were making their way to Oxford, just as it was becoming impossible for home students to go the other way as the war between France and England intensified in the 1190s.[29]

* * * * *

In the Saxon period the priory precinct was large, stretching from the present wall separating Christ Church from Corpus Christi College as far as

Details of some of the Romanesque capitals in the cathedral.

the west end of St Ebbe's Church, but the buildings were probably simple and small. The main street through Oxford ran through the centre, bringing the priory and the early townsfolk of Oxford into direct and continuous contact. During the twelfth century, as the precinct began to shrink, the buildings grew in size and grandeur.

Soon after the confirmation charter of 1122 had been received, the canons, under Guimond's governance, began to close themselves off from the burgeoning town. First, they took advantage of Henry I's permission to build over the street that ran around the inside of the town's defences to the south of the priory church. All the entrances were gated, and the precinct was, for the first time, fully enclosed.[30] Houses could now be built on the street towards the ford and around the north side of the priory, gradually hemming the canons into an increasingly private place.

St Frideswide's was not a wealthy house, and it would appear that there had been very little new building, if any, between 1004 and the refoundation.[31] The 1004 church would probably have been constructed in stone, and the Augustinian canons would have used this, perhaps altering the east end to allow for their liturgy. According to the miracle stories surrounding the discovery of Frideswide's bones before her translation, the old church had a tower.[32] Fragments of early footings were revealed during archaeological investigations in 1962–3 which may show the extent of the early twelfth-century transepts and, comparing examples from other Augustinian houses, may give some clues to the floor plan of the eleventh- and early twelfth-century church.[33]

That the church was on roughly the same site as the present one is endorsed by the location of the Chapter House and slype (the passage between the Chapter House and the south transept). The Chapter House doorway, with its zigzag motif, and masonry fragments (including scallop-shaped capitals from a blind arcade uncovered when George Gilbert Scott reclaimed the north cloister walk in 1871 from its eighteenth-century reworking as a muniment room) show local Romanesque work from the mid-twelfth century. Some fragments survive, but others were drawn by John Buckler as they were removed.[34] Most of the decoration of the Chapter House doorway and the window openings to either side are so similar to examples at Reading Abbey as to suggest the same masons. These men were working at Reading around 1125 to 1140, and may have influenced a school in Oxford working not just at St Frideswide's but also at St Peter's in the East and at St Ebbe's, and a bit later at Iffley.[35]

So some work was going on, at least around, if not in, the church, but it is most unlikely that this would have taken place before the death of Roger, bishop of Salisbury, in 1139 and the return of the temporalities that he had purloined for his own profit. Except, perhaps, for the laying of a new Purbeck marble grave slab, found during the nineteenth-century restoration of the cathedral, which may have been brought from Dorset by the priory's patron, Roger of Salisbury, to mark the site of St Frideswide's burial.[36] Neither could the work be done until after the threat from the civil wars of Stephen and

The Norman doorway to the Chapter House, which, with its round-headed windows on either side, was retained when the Chapter House was rebuilt in the mid-thirteenth century.

Matilda had subsided in the early 1140s. If the city wall ran as close to the priory church as has been suggested, possibly running under the line of the existing south cloister walk, then the alterations to the cloister and the enlargement of the precinct could not have taken place until it was safe to take down the wall.[37]

So it must have been under the second prior, Robert of Cricklade, that work began on rebuilding the dilapidated eleventh-century church. Stylistically, the chancel dates from 1165–70. Robert had travelled abroad – in Italy, Sicily and France – and around the British Isles. He had seen Romanesque architecture and would no doubt have wanted to replace the old-fashioned Saxon church with something grander and more in keeping with the times. From his home in the west of England to Jedburgh in Scotland,

> A date for the twelfth-century reconstruction of the priory church has long been debated. Pevsner suggested 1190, based on the styles of the capitals; the *Victoria County History* also chose the 1190s, based on the accounts of the fire, although both believed that there was some rebuilding very soon after 1122 and that fragments survive in the triforium windows in the west wall of the south transept. The Royal Commission for Historic Monuments opted for a period later than 1170.
>
> More recently, a date in the mid-twelfth century has been settled on, with some work happening before the translation of the relics of St Frideswide into a new shrine in 1180, and some following on soon afterwards.
>
> Sherwood and Pevsner (1974), 113–18; VCH Oxon, iv 91979), 364, 369; RCHME Oxford (1939), 35; Halsey, in Blair (1990), 116–17

Robert may well have seen the giant order developed and wanted the same for St Frideswide's.[38] The old church – to the north of the present one, with its central axis probably running in a line through the present Latin chapel and north transept – would have been left in place to allow worship to continue while the new (grander and much larger) building was constructed. Beginning with the east side of the cloister and the chancel (constructing from east to west) would have allowed the canons to continue living and working there, albeit in temporarily constrained and difficult conditions. The new cloister was built over an old graveyard and rubbish tip, and extended southwards within the lines of the new wall and over the old road. The Chapter House, the slype and the earliest parts of the dormitory would have been constructed at the same time.[39] The chancel would have been ready in time for the translation of the relics of Frideswide into the raised shrine in 1180.

Prior Philip must have made tremendous efforts to make the chancel and the new site for the shrine look respectable for the visit of the grandees. It is easy to imagine scaffolding and building materials screened and covered, and hurried decorating to provide a stage suitable for such an important occasion. But, as soon as the visitors had departed, Philip would have picked up the task, and he rapidly completed the transepts and the crossing tower during the 1180s.[40]

Things are seldom straightforward, however, and in 1190 a fire swept through Oxford and the priory. The full extent of the damage is unknown, but it cannot have been as bad as some reports suggest. The suggestion that everything was destroyed has come from two documentary sources: a sermon by Alexander Neckam preached on Ascension Day in either 1191 or 1192, which describes the roofless state of the church at the time, and a papal bull issued by Celestine III in 1194 appealing for alms to help rebuild the church after *vehementis ignis incendio combusta*.[41] There is no archaeological or documentary evidence that the town suffered much damage, and it seems likely either that the accounts of the state of the priory were exaggerated in order to bring in funds for the building project or that Neckam was describing the church in the middle of the construction programme or that there was some damage to the roofs only. If there had been damage to the new shrine, Prior Philip, who had overseen the translation, would surely have made some account of this and launched a fundraising appeal.[42]

The north chapels would have been important, as they were associated with the shrine of the saint. The choir aisle and the first shrine chapel were aligned on the chancel, and were built before the translation of the remains in 1180, with an almost solid wall between the aisle and the chancel. Archaeology suggests that the choir aisle was four bays long, with the shrine chapel constructed as a four-bay square to the north of the aisle's two western bays.[43]

The nave was completed after the 1190 fire, and it is possible that the eastern bay of the chancel was rebuilt at same time.[44] The cloister and Chapter House saw some changes at this period too, with the walks and garth (the area enclosed by the cloister walks) lowered by about 110 cm.[45]

As the cult developed, so the plans for the priory church were expanded, with aisled transepts forming part of the rethought design. The bays of the choir aisle and the shrine chapel adjoining the new north transept had to be distorted to fit, but that side of the church was now better able to cope with pilgrims visiting the shrine in the decades after the translation.[46] The giant order

> ## The medieval diocese
>
> During the Saxon period, from the arrival of Birinus (the first bishop of Dorchester, commissioned by Pope Honorius I to convert the West Saxons) in 634, Oxford fell within the diocese of Dorchester on Thames. The diocese had mixed fortunes, not least because the Thames Valley was variously under the control of Wessex or Mercia. It came to an end in 663 and was possibly revived briefly, but definitely ceased to exist from 686 until 886. By that date Oxford had become part of the diocese of Leicester, after the Battle of Bensington (Benson) in 777, but for safety's sake, as the Danes were over-running the Midlands, the bishop returned the see to Dorchester.
>
> The diocese of Leicester survived the Conquest briefly, but in 1070 it was incorporated into the diocese of Lincoln. Oxfordshire became an archdeaconry. The move was evidently not popular in Oxfordshire; no gifts are recorded from the county to the new cathedral.
>
> The first suggestion of a more local diocese came in 1539, after the dissolution, when a bishopric of Oseney and Thames was proposed, with its cathedral at Oseney. The scheme was carried out in 1542, but with the title being just Bishop of Oxford. Robert King was appointed the first bishop and was given Gloucester Hall as his episcopal palace. Dean John London and six canons ran the cathedral.
>
> On 20 May 1545, King Henry VIII College (the collegiate church that had succeeded Cardinal College) and Oseney Abbey surrendered to the Crown, and the new diocesan seat at Christ Church was founded on 4 November 1546 under the leadership of Dean Cox, who had succeeded London as dean of Oseney, aided by eight canons, four of whom had come with him from Oseney.
>
> *VCH Oxon*, ii (1907), 1–63

gives the small church a sense of height and grandeur, giving an appearance of three storeys within only two. Similar forms were probably built at Reading and Abingdon, and in other churches in the south and west of the country, subsequently lost either to the dissolution or to later rebuilding.[47] Over the chancel and the transepts, and possibly the nave, would have been a rib vault.

The south transept is equally complicated, if not more so. The Chapter House and the slype were already in place before the rebuilding of the priory church in the later twelfth century. To build both transepts to match, it would have been necessary to absorb the slype into the church. But it was nearly new, and its destruction would have been an unlikely path to follow. So the third bay of the south transept flies over the slype and exists only at 'first-floor' level. If there was a night stair from the dormitory in the east range of the cloister, then the canons would have come through the room over the slype, and down an earlier version of the present stairs into the south transept.[48] This left the south transept as an oddly truncated version of the north, with only two bays, a single-bay east aisle and, possibly, a single-bay west aisle with an unusual doorway out to the east cloister walk. The east aisle survives as the Lucy Chapel, but the west, if it was ever built, was demolished during the fifteenth-century alterations to the cloister.[49] Aisled transepts were unusual in England until about 1180 but had been common in French Romanesque churches. Around 1180, though, they appear not just in Oxford but also at Wells Cathedral and Byland Abbey, shortly followed by York Minster, Beverley Minster and Westminster Abbey. At St Frideswide's the introduction of aisled transepts was most likely to do with the enhanced status of the cult of the saint.[50]

The church progressed from east to west, with the western crossing piers constructed in line with the Chapter House doorway, and the eastern end as close to the city wall as it could go, allowing for the roadway inside the wall.[51] By about 1200 the church, which straddles the end of the Romanesque period and the beginning of Early English Gothic, must have been largely complete, but the fire of 1190 seems to have knocked the stuffing out of the prior and canons, and the decoration of the westward capitals is of far poorer quality.[52] The good work has a strong French influence, and the stone spire too appears to be based on examples from northern France.[53] The speed of Cardinal Wolsey's demolition men working in 1525 suggests that the west end was a simple construction with no large towers. The generally accepted view is that three nave bays were taken down to construct the eastern side of Tom Quad, but it could possibly have been four.[54]

3

Crown and convent: the thirteenth century

The future looked very promising for the emerging University until the reign of John and the papal interdict of 1208 all but knocked things on the head. Scholars were already departing Oxford before an incident in December 1209 when a student killed his mistress and fled the scene. The student's two room-mates were arrested and hanged as complicit in the crime. Oxford's scholars were horrified at this: their immunity from the town's jurisdiction had been questioned, and so they left the town in large numbers for Cambridge, Paris or Reading. For some years there were no schools in Oxford, and it looked for a while as though the University was dead before it had ever really been born. In fact, things worked out very differently.

The settlement to bring the scholars back to Oxford was tied up with the armistice over the interdict. It took some years to negotiate a means to establish ecclesiastical control, but in 1214 the papal legate laid down rules establishing a pre-eminence of the teaching masters – guided by a chancellor appointed by the bishop of Lincoln – over the town burgesses.[1]

None of the religious institutions in Oxford had any direct relationship with the nascent body of scholars except St Frideswide's. The priory was charged with the safety of the first of the University's chests. Bishop Grosseteste stipulated in 1240 that one of the canons of the priory, with two regent masters, should act as keeper of the chest, which was to hold the annual

> ## Priors of the thirteenth century
>
> | | | | |
> |---|---|---|---|
> | Simon | c.1195 | Robert of Olney | 1260 |
> | Elias (Scotus) | 1228 | John of Lewknor | 1278 |
> | William of Gloucester | 1236 | Robert of Ewelme | 1284 |
> | Robert of Weston | 1249 | Alexander of Sutton | 1294 |
>
> Nearly all the priors from Robert of Weston onwards held a canonry at St Frideswide's before their promotion, except William Chedill (1501). Only the last prior, John Burton (1513–24), appears to have held a university degree.
>
> Smith and London (2001), 443–5; Smith (2008), 501–2; Emden (1974)

payment of 52 shillings from the burgesses for the support of poor scholars, one of the conditions laid down in 1214. University business and examinations were, on occasions, conducted in the Chapter House at the priory.[2] The election of Thomas Chaundler as University Chancellor was held there in 1457; and the priory bell, too, was used to determine the start and finish of afternoon disputations between lunch and compline.[3] Some of the early academic halls – the Civil Law School, St Patrick's Schools, Urban Hall and Bekes Hall, for example – belonged to the priory, although it is doubtful whether the priors and canons had much input or influence over teaching or administration.[4]

The management of priory affairs did not always run smoothly. Its relationship with Oseney Abbey remained troubled as the 1145 dispute over the church of St Mary Magdalen rumbled on for years and there were further disputes over the tithes of Norham, Berechcroft and Bradmore, to the north of Oxford, and of Water Eaton, with Oseney accusing the priory, perhaps justifiably, of forging property deeds. Oseney usually won. The legality of the gift of the estate at Piddington by Malcolm of Scotland in 1160 was under debate for two centuries, and the donation of the church at Oakley in 1142 – by Empress Matilda – was revoked in 1221 by Henry III. He claimed possession, in spite of the fact that Matilda's grant had been confirmed by Robert, Earl of Gloucester, Stephen and Henry II, and a verdict in his favour was made by a civil court. The canons took their case to Pope Honorius III, and the king appealed to the papal legate, Pandulf.[5] Although the case presented to the pope and consequent letters of confirmation are recorded in the cartulary, it is not until a presentation of a vicar to the church is listed in 1316 that it is possible to be certain that St Frideswide's won its case.[6]

Philip remained in place until 1191, but being a prior can have been no easy thing. He had overseen the translation of the bones of the saint, and put the priory onto a good footing as a place of pilgrimage.[7] Prior Simon followed in Philip's place and must have found life in Oxford – with the trouble surrounding the scholars and the interdict, and the constant legal nit-picking with Oseney – too much to bear, and he handed in his notice in 1228.[8]

In Simon's place came Elias, who caused an upset in 1234 when he borrowed £43 from Simon and Copin, two Jewish moneylenders who leased property on St Aldate's from the priory, part of which may have been used as a synagogue until the expulsion of the Jews from England in 1290.[9] Bishop Grosseteste was horrified and immediately called for Elias's resignation.[10] Elias appealed, and a tribunal, headed by the prior of Bolton, reversed Grosseteste's decision and imposed on the bishop's court charges of 140 marks.[11] Grosseteste, in his turn, appealed to the pope, who came down firmly on the bishop's side. Elias departed and was replaced by William of Gloucester, who was appointed by the bishop on the authority of the Lateran Council.

Elias's financial misdemeanour took place in the same year that a General Chapter of the Augustinian order was held at St Frideswide's. These took place every three years on the first Sunday after Trinity, on the order of the Lateran Council of 1215. The abbots and priors of all the houses in the province were to attend to present the certificates of the Visitations that had taken place, and to deal with any other business. The Chapters held at St Frideswide's were under the presidency of the abbot of Oseney, John of Reading, and the prior of Barnwell, Laurence de Stanesfeld. The proceedings began with all the participants – possibly around 150 men – processing behind a cross from Oseney to St Frideswide's. Mass would have been held in the priory church, followed by a sermon and prayers in the Chapter House. Then any strangers were excluded and the work would have begun. No details of this General Chapter survive, so it is difficult to say whether Elias was brought to task there and then. Perhaps he had borrowed the money to pay for the Chapter's visit; a day of church services and important discussion would have needed considerable quantities of food and drink.[12]

William came to St Frideswide's from Dunstable Priory, where he had been the cellarer, and proved a good choice.[13] During his time at the priory (1235–48) new benefactions were received, some to help the infirmary; Ralph of Brackley gave 3 shillings a year from his property in the parish of St Mary Magdalen, and William FitzWalter donated 2 shillings towards the upkeep of a lamp.[14] Another benefaction was to keep a lamp burning in St Lucy's Chapel during Mass.[15] Other gifts were more practical: Reginald the mason bequeathed a mazer (a wooden cup, usually of maple and sometimes mounted with silver) for high table, and one of the town burgesses, John Courcy, gave an annual rent of 4 shillings for the upkeep of the towels used in the refectory.[16] Practicality seems to have been the order of the day in the mid-thirteenth century: in 1258 Pope Alexander IV granted the canons a faculty to wear caps at divine services as it was so cold in the church.[17] It was also during William's tenure that Ralph Peckwether, or Peckwater, conveyed all his property in Oxford to the priory.[18] The administration of the priory and its growing estates settled down and flourished under the leadership of William and his successors, Robert of Weston and Robert of Olney.

Olney was prior for eighteen years, from 1260 to 1278, through a period of both national and local turmoil. In 1263 the country found itself once more embroiled in civil war, with Henry III at loggerheads with Simon de Montfort. Five years earlier the town had hosted the Parliament from which emerged the ill-fated Provisions of Oxford. The seeds of war were sown, and in 1263 Henry made Oxford his headquarters. He did not stay at the priory but did make a visit to Frideswide's shrine, giving 100 shillings for the maintenance of a chaplain who was charged with saying a daily Mass for the saint, for the king's ancestors and successors. Henry promised more if he were successful on the battlefield.[19] It was not just the king who made use of the priory; de Montfort asked, in 1264, for 1,000 marks to be brought up from London and deposited at St Frideswide's until they could be collected by his son on his way west to relieve him.[20]

Just three years later de Montfort had been brought down, but the country was still at risk from some of his follower barons who remained at large. Oxford was put into a state of defence, which included deepening the ford below the priory. The prior, Robert of Olney, was employed by the king on a number of occasions, often travelling considerable distances around the country and for extended periods. When he wrote to Henry explaining that he was unable to undertake one particular task because it would take him away from his duties as prior, the king's attitude to Robert cooled. From this point he would occasionally send old, retired retainers to the priory to be housed, at the expense of the prior and canons. After he had sent his old serjeant, Richard Andrew, the king did promise not to send any more, but he appears to have made no attempt at all to help with a pension or other expenses.[21]

In 1268, during the Ascension Day celebrations, it is said that some of the town's Jews, possessed by demons, seized the cross that was being carried at the head of the procession. They broke it up and threw the fragments on the ground. As with any such occurrence, the news spread quickly, soon reaching the king and the prince of Wales, who were staying

The expulsion of the Jews

This was a period of increasing anti-Semitism for both religious and fiscal reasons. Henry III demanded ever higher levies from the Jewish community in England. In order to fund these, the Jewish moneylenders (who had always been invaluable to the Crown in this respect and, for many years, protected) sold the debts of Christian borrowers. The new owners increased the pressure to repay, and it was the Jews who were given the blame. In 1275 Edward I was in dire need of money but was unable to raise taxes without Parliamentary approval. In order to persuade Parliament, Edward gave them, in 1290, what they had wanted for some time: the expulsion of the Jews.

The plants carved on the shrine are symbolic of Frideswide's healing powers but also have religious meanings. Vines represent the Eucharist, and columbine the Holy Spirit, for example.

at the palace in Woodstock. On his return to Windsor, Henry sent a letter ordering the miscreants to make two new crosses, at their own expense – one in silver to be carried in processions and one in marble to be a fixture in the priory church. There was to be a gold plaque erected somewhere prominent between the priory and the Jewish quarter explaining why the crosses had been made.[22]

> ## The shrine carvings
>
> Vines – symbolic of the Eucharist.
> Fig – a plant with healing properties particularly for boils.
> Ivy – an evergreen representing eternal life.
> Hawthorn – representing Holy Innocence, and used as a tranquilliser.
> White bryony – a very poisonous but medicinal herb used as a purgative or for skin problems; the roots sometimes used as a substitute for mandrake.
> Greater celandine – a poisonous plant used for problems with sight, and particularly common in Oxford.
> Columbine – a symbol of the Holy Spirit, and used as a cure for hysteria.
>
> Mabey (1996 and 2012); Wickham (1981)

After Olney's death, the sub-prior, John of Lewknor, was elected in his stead. He resigned just five years later, and Robert of Ewelme took over. During Ewelme's time came one of the greatest events in the priory's history: the second and last official translation of St Frideswide's remains into an even more beautiful and elaborate shrine.[23] The prior must have been working on the preparations from the time he arrived in Oxford in 1284; certainly, a John of Elsfield conveyed land on St John's Street near the east gate to the priory to help pay for the new feretory, and the new shrine platform must have taken some years to carve.[24] There is no record of the mason, but the skill of his hand is evident in the depiction of Frideswide and her ladies peering out from a selection of local plants, all of which have links to the legend of the saint.[25]

The shrine base was of a hard limestone, and the extension to the chapel was undoubtedly built to accommodate this, with its stained-glass windows showing Frideswide and other saints looking down on the scene below.

The ceremony, held in September 1289 – a much more convenient time of the year for future pilgrims than the February of the first translation

– was attended by William de la Corner, bishop of Salisbury, and Edmund, Earl of Cornwall.[26] It has been said that this was not quite the stellar cast of the first translation a century earlier, but Cornwall had acted as regent during Edward I's campaigns in Wales and France. His presence, even if it was just during a stop-over between his new chapel at Abingdon Abbey and Westminster, must have been a matter of pride to the convent.[27] Although there are no records of the celebrations, translations could be exciting events for the whole community. Frideswide was not a saint of national importance, but the spectacle of the morning procession of the canons in their best vestments and the aristocratic visitors in all their splendour, with music and incense, must still have made an exciting diversion. The beautiful new shrine base would have received the bejewelled feretory and a service of consecration and dedication conducted probably by the visiting bishop of Salisbury with the prior in attendance.[28] New pilgrims would, the priory

The parish church of St Frideswide

From early times, the priory church had a parish church attached to it. The parish was first recorded in the 1170s, but the church was probably built soon after the priory was refounded in 1122, to ensure that the parochial functions of the Saxon minster church were maintained. There was just enough income to support a vicar's food, lodgings, clothes and fees, but additional costs were met by the priory.

In 1298 the parish of St Edward was deemed to be too small to support its minister and so was amalgamated with St Frideswide's. But it was St Frideswide's that ceased to exist; its vicar was transferred to St Edward's, but he continued to receive his stipend from the priory. The parochial activities were a nuisance to the services at the shrine and in the conventual church more generally.

No one knows exactly where the parish church lay, except that it was very close to the priory church, possibly right alongside the present building. It may even have been a parish altar within the priory church, probably roughly under the present north transept, close to the shrine chapel.

Warner (1924), 206; *VCH Oxon*, iv (1979), 381; Blair (1990), 256–8

Alexander of Sutton was appointed prior in 1294 and remained in post until 1316. The burial of a prior inside his church was unusual, but it may have been Sutton who oversaw the extension to the Latin chapel and, as such, earned himself the honour of being buried close to the saint: in fact, on the site of the original shrine.

hoped, be flocking to venerate the saint and to be astonished by her splendid new surroundings.

* * * * *

For a few decades after the fire of 1190, the priory church was enjoyed by the canons, but around 1230 the Lady Chapel – fully Early English Gothic – was constructed alongside the north chancel aisle.[29] Its two westernmost bays would have caused a remodelling of the square shrine chapel, essentially reducing that chapel to half its original size, which must have been a tremendous nuisance for managing the flow of pilgrims, but the arch under which the shrine stood was remodelled as the Lady Chapel was constructed to provide a more imposing setting.[30] Then, in the last decade of the

Crown and convent: the thirteenth century

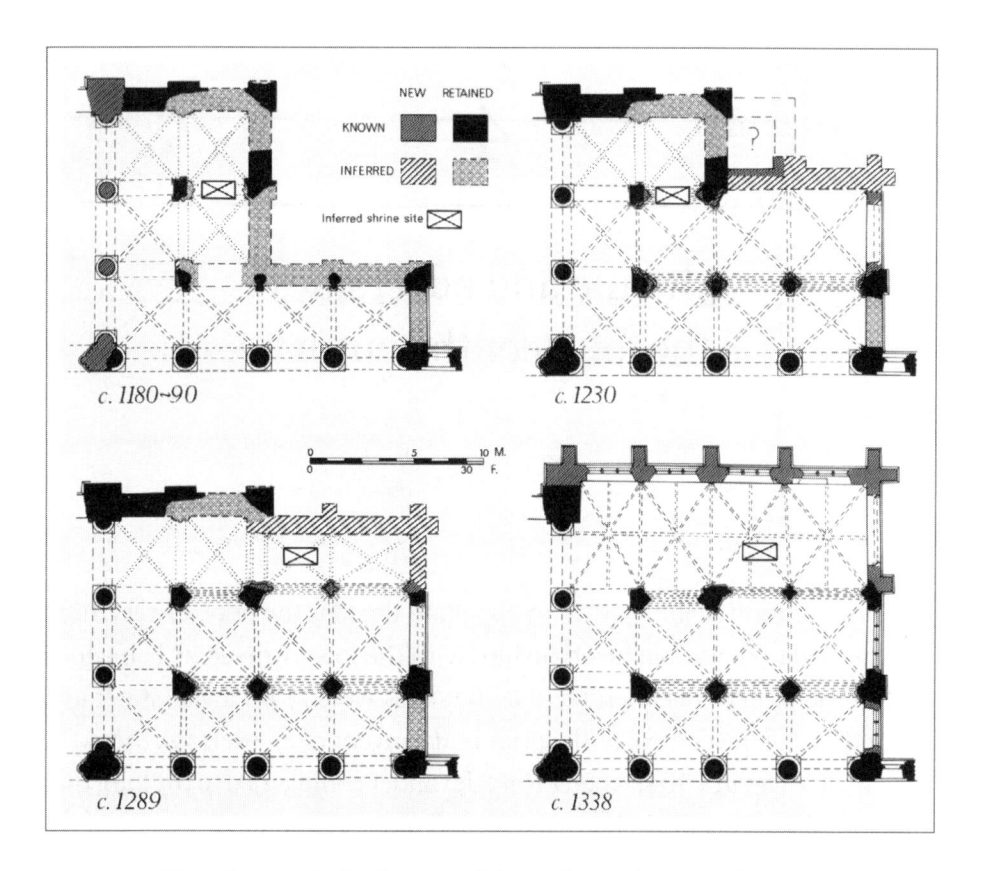

Plans showing the development of the north-east chapels in the priory around Frideswide's shrine. After the Reformation, and then the muddle surrounding the burial of Catherine Vermigli (see Chapter 6), the site of the shrine appears to have been largely forgotten. Its present location in the Latin Chapel is based on archaeological and historical research.

thirteenth century – or perhaps just before, when the second translation of Frideswide's remains took place – the stub of the shrine chapel was extended alongside the full length of the Lady Chapel.[31] This odd extension, which was narrower than the original square chapel, must have been created to allow for the new shrine, probably placed in the second bay of the chapel, and to make veneration easier than it had been for half a century or so.

4

'Misrule and adversities': the fourteenth century

The fourteenth century was an appalling time for the priory. Everything seemed to go wrong. Relationships with the town worsened; behaviour within the priory was often terrible; finances were in an awful state; and events beyond the control of the prior and convent often overtook them.

It all began in 1304, when Prior Alexander complained to the king that some unnamed people had broken in and assaulted some of the servants, killed some cattle and thrown them into the Cherwell.[1] And in 1308 two of the priory servants – John of Sutton, the porter, and the sub-sacrist, John Tykeys – stole 12 marks from the chest.[2]

Edward II had continued the habit of his ancestors by imposing old servants on the priory for care in their retirement. One of these men, Robert Tackley, had been a drain on the canons' purse for some time, but no sooner had he been buried than the king produced another, Geoffrey de la Naperye.[3] Other men bought themselves board and lodging within the walls of the priory. Henry de Creton had paid £100 as a corrody (an allowance for maintenance, or a pension) to Prior Alexander in return for places for himself and his groom. The arrangement was probably to mutual satisfaction; a regular payment into the priory coffers in exchange for hospitality. But in 1318 Henry complained that the prior and canons had broken into his rooms, stealing his goods and the papers that proved his right to be there. There is no record of any redress, or even whether the accusation was true, but Prior

> ## Priors of the fourteenth century
>
> Alexander of Sutton   1294   died
> Robert of Thorveston   1316   resigned
> John of Littlemore   1338   died
> Nicholas of Hungerford   1349   died
> John of Wallingford   1362   resigned
> John of Dodford   1374   died
> Thomas Bradwell   1391
>
> Smith and London (2001), 443–5; Smith (2008), 501–2

Robert of Thorveston certainly remained in office until around 1337, one of the longest-serving heads of house.[4]

Robert had also had a run-in with the local sheriff. In 1329 Edward III had issued a writ to the mayor and bailiffs of Oxford directing them to make sure that all the rights of the fair, including their control of the town, were allowed to the priory.[5] It was a long and full document, not just a quick note reminding the town of St Frideswide's rights. So when, during the fair the following year, the sheriff's bailiffs arrested one Thomas de Legton, from Abingdon, and imprisoned him for felony, Prior Robert took exception and had a writ issued to ensure Legton's release. The cynic might wonder whether Legton had offered to help fill the priory's empty coffers, but it is quite likely that the prior was really upset about the infringement to his rights during this one exceptional week of the year.[6]

St Frideswide's was certainly in dire financial straits. By the 1330s the desperate position was acknowledged; the priory was in debt to Florentine moneylenders to the tune of £1,200.[7] As the financial situation grew worse, so did relations with the town. The priory's control over the town during the fair was the biggest bone of contention. Robberies seem to have been frequent, but the citizens became violent in 1336, when they seized the prior and canons and threatened them with torture or even death by burning if they did not observe the statutes of the town.

The townsmen looted the priory, taking cartloads of grain and stealing fifty of their pigs.[8]

It was in 1337, in the midst of all these difficulties, that another General Chapter was held at the priory. Little is recorded of the business discussed or the decrees issued except that it was ordered that no canon should take part in archery with secular persons. Three years later the heads of nine houses were summoned to appear at the Chapter in 1340 to answer for some disobedience. Perhaps they had been sharpening their skills with bow and arrows in the wrong company![9]

The choices of priors during the century were odd at times, to say the least. Robert's successor in the priory house was John of Littlemore. John had at first looked a promising candidate; in 1341 he had been collector of wool in the county for the king, but then he was accused of failing to carry out his duties satisfactorily – was he using the king's money to supplement the priory coffers, or even lining his own pockets? Whatever it was that he had done wrong, John ended up in prison. Somehow, though, he either redeemed himself or talked himself out of gaol and was rewarded, bizarrely, with the position of collector of the king's tenth from the clergy in the diocese.[10] Surely almost a temptation too far for the head of a bankrupt convent that had, allegedly, had its profits from the 1344 and 1346 fairs – perhaps as much as £1,000 – seized by the mayor and his bailiffs.[11] But there are no records that John's misdemeanours were repeated, and he remained in place until his death in 1349.

It was under John that St Frideswide's received one of its most enduring gifts: that of Stockwell Mead from Lady Elizabeth Montacute (or Montagu) in 1346.[12] She gave the 46 acres of meadow between that already owned by the priory to the north and the Thames to the south to fund two chantries to the memory of her husband, and probably of her son, both called William.

In June 1348 the Black Death arrived in England, at Weymouth, from where it travelled to London by the autumn of that year. Oxford began to experience its horrors in November, the disease probably having been carried by tradesmen and merchants from Winchester and along the Thames. It may be no coincidence that a guild of barber–surgeons was incorporated at

Oxford in 1348 and maintained a light in the Lady Chapel.[13] We know little about the fate of the priory during the Black Death; Prior John may have been a victim – he died between January and April 1349, when, according to the number of wills registered, the plague was at its worst in the town – but it is likely that the canons of the priory were largely untouched by it; better and secluded living conditions would have protected them from the worst.[14] The number of casualties in the colleges and the monastic houses was low compared with that of the town, which suffered a different fate.[15]

The next prior, Nicholas of Hungerford, seems to have been an even odder choice than his immediate predecessors. His appointment, in 1349, was marked by the usual formalities of fealty to the Crown and the handing over of the temporalities (the secular profits due to the prior and convent), but the bishop of Lincoln, John Gynwell, was evidently troubled for some reason and tried to quash the election.[16] The bishop was unsuccessful, and Hungerford took office. Whatever it was that had concerned Gynwell, his misgivings were soon justified. Hungerford was not a religious man, and he was soon treating the priory more like a hunting lodge than a religious house, and its possessions and treasures as his own.[17] The statutes of the house were blatantly ignored by Hungerford and his town cronies, and some of the canons wandered about the town with little regard for the basic rules of discipline.[18] The sub-prior was in despair. What little money the priory had left was being pilfered by the prior, and the canons were evidently suffering from the lowest morale. After five miserable years, things came to a head in 1354, when Hungerford, supported by a group of thugs from the town, actually broke into the priory church and attacked the sub-prior and the canons in the middle of a service. Bishop Gynwell had the unpleasant task of holding an enquiry. Although the priory was never popular with the town, it seems – at least according to Hungerford's own story – that a little later, violent men from the town entered the priory armed with clubs and swords with a view to killing him. Perhaps the townsfolk had more sympathy with the plight of the canons than they did with a prior who was evidently a violent, unscrupulous thief.[19] Hungerford fled Oxford, although it seems that he was not removed from his position.

In 1354 the king stepped in. Through 'misrule and adversities' the priory had found itself so far in debt that Edward III took the place into special protection and gave it into the hands of receivers. After providing maintenance for the canons and other residents, the remainder of income was to be used to maintain the buildings and to deal with the debts.[20] Alongside the king's accountants, the sub-prior must have tried to pick up the pieces. Together they would have worked through the accounts and been shocked to find the state of the priory finances. The sub-prior may have smiled ruefully when, in 1361, William Doune, the archdeacon of Leicester, left 5 marks to repair the church and cloister of St Frideswide's, a further 10 marks for the maintenance of its living quarters and £10 to the priory, on the condition that it should not be pocketed by the prior.

Bizarrely, Hungerford was allowed to return. But soon, in 1362, the priory complained to Archbishop Simon Islip that Nicholas was leading a dissolute life and had gone back to squandering the priory's goods.[21] Islip, who was renowned for supporting clerical privilege, held an enquiry and even conducted a Visitation, but nothing was done to sanction Hungerford. It is possible that the prior had royal support in the person of the prince of Wales.

In 1357 John of Dodford, one of the canons of St Frideswide's, received letters from the pope granting him the vicarage of Whittingham in Northumberland. Just a few years later John changed his mind about being a vicar and was granted permission by the bishop of Durham to come to Oxford to study. Once in Oxford, he somehow convinced Hungerford to swap his office of prior for the vicarage of Whittingham, and received papal approval for the exchange. Why Hungerford, who seems to have been pretty worldly, would fall for this can only be surmised. Perhaps Dodford made it worth his while, paying Hungerford for the change and thus resulting in a charge of simony, but the case came before Pope Urban V. Hungerford pleaded that he was only a simple man and that Dodford had deceived him. The pope was having none of it and deprived Hungerford of both vicarage and priory. But the prince, to whom Hungerford had once been chaplain, stepped in and requested a rethink. Nicholas was reinstated and remained prior until his death in 1370. It would seem reasonable to assume that the prior counted his lucky stars and behaved impeccably for the remainder of his time at St Frideswide's, but no; in 1367 he went abroad for two years, leaving two attorneys to conduct priory business while he was away. To the horror of the canons they discovered that in the year between his reinstatement and his departure for foreign climes Hungerford had put the house into such a state of indebtedness to overseas lenders that the canons were unable to support themselves or to fulfil any of their obligations. Once again the king brought in the receivers and put the convent under the control of commissioners, John of Nowers and John of Baldington.[22]

After Nicholas's death there was some confusion about his successor. John of Dodford, who had allegedly been sold the prior's position in 1362, claimed that he was next in line, but the chosen prior was John of Wallingford. Wallingford's election received royal assent on 1 February 1370, but the Dodford affair would not lie down. Dodford took possession of the priory. Orders were given for his arrest, but he contested it, and the bishop of Lincoln gave orders for his installation. At this point the Crown stepped in again. The king's rights as patron of the priory were being usurped; the temporalities were seized and another order for Dodford's arrest issued. After considerable shenanigans, involving a petition and correspondence administered by the abbot of Oseney – no friend of St Frideswide's – Dodford managed to secure Wallingford's resignation in 1374, and eventually stepped into the priory house himself in 1376, having assured the king that there was nothing prejudicial to the monarch.[23]

Hardly surprisingly, Dodford did not turn out to be the ideal prior either. In 1376 he was imprisoned in the Tower of London, leaving a steward, Richard Segworth, to manage his affairs at St Frideswide's, contrary to the arrangements laid down by Edward III in 1335 in a charter that specifically gave the government of the convent to the sub-prior and the canons during any vacancy.[24] Wallingford, presumably a reluctant canon at this point, took his chance for revenge. With some of the canons he attacked Segworth, robbed him and imprisoned him.[25] Dodford heard about the crime, and appealed to the king from the Tower. The king ordered the release of

Segworth and the arrest, by the civic authorities in Oxford, of the perpetrators. This must have been seen as the very worst form of punishment. Dodford too was freed – although he was confined for a short period in the Marshalsea prison in 1378 for an unknown offence – and for a while the priory appears to have settled to a form of peace.[26]

But it was short-lived. The long-running dispute between the town and priory about the site of the town's stalls at St Frideswide's Fair erupted again in the 1380s. The University had won control over the twice-weekly street markets after the St Scholastica's Day riots in 1355, and then tried to do the same over the fair as well. In 1380 scholars and possibly the University officers themselves, pulled down the merchants' tents, cut their ropes and deliberately provoked a riot to disrupt the fair and, they hoped, to see themselves granted control. It backfired, and in 1383 the University had to concede that the priory had control over all commercial activity within its own precinct.[27] And then in 1382 Wallingford, evidently released from gaol, decided to have another go at Dodford. Gathering around him a gang of local ne'er-do-wells, he lay in wait for Dodford as he was travelling to one of the priory's parish churches. They assaulted the prior, perhaps leaving him in a poor state at the side of the road, and carried on to the priory's manor at Bolles, in St Clement's, and plundered it of corn, cattle and seventeen pairs of swans. Apart from the usual order for the arrest of the perpetrators, nothing more is known of the fate of Wallingford and his cronies.[28]

Dodford must have survived the attack as, later in the year, he hosted a convocation of the southern province at the priory. The meeting was largely to deal with Wycliffe and heresy in the University, with the king and the church determined to stamp their authority firmly over the Chancellor and the regent masters.[29] But a few years later Dodford was once again in trouble and absent from the priory. He may have been in prison again, as in 1387 he was pardoned of trespasses of 'vert and venison' in the royal forest of Bernwood and Stowe on the edge of Oxfordshire and Buckinghamshire, where the priory held land.[30] There is no record of exactly what Dodford had been charged with; it could have been poaching of deer or boar but is more likely to have been the enclosing, or taking in, of land that was governed by forest law. It is just possible that Dodford was, for once, innocent, and the land may have been his to enclose. The Great Perambulation of 1300 had reduced the quantity of land under stringent and punitive forest law, but successive monarchs had tried to reclaim it. Certainly, he seems to have received some compensation when he was made governor of Wallingford Castle.

John of Dodford died in 1391, and the election of Thomas Bradwell, previously the priory's sacrist, drew the ill-fated fourteenth century to its close.[31] The priory was still in a sad financial state – so much so that when Thomas, Duke of Gloucester, stayed at St Frideswide's in 1392, the food and drink bill of 27 shillings and 4 pence was met by the town.[32] In the early years of the fifteenth century the Crown was still managing the priory's secular properties, and at a Visitation in 1423 the bishop of Lincoln, Richard Fleming, put in place strict financial constraints: no corrodies could be sold or granted; no serious business could take place without the agreement of the whole house; the resident canon at Binsey must have a proper stipend; jewels were to be redeemed from the pawnbrokers; no sporting dogs could be kept in the priory; the canons were not permitted to take part in archery meetings or any other social gatherings with townsfolk; there was to be no

---

Alexander V, a Franciscan friar from Crete, graduated from Oxford as a Bachelor of Theology before moving on to Paris. He is the only member of the University of Oxford to have become pope. Alexander only held the papacy for ten months, and even then his position was disputed by rival claimants.

During his short period of office Alexander tried to promote reform and to heal the Western Schism. He seems to have had a particular concern for the Augustinians and minor orders.

Alexander is said to have favoured friends and allies, and the privilege of the indult (permission to veer from normal canon law in certain circumstances) was granted to the prior of St Frideswide's almost immediately after he had been elected pope.

Dictionnaire d'histoire et de géographie ecclésiastiques, ii (Paris, 1914), cols. 216–18; Cross and Livingstone (2005); Emden (1957), 345–6

drinking or gossiping after compline; and no one was to leave the dormitory, except for matins, between compline and seven in the morning.[33]

On the whole, though, the behaviour of the members of the priory, not least its priors, improved. In the 1390s some of the canons were rewarded with papal chaplaincies, including John Bannyge, Richard Godyngton and John Woodstock.[34] Not all treated the honour with the respect it was due; Woodstock was stripped of his chaplaincy when the pope heard that he had left the priory and was leading a rather dissolute life, but things were definitely far better than they had been.[35] So much so that in 1409 Pope Alexander V granted an indult for the priors, beginning with Richard Oxenford, to wear the mitre, ring and other pontifical insignia, and to give solemn benediction at Mass, vespers and matins.[36] Also in that year Richard was appointed a collector of part of the tenth that had been granted to the king. So unlike his fourteenth-century predecessors was he that, when he found some of the money had gone missing, he made up the £8 6s. 8d. from his own pocket.[37]

* * * * *

The fourteenth century saw changes in the fabric of the priory church. By the 1330s, the late thirteenth-century extension to the shrine chapel was evidently insufficient in both size and grandeur. Around 1338, when a chantry was established for the bishop of Lincoln, Henry Burghersh, the two new bays were taken down and the whole chapel given a new north wall and windows showing several female saints.[38] Burghersh's chantry required that Masses were to be celebrated before the altar of St Frideswide, and a licence was issued for the dedication of new altars in August 1338.[39] It was also around this time that the figure of St Frideswide was erected on the north-west corner of the north transept.[40] Some years later Lady Montacute's tomb was erected close to the chantry established by her in 1346, probably beneath the decorated vault in the Lady Chapel.[41] Her gift specifically requested that the chantry should be in the Lady Chapel close to the feretory of St Frideswide. Prior Sutton had died in 1316 and was buried in an elaborate tomb between the Lady and Latin chapels, on the 1180 site of the shrine.[42] Later important donors such as Thomas Bloxham and Dr Boteler,

> ## Latin chapel windows
>
> The windows, which appear to have been designed for the chapel, were moved around the cathedral (to the west end and then the north transept) and then back to the Latin Chapel in the later nineteenth century. They show: St Catherine of Alexandria (twice), who in the foundation legend is said to have tutored Frideswide; the Madonna and Child, with the Christ child holding an orb decorated with a church, a thorn tree and a river – obvious symbols from the legend; St Hilda (the abbess of Whitby, who died in the year of Frideswide's birth) or St Ethelreda (queen and founder of Ely Abbey); the angel Gabriel; an archbishop; the Virgin Mary; St Margaret of Antioch, to whom the church in Binsey is dedicated; and St Frideswide herself. The fourth window in the Latin Chapel is a poor imitation from the 1870s.

whose graves are now lost, and George (or John) Nowers, whose tomb is in the third bay of the arcade, requested the same.[43]

The proximity of St Frideswide's shrine must have been the principal reason for the siting of the 'watching loft' at the eastern end of the Lady Chapel/Latin Chapel arcade. Once labelled, as late as the eighteenth century, as the tomb of Frideswide's parents, Didan and Safrida, the fifteenth-century Perpendicular tomb – in fact, probably of the first wife of Sir Robert Danvers, Justice of the Common Pleas – has a timber loft above to serve as a chantry chapel or to give a priest a perfect view to watch over the shrine.[44]

And so the priory church was just about in its present state by the middle of the fourteenth century, and it remained almost untouched for 150 years. It was only a small church, if quite large enough for its community, but the form was exactly what would have been expected, with the usual pattern of three vertical stages of arcade, triforium and clerestory, albeit arranged in an unusual grand order – with the triforium contained within the arcade – to give an impression of height in a building that is actually quite low by contemporary monastic standards.

On the other side of the church, around 1320, the eastern wall of

The Lady Chapel, watching loft and Montacute and Sutton tombs. The screens installed by Brian Duppa in the 1630s are visible, separating the chapels from the north transept.

the Lucy Chapel was rebuilt to allow for the installation of a new window showing the murder of Thomas Becket. This was the date when St Frideswide's chest was removed from the priory to St Mary's; perhaps the chapel had been the repository for the chest, and once it had been removed, the chance was taken to remodel.[45] But 1320 was also one of the recognised 'jubilee' years celebrating Becket's death, and the pope granted a plenary indulgence for all those visiting his shrine that year. Perhaps a wealthy benefactor saw the gift to the priory as his route to heaven.

The Chapter House was rebuilt in the second quarter of the thirteenth century, around the same time as the Lady Chapel and in the same Early English Gothic style, with its tall, linear lines, retaining the old Romanesque doorway and west wall.[46]

Until very recently it has been thought that the beautiful stone lierne vaulting and elaborate pierced pendants of the choir dated from the very end of the fifteenth or even the early years of the sixteenth century, and that the work was executed by William Orchard, master mason.[47] But the style of the vault has been reviewed, and opinion now is that it was constructed perhaps a century earlier. Rather than being a successor to the Divinity School, it was instead an influence on it, as it may also have been on the ceiling of Henry VII's chapel at Westminster Abbey.[48] It seems an odd time for there to have been such major and elaborate alterations to the choir – the priory was in dire financial straits towards the end of the fourteenth century, and most of the priors do not appear to have been men who would have cared

The priory's domestic buildings

The location of most of the domestic buildings of the priory church is unknown, although it is assumed that the arrangement of the buildings up until the construction of Meadow Buildings in 1863 largely reflects the original arrangement, with the refectory on the south side of the cloister, the kitchen probably underneath its Wolseian replacement and the infirmary under the western end of Meadow Buildings. The monks' dormitory would have been immediately to the south of the Chapter House, with its day stair from the cloister. The prior's lodgings were alongside, extended and altered in the late fifteenth century.

Other administrative offices would have closed the refectory/kitchen/infirmary quadrangle on the east. There may have been a gatehouse, and somewhere there would have been guest lodgings, possibly close to the west end of the church, where a well-built stone garderobe was discovered in recent excavations.

The lesser buildings seem to have been neglected at times; in 1316 the king granted the canons part of the royal quarry at Wheatley. The stone would be used not just for the priory buildings but also for priory properties in the town.

The grange and fishponds were to the east of the priory in and around Merton Field.

Curthoys (2017), 5–11

much for the beautifying of the fabric. However, in 1398 Henry Beaufort, newly appointed University Chancellor and at the beginning of an extraordinary career, acknowledged Frideswide as patron saint of both Oxford and the University.[49] Her day was to be celebrated throughout the University, and an indulgence could be offered to all those visiting the shrine.[50] Every term there was a solemn procession to St Frideswide's, where Mass was said on behalf of the University's benefactors, the royal family, and for the peace of the University. Another procession took place on 16 November – the feast day of St Edmund of Abingdon, and the anniversary of the death of Henry III.[51] Perhaps the work on the choir vault was funded to commemorate this event by a generous benefactor whose name is unknown.

5

Finance and finality: the fifteenth and early sixteenth centuries

By the middle of the fifteenth century, when the bishop conducted a Visitation, the priory's finances were on a slightly more even footing. The prior and eleven of the canons were present, with the others, perhaps six, out serving their churches. The income was only £160 per annum, but it was enough to meet basic expenses. All the Visitors could find to complain about was that the prior's family came to visit rather too frequently, and that the prior did not consult the canons sufficiently on business matters. Certainly things were tightened up under Prior George Norton; the rents due to the priory were listed, and receipts issued to the colleges and other institutions that owed rent, during 1480 and 1481.[1] By 1482 the income of the previous three years was up to £940 2s. 8d., double what it had been only forty years earlier. The priory was almost breaking even – expenditure was just over £1,006 in the same period. The account records all the outgoings of the priory, including the stipends and liveries of the carpenters, masons and other servants, and payments to the man who brought the salt fish as well as the bigger obligations of the tenths to the king and the repair bills for the buildings. It also lists the farm animals that would have been kept on the meadow: one bull, seven cows, twelve cart-horses, four mares, one hen and one cockerel, eight pigs and piglets, seven sheep and a lamb.[2]

This sudden accounting may have been associated with the

> ## Priors of the fifteenth and early sixteenth centuries
>
> | | | | |
> |---|---|---|---|
> | Thomas Bradwell | 1391 | George Norton | 1479 |
> | Richard of Oxford | 1405 | RichardWalker | 1484 |
> | Edmund Andever | 1434 | Thomas Ware | 1496 |
> | Robert Downham | 1439 | William Chedill | 1501 |
> | John Westbury | 1458 | John Burton | 1513–24 |
>
> Smith and London (2001), 443–5; Smith (2008), 501–2

canonisation of Frideswide in 1481. During the fifteenth century the services surrounding Frideswide appear to have been regularised. In 1434 Archbishop Henry Chichele, who was at the beginning of his close association with the University, passed a constitution for her feast to be celebrated throughout the southern province. St Frideswide's Day was to be celebrated with nine lessons and music according to the Use of Sarum. The lessons were probably the nine extracts from St Augustine and St Gregory to be read at the Common of a Virgin.[3] Later, special readings were devised for Frideswide, again probably in preparation for her canonisation.

* * * * *

Evidence in the masonry shows that the intention was to carry the late fourteenth-century choir vault, or at least something similar, over the transepts and probably over the crossing. Springers were in place, old shafts removed and the wall surfaces prepared, and in the north transept work on the clerestory had already begun. This may have been considerably later, however, than the creation of the choir roof. James Zouch, whose memorial is in the north transept, left a bequest in 1503 to the priory, explicitly for the continuation of the vaulting.[4] Even at this point the finances of the priory were not in a good state, certainly not sufficient for major improvements and

James Zouch left £30 in 1503 towards continuing the stone vault of the choir into the north transept. Work was begun but it ceased before more than a single bay and some preparatory work were completed. Dendrochronology has shown that at least part of the timber for the roof was felled in the winter of 1506–7. Zouch also left 40 shillings for his tomb, which is located in the north transept under the Victorian St Michael window.

embellishments to the fabric. Perhaps William Orchard had been commissioned to continue the work begun a century earlier, but he died in 1504. The loss of a master craftsman, the death of a major benefactor and the priory's poor financial position stopped any work in its tracks. So in the winter of 1506–7, trees were felled for a timber roof over the north transept.[5]

But there were some changes at the end of the fifteenth century and very early in the sixteenth. Under the priorships of Thomas Ware and William Chedill the cloister was rebuilt (this time possibly by Orchard, funded by Robert Sherborne), and a new refectory was constructed on the south side of the cloister.[6]

* * * * *

> The master mason William Orchard was responsible for the building of Magdalen College from 1468, and although there is no documentary proof, it is thought that he also constructed at least the vault of the Divinity School.
>
> As a quarryman, Orchard supplied stone for St Bernard's College (now St John's) and Eton College.
>
> He died in 1504, having requested burial at St Frideswide's.
>
> ODNB

Almost nothing is known of the priory in the last few decades before its dissolution. George Norton resigned the priorship in 1484, and Richard Walker, one of the few outsiders to be elected, arrived in August of that year.[7] Walker was evidently not one of the better holders of the post; a commission was launched in 1495 to investigate the crimes and excesses of the prior and the canons. What those crimes were is unknown, but Walker died in 1496 and the priory passed, for the next five years, into the hands of Thomas Ware and then to William Chedill. During Chedill's occupation of the Priory House, a pardon was granted to both prior and convent in 1509, which may well have been associated with the 1495 commission. Certainly Chedill was granted a pension by the bishop when he resigned his office in 1513. Was the writing on the wall when John Burton, the only prior to have a degree from the University, took over the priory?[8] Probably not quite – in 1512 Henry VIII had sent Reginald Pole to the priory to be accommodated during his first student years in Oxford; in 1517 all that the Visitors could find to complain about was the lack of a grammar master, and in 1518 it was decided that the 1521 General Chapter would take place at St Frideswide's. It was Cardinal Wolsey who issued the statutes that were to be examined there,[9] but Wolsey was already beginning to look towards Oxford to pursue his passion for education.[10]

The statutes that Wolsey had first mooted at the 1518 General Chapter were probably designed to reform the monasteries: to instruct them to return to a life of ascetism. In 1520 he issued orders and statutes that included demands that unsuitable people and women were not to be permitted in the monasteries, that monks were not to leave the precinct, that they were not to hunt or go hawking, wear furs or shoes like those of the laity and that they were to keep canonical hours. But the monks and canons were frank with the cardinal, telling him that this would not go down well; new recruits would be hard to find, and the present members would rise up against such an idea. They were probably playing straight into Wolsey's hands.[11] On the financial front Wolsey had tried to make taxation fairer (compared with the old ratings system, which dated from 1291) for both laity and clergy when the subsidy of 1523 was demanded; a new valuation allowed the tax to be graduated according to wealth. St Frideswide's, in spite of its financial troubles still one of the richer houses dissolved to fund Cardinal College, was taxed on a net income of £148 16s. 9½d.[12] Some of the suppressions for the college were of very definitely decayed houses with few resident canons, monks or nuns, and some were undoubtedly poor. But there were odd inclusions, such as Daventry, with a gross income of £236, and Lesnes in Kent, with £189.[13]

Wolsey's scheme was undoubtedly to provide funds for his proposed new college, but the notion of dissolving very small, impoverished or ill-disciplined monastic houses was neither new nor particularly questionable. Many bishops in the early sixteenth century were concerned about the condition of the monasteries, and converting monastic houses – or diverting their resources – into colleges or schools, with the canons re-employed as parish priests, was seen as the right way forward.[14] Bishop William Waynflete had acquired Selborne Priory in Hampshire for Magdalen College, and John Alcock, the bishop of Ely, had suppressed St Radegund's in Cambridge to use the site for St John's College. There were many other examples. And reform of monastic life was not just a preoccupation of the English: there were movements in Spain, France and even Sweden.

The mechanism for suppression was fiddly, but surprisingly fast. A papal bull had to be obtained, followed by royal approval. A local jury was required to confirm that the house was indeed of royal foundation (a stipulation laid down by the pope), after which the property would be surrendered 'voluntarily' to the Crown. Once these stages had been achieved, a

Monastic houses repressed to fund Cardinal College

	Value	Numbers	Date	Order
St Frideswide, Oxford	£220	15	1524	Augustinian
Bayham, Sussex	£125	10	1525	Premonstratensian
Blackmore, Essex	£85	4	1525	Augustinian
Bradwell, Buckinghamshire	£47	3 or 4	1524–5	Benedictine
Canwell, Staffordshire	£25	1	1525	Benedictine
Daventry, Northamptonshire	£236	10	1525	Benedictine
Dodnash, Suffolk	£44	4	1525	Augustinian
Felixstowe, Suffolk	£40	3	1528	Benedictine
Horkesley, Essex	£27	2	1524–5	Benedictine (Cluniac)
Ipswich, Suffolk	£80	7	1527	Augustinian
Lesnes, Kent	£189	6 or 11	1525	Augustinian
Littlemore, Oxfordshire	£33	5	1525	Benedictine (nuns)
Poughley, Berkshire	£71	4	1525	Augustinian
Pré, Hertfordshire	£65	3	1528	Benedictine (nuns)
Pynham (Calceto), Sussex	£43	1	1525	Augustinian
Ravenstone, Buckinghamshire	£66	2 or 5	1525	Augustinian
Rumburgh, Suffolk	£30	3	1528	Benedictine
Sandwell, Staffordshire	£38	1 or 2	1525	Benedictine
Snape, Suffolk	£99	uncertain	1527–8	Benedictine
Stansgate, Essex	£43	3	1525	Benedictine
Thoby, Essex	£75	3	1525	Augustinian
Tickford, Buckinghamshire	£57	6	1524	Benedictine
Tiptree, Essex	£22	2	1525	Augustinian
Tonbridge, Kent	£169	8	1525	Augustinian
Wallingford, Oxfordshire	£134	5	1528	Benedictine
Wykes, Essex	£92	4	1525	Benedictine (nuns)

conveyance under the Great Seal and a licence would be granted to the cardinal to proceed with the foundation of his college.[15] An inspeximus or reaffirmation of a papal bull issued by Clement VII permitting the suppression of the monastery was signed on 19 April 1524. It duly received the royal assent, and Wolsey sent a commissioner to oversee the handover just two

Finance and finality: the fifteenth and early sixteenth centuries

The first page of a valuation of the monastic institutions that were dissolved to fund Cardinal College, showing the temporalities and spiritualities of St Frideswide's Priory.

days later. Prior John Burton surrendered the priory on 24 April. Conversion to a college had already been approved three weeks earlier, on 3 April, by the pope, but it was early May before the prior and the fifteen canons knew that they were to be moved to other priories or given small pensions.[16] Burton was transferred to Oseney – a decent promotion – to be abbot there until he died in 1537, fully aware that the abbey was heading for the same fate. The final grant of the priory to Wolsey was dated 1 July 1525, but the work on his new college was already well under way and the site was ready for the laying of the foundation stone on 17 July.[17]

In towns other than Oxford, the loss of their monastic houses to Wolsey's grand scheme was met with some anger or disbelief. The citizens of Tonbridge, for example, were offered a school – with places guaranteed for boys to come to Cardinal College – to replace their priory, which was closed in February 1525. A meeting was held in the town in June 1525, with the scheme explained by no less a personage than the archbishop of Canterbury, William Warham. The prelate's powers of persuasion were lacking, and the townsmen expressed a preference to retain the priory, but the end was coming, regardless. Needless to say, Tonbridge Priory was not to be refounded and so the town lost out completely.[18] The suppression of St Frideswide's appears to have been received with greater ambivalence, but then it had never been popular.[19]

Interlude

From priory to cathedral

The dissolution of St Frideswide's Priory was quickly done. Even before the formal papers had been completed, Thomas Wolsey had begun the clearance of the site for his new college. There would be a chapel in Cardinal College, of course, and services were to be maintained in the old priory church until the new dean and canons were *in situ* and the new building ready for worship. A priest, Davy Griffiths, was paid £7 in 1528 to say services and to oversee the workmen for a period of around thirteen months.[1]

Why Dean?

A dean is usually understood to be the head of a chapter in a collegiate or cathedral church. After 1546, when Christ Church was founded as a joint institution of college and cathedral, the use of the title 'dean' for the head of house made perfect sense. But why did Wolsey choose to use the title for the head of his college in 1525?

A dean could be the head of a group of monks in a Benedictine monastery but could (and can) also be the fellow in charge of the studies and discipline of junior members of Oxford and Cambridge colleges. Wolsey's use of the term demonstrates that he saw his new foundation as a natural successor to the monastery, not as a usurper. Wolsey was quietly but publicly demonstrating his commitment to the church and to education.

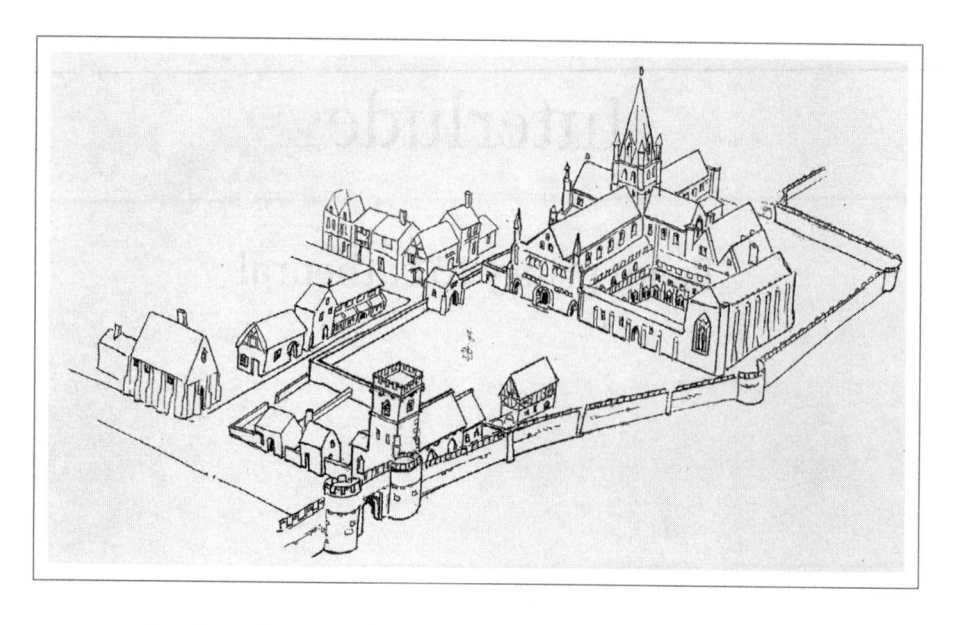

A conjectural drawing of the priory immediately before its dissolution.

The Great Quadrangle (now Tom Quad) was erected with extraordinary speed, with most of the south, west and east sides completed at least to first-floor level by the end of 1526. Three or four of the westernmost bays of the priory church must have been demolished almost as soon as the prior left the premises, and the west end – now just a few feet from the east wall of the new quadrangle – was closed with wooden shuttering.[2]

Wolsey's plans for the church have long been debated, but it seems unlikely that he intended to keep it.[3] The footings and first stone courses of a vast chapel along the north side of the quadrangle, probably to resemble that of King's College in Cambridge, had already been laid within eighteen months of the official founding of Cardinal College, and a roof was being constructed off-site at Sonning.[4] It is possible, too, that stained glass and furniture were already in preparation – the Passion windows in Balliol College chapel may have been painted by James Nicholson for Wolsey but given to Balliol by Dean Higden when Wolsey fell, and the stalls now in the Latin Chapel appear to date from Wolsey's time.[5] Why would Wolsey have needed two large chapels? The cloister had already lost its west walk to make way for the Hall staircase, and a temporary belfry was begun in the cloister garth.[6] Cardinal College was dedicated to the Holy Trinity, the Virgin Mary and St Frideswide, and the first service held at the college was deferred from 25 March 1526 (Lady Day) until 19 October (St Frideswide's Day), but neither of these facts really suggests that Wolsey was intending to keep the priory church; they may just indicate that he was acknowledging the original establishment.[7] Besides, where else – until the new chapel was complete – would he have held the celebrations? He may well have been intending to dedicate his new chapel similarly, moving the shrine to a prominent place there.

The statutes for the new college called for choristers and a master of music, a precentor and a sacristan. It is easy to forget that this was still Catholic England, but the statutes decreed that there should be prayers on rising and retiring, seven daily Masses and three special Masses each week to commemorate the founder. These must have been conducted in the ancient priory church, with its nearly new choir roof at one end and a demolition gang working at the other. The first man approached for the position of master of music was Hugh Aston, the celebrated master at St Mary Newarke in Leicester. The bishop of Lincoln, John Longland, who was managing the recruitment on Wolsey's behalf, found negotiations difficult. Aston prevaricated and haggled over pay, eventually turning down the position. So the bishop turned his attentions to John Taverner, of Tattershall College in Lincolnshire.[8] Taverner, too, appeared reluctant to leave a prestigious and well-paid job, but Longland prevailed and Taverner was on the payroll of Cardinal College by the end of March 1526. By late spring, organist and bishop were working to put together a choir of some reputation in time for the opening ceremony.[9] It was Longland's difficulties with his chosen candidates for the position of music master that caused the deferment of the celebrations, rather than any attachment to the priory church; Wolsey was determined that everything would be ready, and when delay was inevitable, he chose a date of local significance.[10] The cardinal also commissioned many precious items for the chapel from the court goldsmith, Robert Amadas, including: a silver-gilt enamelled crucifix depicting Mary and John, and weighing 117

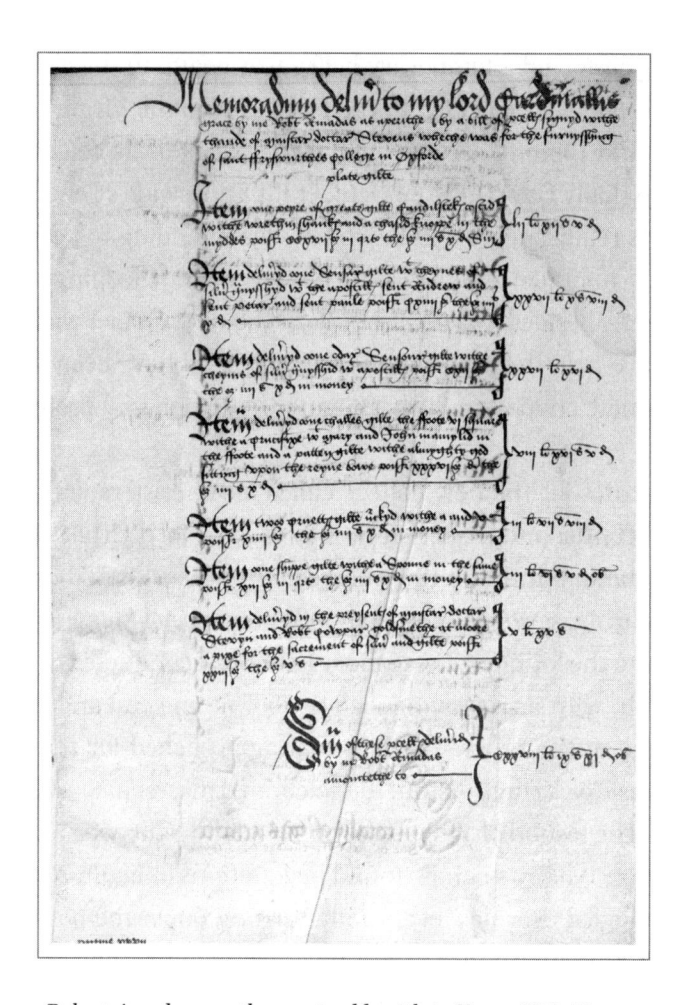

Robert Amadas was the court goldsmith to Henry VIII. He was commissioned by Cardinal Wolsey to produce jewels and plate for Ipswich College, St Albans Abbey and St Frideswide's College, as Cardinal College was sometimes known. This page, from his account of work done for Cardinal Wolsey, shows Amadas's delivery of gilt candlesticks, chalices, censers and a pyx for the chapel, among more secular items.

ounces; an embellished coconut with a gilt cover decorated with an image of St Frideswide; gold and silver chalices; mazers; a staff with a silver-gilt cross; and a silver-gilt censer.[11]

These elaborate and valuable gifts for Catholic worship would not have gone down well with some of Wolsey's chosen students, who were discovered, probably much to the public embarrassment of the Dean and Chapter, to be reading Zwingli, Wycliffe and Bucer, and discussing Lutheran ideas. The young men were rounded up, and some were imprisoned in a cellar, where they sickened and eventually died.[12]

But Wolsey's fate is well known. He fell from grace in 1529 for failing to deal with Henry VIII's 'great matter', was charged with *praemunire* and died the following year. (*Praemunire* was the title of statutes designed to protect the English Crown against encroachment by the Papacy.) His college almost fell with him, but was reprieved, in a much-reduced form, through the supplication of the dean, John Higden. Henry VIII evidently rather liked the idea of his own college in Oxford, and King Henry VIII's College, formally founded in July 1532, kept the site operational as a collegiate church. What happened to all the Cardinal College students is unknown, and there is no record of any provision being made for them, but Henry must already have been thinking ahead.[13]

There were twelve canons with the new dean at King Henry VIII's College, four of whom had stayed on from Cardinal College, and a much-reduced staff, including eight chaplains, eight lay clerks and ten choristers to sing divine service.[14] The Sarum rite – which was to become the backbone of the Book of Common Prayer – would be followed. This small group of men were to witness great change.

The dean of the new collegiate church was John Oliver.[15] He was an Oxford-educated man, a moderate reformer, who (despite not being ordained) had previously held and who continued to hold a few incumbencies after his appointment to King Henry VIII's College in 1533, but his main employment was as a prominent civil lawyer. He worked with Wolsey, and then with Cromwell advising the king on the break with Rome. He was favoured by Richard Rich and sat on various legal commissions including the commission that tried Stephen Gardiner and the party that worked to secure a royal French bride for Edward VI. Oliver remained in post until the surrender of the college to the king on 20 May 1545, preparatory to the foundation of Christ Church.[16]

The college, though much smaller than Cardinal College, was not poor.[17] It had been granted all the property that had belonged to the priory, along with income from other suppressed monastic houses, notably Daventry Abbey.[18] But the dean and canons had been left to manage a building site that was far bigger than their needs and beyond their income to complete. They appealed to the king for help, and at least one canon, Richard Croke, contributed twenty nobles towards the finishing of his own lodgings.[19]

But it was during Oliver's short deanery that lasting changes were to be made to the church fabric. A proclamation of 1538 made the king's views clear. Henry VIII's dislike of Thomas Becket, who had stood up for the rights of the church over the state, was made manifest in his destruction, in 1538, of the shrine to the saint at Canterbury and the appropriation of the gold and jewels that decorated the feretory.[20] Other shrines, to other saints, suffered a similar fate, including St Frideswide's. The shrine was broken up and scattered, its pieces used to line a well and incorporated into the new west wall of the church.[21] The relics of the saint were rescued and concealed somewhere against a change in the times.[22] Statuary and images of other saints would have been removed, along with the candles and votive offerings that would have surrounded them. The king wanted no more superstition.[23]

One of the mitigating reasons given for the dissolution of the monasteries was to fund better and more universal education by founding schools and colleges attached to the dioceses across the country. But Henry's plans were broader than just the creation of new educational establishments; he was concerned about the health of monastic institutions and the size and number of English dioceses. As early as 1528 Wolsey was given powers, through papal bulls, to suppress certain monasteries and to use their revenues and buildings to create new cathedrals and dioceses.[24] The king did not intend to go down the German route and abandon cathedrals and bishops altogether; in fact, he was concerned to protect them during the dissolution.[25]

Wolsey's first decision was over the form of the new and old cathedrals. Would the existing monastic institutions be permitted to stay monastic, or should there be a mix of secular and religious canons, or should they all be purely secular? He opted for the last, reorganising the existing monastic cathedrals and creating new ones, using St George's, Windsor – the king's chapel – as a model.²⁶ There were all sorts of reasons why this was difficult and likely to be unpopular – not least the loss of revenues for the bishops whose dioceses were to be reduced in size.²⁷ But there were also those in favour, and Wolsey trod a difficult path, unable to please everyone.²⁸ The cardinal's fall and death brought the plans temporarily to a halt, but they were revived in the late 1530s, when Stephen Gardiner, bishop of Winchester and Wolsey's successor as royal secretary, and Richard Sampson, then bishop of Chichester, were charged with drawing up a proposal that must have drawn heavily on Wolsey's original.²⁹ Gardiner proposed sixteen new dioceses; the king suggested thirteen, all aligned on county boundaries. The scheme was to include provisions for readers in humanities and divinity.

The proposal for Oxford, originally called the diocese of Oseney and Thame, paralleled that of other cathedrals and included a bishop, a president (or dean), eight canons, four petty canons (to sing in the choir), eight lay singers, eight choristers, a school master, a gospeller, an epistoler, two sextons, six students of divinity (three to be at Oxford University and three at Cambridge), ten almsmen, an estates steward, a porter, a butler, a caterer, a cook and an under-cook.³⁰ Interestingly, the proposal for Oxford did not include readers, presumably because the university was already providing these.³¹

Henry's last French war had a huge impact on the finances available to

The bishop's residence

Robert King was given the former Benedictine Gloucester Hall (now Worcester College) as his episcopal palace, but it only remained as such until the accession of Edward VI, when it reverted to the Crown.

By tradition, King built the house in St Aldate's, known as the Bishop's (or Old) Palace, but there is no evidence that he lived there, and the existing house is from the seventeenth century.

In 1634 a palace was constructed for Bishop John Bancroft at Cuddesdon, a few miles to the south east of the city. It remained the episcopal residence until 1937.

fund the new cathedrals scheme, and only six of the proposed new dioceses were actually created, most of which did not follow the county boundary idea (and one of those, the diocese of Middlesex centred on Westminster, was soon abandoned), but it was still a reform of some note.[32] According to Cole, who edited King Henry's scheme for the reform of old bishoprics and the creation of new, it was 'the disposal of the ecclesiastical confiscations at the King's caprice, and the execution of Cromwell' that caused the proposals to fall short of the original intentions.[33]

On 1 September 1542 the bishopric of Oxford was formally created with the name 'The Cathedral Church of Christ and the Blessed Virgin Mary'. The see was at Oseney Abbey, which had been surrendered to the Crown in November 1539. Its church was undoubtedly splendid – 332 feet long, with a nave with double aisles on both sides, numerous chapels and two towers – but very isolated, in a rather marshy bit of countryside to the west of the city: an ideal location for a monastery, perhaps, but not for a cathedral.[34] The bishop was Robert King, and the first dean was John London.

King was a local man and had studied at both Rewley Abbey and at St Bernard's College in Oxford. Under the patronage of John Longland, the bishop of Lincoln, he was made abbot at Thame in 1527 and then of Oseney a decade later. King's appointment to Oseney had facilitated the dissolution of the abbey – he was related by marriage to Cromwell – and he was rewarded with the new bishopric, a position he held until his death in 1557.

London was another local, educated at, and later warden of, New College. He was an ardent reformer, about whom opinions are divided; he worked with Longland and later with Gardiner, and was active in the dissolution of local monasteries.[35] He held the deanery for a very short time, dying in 1543.

Statutes were drawn up for most of the new cathedrals in 1544, with the panel headed by Richard Cox, the new dean of Oxford Cathedral, appointed in January 1544.[36] Archbishop Cranmer achieved much, although Henry VIII was determined that choral services would continue as before. However, night-time services were abandoned, and said – rather than sung – services were permitted to save time when a sermon was to be preached. An English litany – with references to saints removed – was introduced into services from 1542 in parish churches and so into cathedrals.[37]

But Henry's financial woes were to render the cathedral at Oseney very short-lived. A cathedral in the centre of the city based on King Henry VIII's College was already on Henry's agenda early in 1545.[38] After all, it was a foolish waste of money to have two establishments of dean and canons so close together, and he appears to have wanted the cathedral in a more central location. In May 1545 both the cathedral at Oseney and the college in Oxford were seized by the Crown. The lands and other property of both were put up for sale, and an inventory taken of the treasures of the old priory church, which still had its nine altars and associated hangings, vestments, palls, plate, candlesticks, song books, Mass books and sacring bells.[39]

However, something bigger than just a better location for the cathedral appears to have been in the offing. Peckwater Inn, which had been in the hands of New College after the collapse of Cardinal College, was surrendered to Henry, as was Canterbury College (in November 1545).[40] Some of the men of the cathedral at Oseney, while officially no longer employed, were in fact still active in preparing for the move across town. The roads and bridges between the two sites were repaired to ease the passage of all the materials, such as lead and stone, which the king had decreed could be moved and reused. Fixtures and fittings as well as men and boys were settled into their new home. The bells of the old abbey, including Great Tom, took sixteen days to take down, cart across town and rehang in the steeple of the even older priory church. An oak platform was installed in the tower to aid the hanging of the bells, and a new sanctus bell was cast. A holy water sprinkler was purchased, and the cathedral clock was given new pulleys and ropes. All sorts of repairs and cleaning were taking place; new timber was brought in from Sugworth, near Abingdon, to supplement the recycled stock from the abbey, and a glazier repaired and installed the church glass.[41]

A fairly substantial body of men was being paid from June 1545 and, significantly, fifty scholars received exhibitions. Henry's original scheme for the reorganised dioceses of England included provision for scholars from each diocese to attend Oxford or Cambridge, funded by their cathedrals.

A page from the accounts dealing with the interim period between the creation of the diocese and the foundation of Christ Church, showing the wages paid to the dean and four canons, the schoolmasters, petty canons, the gospeller and the epistoler.

Oxford, as we have seen, was charged with the support of six students. College accounts suggest that all the boys appointed as students by the dioceses would be coming to one single residential college rather than being scattered to different halls and colleges.[42] The lands that each cathedral would have used to pay for the boys' keep while they were at university was surrendered to the Crown, in some cases on the very day that Oseney and King Henry VIII's College were also suppressed.[43] Everything points to Christ Church having been very definitely planned from the spring of 1545 at the

An account book in the Christ Church archives records the income from estates and expenditure, including stipends, during the interim period between the suppression of Oseney Abbey and the formal foundation of Christ Church. The list of men and boys receiving stipends during the eighteen-month period covered by the interim accounts includes:

The dean: Richard Cox;
Four canons: William Haynes, Thomas Day, John Dyar and Alexander Belsyre;
John Candelar – schoolmaster, along with an usher and twenty schoolboys;
Petty canons, some with specific tasks, such as the chaunter, the gospeller and the epistoler;
Twelve choristers; and
Senior staff, including a porter, a caterer, a butler, a barber, two cooks and a carter.

Haynes, Day and Belsyre all stayed on as canons of Christ Church, and a Mr Candler, from Norfolk, is listed briefly among the second rank of Students in 1548. A number of the senior staff also continued in employment after the foundation in 1546, including Thomas Williams (caterer) and Robert Jones (porter). Even one of the almsmen, William Webster, was already in place.

There were also the fifty scholars listed under the headings of the various diocese, beginning with Canterbury (12 men), then Westminster (10), Rochester (2), Oseney (2), Winchester (6), Gloucester (1), Worcester (6), Chester (2), Ely (1), Durham (6) and Peterborough (2). The diocesan system did not survive the foundation of Christ Church, nor did the grammar school, which was laid down in some early covenants for Christ Church, but existed only briefly.

CCA iii.b.99; Orme (2017), 106–7; CCA DP xii.c.5, fols 35v & and 36

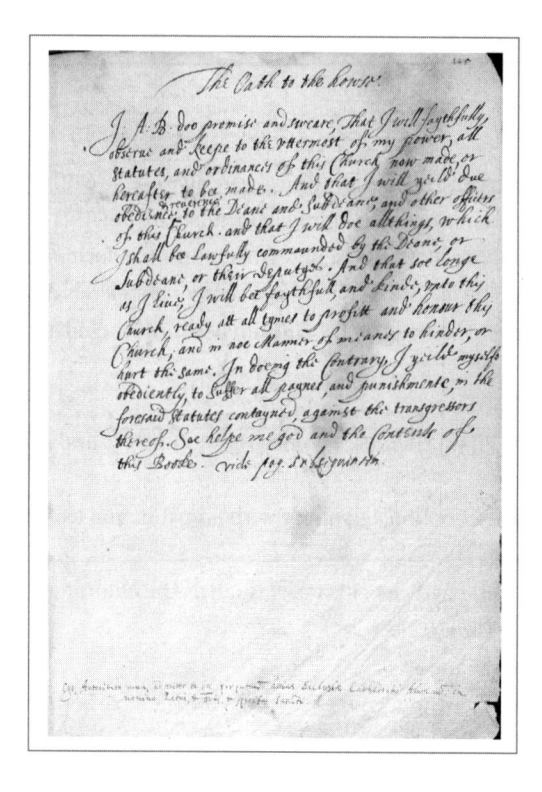

A later copy of the oath to the House sworn by all new undergraduates at matriculation, probably dating to the end of the reign of Elizabeth, between 1595 and 1603.

latest, and the tradition that it was the cleverness of Matthew Parker, the Vice-Chancellor of Cambridge University, which convinced the king to save Oxford and Cambridge colleges from the threat of the Chantries Act (which sought to acquire gifts for prayers for the dead for the king's coffers) seems to have been founded on sand.

A draft of the foundation charter of a new cathedral was drawn up in November 1545, and the letters patent were prepared by 26 January 1546. But the final step of enrolment did not take place immediately, in spite of the fact that the college was almost up and running. It took time for the buildings, most of which had seen little attention since 1529, to be brought into a habitable state, and it was not until 4 November 1546 that the foundation charter was finally enrolled. It was followed a month later, on 11 December, by the Charter of Dotation, which gave Christ Church its endowment promising an annual income of £2,200. The first students, barely even hinted at in the foundation charter, took their oath to the House on 14 January 1547.

Part II
THE CATHEDRAL

6

Trouble and turmoil: the later Tudors

There was never any intention that college and cathedral would operate separately. Statutes were always on the cards, and the drafts that survive in the archive begin with an annotated version of Henry VIII's statutes for his new cathedral foundations. But the king died before any document could be finalised, let alone ratified.[1] The absence of statutes, for college and cathedral, was to be a defining characteristic of the foundation until the middle of the nineteenth century.

The cathedral establishment was, at least at its head, intrinsic with that of the educational body. The dean was head of both, and the eight canons formed the governing body.[2] There were, of course, the one hundred Students and, very swiftly, fee-paying commoners, but the rest of the foundation – those paid from the endowment – were cathedral men: chaplains, lay clerks, choristers, vergers and the sacristan. A few covenants, signed by Edward North, chancellor of the Court of Augmentations, made sure that these men were included in the grand scheme, even the twenty-four almsmen who were part of the scheme for all of Henry VIII's new cathedrals.[3] Other servants were needed for both 'sides': not least the barber, whose time would have been occupied maintaining neat tonsures in a large establishment full of future and present clerics.[4]

* * * * *

Edward VI succeeded his father at the end of January 1547, and almost immediately a royal commission was set up to visit parish churches and cathedrals alike. The new cathedrals were little touched as Cranmer, the reforming archbishop, had already set these up much as he wanted them, but services increasingly became daytime events, and static rather than processional. Sermons were to be given every Sunday and on holy days, not just during the fasting periods of Lent and Advent.[5] English Bibles were to be provided both in the choir (for the clergy) and in the nave (for the public).

Chantries and religious guilds were abolished at the end of 1547. It is impossible to say whether the Montacute chantry was still functioning or whether the chantry priest was still using the chapel in the watching loft, but if they had survived 1524 and 1532, they certainly would have been moved on by Easter 1548, when the Act came into effect.

More change came in 1549, when Edward VI imposed the Book of Common Prayer. Services were now standard across the country and had to be in English, although Christ Church, as an educational establishment, was exempt and could continue to conduct at least part of its services in Latin.[6] The previously expected eight daily services were reduced to two, and the Mass became 'communion' at a table rather than at a stone altar, which had to be removed. Just three years later, even this was replaced with a more radical prayer book which took out of the service any remaining vestiges of Catholicism.

Cathedral worship under Edward VI became simpler. There was less decoration, less colour, less processional and less music. Cathedrals were encouraged to lead the way in implementing the changes, which were obligatory in parish churches and cathedrals alike.[7] During 1548 money was spent in the cathedral on two service books, ten copies of the psalter, eight copies of the burial service and the chaining of Erasmus's *Paraphrases*, a volume explaining the Gospels and the Epistles that every clergyman and every parish church was required to have under the July Injunctions of Edward VI.[8] All new undergraduates were expected to bring with them a copy of Leo Judas's translation of the Psalms, part of the Zurich or Zwingli Bible.[9] Eight ells of lockram, a course linen, were purchased to make surplices for the choristers. Christ Church's charitable giving, required by Henry VIII's covenants, began almost immediately, with alms for the poor folk of the parishes of the city, fabric to make clothes for the poorer members of staff and medical care for a boy whose arms had been dislocated after ringing the bells, as well as payments to the almsmen.[10] In 1551 all Catholic remnants – altars, images, equipment and books – were removed by order of the Dean and Chapter.[11]

Christ Church was, as a body, conservative in its reforming. At the head, of course, was Richard Cox who had been active on the Protestant side from the 1530s, and was an unsurprising choice for dean, and then for vice-chancellor, to enforce the Edwardian regime in the University. But there were more controversial appointments, not least that of Peter Martyr Vermigli as regius professor of divinity.

Vermigli was an Italian scholar who had been educated in the Catholic tradition, was ordained and rose through the church until he was introduced to the Protestant ideas of Valdès, Bucer and Zwingli, and began to speak against purgatory and in favour of the doctrine of justification by faith alone. Eventually this came to the attention of the curia, and on hearing that there was a warrant for his arrest, Vermigli fled first to Switzerland and then to Strasbourg. But his life became increasingly difficult in mainland Europe, and so, after the fall of Stephen Gardiner and the appointment of Protector Somerset, who allowed open Protestant debate, Archbishop Cranmer invited him to England, and in March 1548 Vermigli was given the regius chair of divinity in place of the conservative Richard Smith.[12] He drew around him a group of supporters from the Chapter at Christ Church but also from further afield, including a number from Switzerland, one of whom – John ab Ulmis – was elected to a Studentship.[13] Vermigli's lectures on 1 Corinthians, which condemned clerical celibacy and the doctrine of purgatory and took issue with the Catholic understanding of the Eucharist, prompted a call by Smith – incensed that he had been required to step down to allow this radical in – and other traditionally leaning members of the University for a disputation. This took place at the end of May 1549, already some months after the publication of the first version of the Book of Common Prayer, in which the

The Protestant Peter Martyr Vermigli was a radical and divisive presence following his appointment as regius professor of divinity in 1548.

doctrine of transubstantiation had no place. Vermigli stood against William Tresham, canon of Christ Church, William Chedsey, who was to become, very briefly, president of Corpus Christi College, and Morgan Phillips, the principal of St Mary Hall. Cox, presiding, announced at the end of proceedings that he was not going to pass judgement on the debate, but it was inevitable that it, and Vermigli himself, would have an impact on the discussions surrounding the 1552 version of the Prayer Book.[14]

Vermigli was not popular in conservative Oxford, even among the townsfolk. When he was made a canon of Christ Church in 1551, following the death of William Haynes, he brought his wife, Catherine Dammartin, to reside with him in his lodgings on the St Aldate's side of the Great Quadrangle. Catherine had been a nun in Metz, and the locals found it too much to bear – a converted nun and a married priest. They rioted outside their windows and forced the couple to move deeper into Christ Church to take up residence in the Priory House safely within the confines of the college walls.[15]

The first men to lead Christ Church were scholars but, considering that their dean was a reforming Protestant, mixed in terms of their religious leanings. In 1548 the dean was Richard Cox, tutor and almoner to Edward VI, an obvious choice. The eight canons included William Haynes, who had been a canon at Oseney, provost of Oriel College and a chaplain to Henry VIII, and William Tresham, the one man who had been appointed at Cardinal and King Henry VIII's colleges as well as to Christ Church, and was conservative in his religion, a fact that would be evident during the brief reign of Mary.[16] Thomas Day had been a canon at Oseney and sub-warden of All Souls College. Then there was Alexander Belsyre, who would become the first president of St John's College, one of two colleges founded during Mary's reign in 1555, James Courthopp, a fellow at Protestant Corpus Christi College, Thomas Bernard, from Cambridge and a chaplain to Archbishop Cranmer, Robert Bankes and Henry Siddall, who stepped into the shoes of John Dyar, who had been a canon at Oseney but who died early in 1547. Siddall had been a canon at Cardinal College and became known for his Protestant sympathies and support for Peter Vermigli.[17]

Apart from Vermigli, the other two public lecturers, or regius professors, were Richard Bruarne, professor of Hebrew, and George Etheridge, medic and professor of Greek, both of whom definitely had Catholic leanings.[18] As Christopher Haigh has put it:

> the first members of Christ Church were a pretty eminent lot. Five would become bishops, three deans, three archdeacons, two heads of colleges and two university chancellors. They included two major Catholic theologians and two Protestant, one of the leading evangelists of the age (Bernard Gilpin), three future presidents of the College of Physicians, one dramatist, two poets, the founder of Anglo-Saxon studies (Lawrence Nowell), and one revolutionary [Christopher Goodman].[19]

Christ Church's constitution, as a unique joint foundation of college and cathedral, was slightly different from that of other cathedrals. The dean and eight canons formed not only the cathedral Chapter but also the

Governing Body of the college. Three of the canons were Treasurers, headed in the earliest days by Alexander Belsyre, who managed the finances of both college and cathedral. Cathedral officers, such as the precentor, the sacristan, the schoolmaster and the choir – including chaplains, lay clerks and choristers – were all paid from the endowment, with no differentiation in the accounts. The two organisations were completely bound together. The one man who probably had very little to do with the new cathedral was its bishop, Robert King. King rolled with the religious changes from his appointment to the see in 1542 until his death in 1557, when he was buried in the cathedral. Apart from a single year in the 1560s and the short period 1589–92 there was no bishop of Oxford until 1604.[20]

But Edward's reign was short; his death and the succession of his Catholic half-sister, Mary, signalled a complete reversal of all that had happened since 1530.

* * * * *

Mary's aim was to push through, quickly, a complete restoration of Catholicism. Her first task was to deal with the clergy who had embraced the Reformation. Cranmer and Robert Holgate, the archbishop of York, were expelled, along with seven bishops, eleven deans and over seventy canons and dignitaries.[21] Some clergy had taken advantage of Edward VI's 1548 decree that they could marry – including Holgate. This was unacceptable to Mary, and she expected these men to leave their wives if they wished to remain in the church. At Christ Church, canons Robert Bankes and Thomas Bernard were deprived of their positions for being married.[22]

But Bankes and Bernard were not alone in having to depart. Vermigli had been placed under house arrest in July, as soon as Mary acceded. In September, as Dean Cox was replaced by Richard Marshall, Cranmer advised Vermigli to leave for the Continent quickly. He left first for Strasbourg and then Zurich.[23] Marshall, an unpopular and by some accounts thoroughly unpleasant man, immediately set to converting or expelling anyone who had supported Vermigli. Most left Oxford, at least, and many, including his Swiss adherents, fled abroad.[24]

Richard Bruarne stepped into Vermigli's canonry; Theodore Newton, a much more junior Student but brother of the deprived dean of Winchester, also left for Geneva; John Pullain took himself only as far as Essex, where he held clandestine Protestant services until things became a bit too hot and he too fled to join John Knox in Switzerland. William Whittingham, who was a skilled linguist and worked for some time as interpreter to Sir John Mason, the English ambassador in Paris, was a staunch supporter of Knox and spent the Marian years in Frankfurt and then in Geneva with another Christ Church exile, Christopher Goodman.[25]

Bishop King, with his background as a Cistercian monk and Augustinian abbot, was a survivor through the Marian period, but other men appointed to the dioceses of the country by Edward VI were not so fortunate. By June 1554 thirteen of the twenty-three bishops in post at Mary's accession had been deprived; four went into exile, and four were burned.[26]

Those men who were clerics or theologians were obviously at risk, but there were others too who thought that making themselves scarce was a good idea. Thomas Randolph, appointed principal of Broadgates Hall in 1549, was a specialist in civil law rather than theology but became the object of complaints, not least because he sheltered John Jewel after Jewel's expulsion from Corpus Christi College.[27] On 28 June 1553 Randolph was given four years' leave to travel, a sort of self-imposed but formally sanctioned exile.[28]

Very few records from the Marian period survive in the archive at Christ Church. Decrees tightening up the roles of ministers and the precentor, with financial penalties for unsatisfactory service, were sent in March 1554.[29] Fines were introduced for non-attendance on Sundays and holy days, and every member of the House had to receive weekly tuition in the catechism in the north chapel.[30] The annual election lists in the Chapter Books are summary documents rather than the full registers of the Edwardian years, but we know from the retrospective deans' admissions books that there was a real exchange of men. Names were 'left out' of the college lists in considerable numbers, to be replaced by those whose faces, and religious convictions, fitted.[31]

One face that definitely did not fit was that of Archbishop Thomas

Cranmer. He had already been found guilty of treason for his support of Lady Jane Grey, but Mary wanted him to answer for his treason against God. Cranmer, Nicholas Ridley and Hugh Latimer were sent to Oxford to dispute with delegations from both Oxford and Cambridge. It was a show trial, which took place in April 1554. At certain points during the debates, which were on the presence of the body of Christ in the Sacrament and on the propitiatory power of the Mass for both the living and the dead, the essential points were translated into English for the benefit of the townsfolk, who were encouraged to shout the defendants down. At the end of the week all three men were condemned as heretics. As soon as the disputation was over, the University received a grant from Mary which tripled its income and allowed the restoration of the Schools, and Christ Church was given the rectory of Tring, in Hertfordshire.[32]

The executions of Ridley and Latimer were delayed a short while until Parliament passed the Act permitting death for heresy. They were tried in the autumn of 1555, stripped of their bishoprics and burned, close to Balliol College, on 16 October. Richard Smith, secure again in his regius professorship after Vermigli's exile, called them 'false martyrs'.

Cranmer's execution was a bit more problematic. Unlike Latimer and Ridley, he had been made bishop by the pope, so it was necessary to wait for approval from Rome. He was permitted to leave the Bocardo gaol, at the north gate of Oxford, for Christmas in 1555, but only into the house of Richard Marshall at Christ Church. Catholic scholars were lined up to debate with him over the holiday, and by the time he was returned to prison he was thinking about retraction. His efforts, including attending Mass, were useless, and the papal sentence was declared in the choir of Christ Church on 14 February. He tried again to recant, and this time it was accepted and a promise made for Masses to be said for his soul, but the sentence stood. Cranmer renounced his recantation publicly in the University church, and died, a Protestant, on 21 March 1556.[33]

It was not just a replacement of undesirable personnel that occupied Queen Mary. She restored the heresy laws that had been abolished by Edward and the ultimate penalty of death by burning, as we have seen.[34]

> CATHAR. VXORIS P. M. 196
>
> pertinet, quam aduersus quendam scio-
> lum coactus est subire, quàm aliquid no-
> ui habeant, præter ea, quæ in excusis eius
> Commentarijs luculenter habentur. Et
> tamen qualiacunque sint, cum opus habue
> ritis, pollicitus est R. D. Cantuariensis se
> daturum. Vale in Domino, & me ut fa-
> cis, in eodem ama: neque interdum pigeat
> de uestris rebus ad me scribere. Salutari
> meo nomine cupio Dn. Bathodium, &
> omnes nostros symmystas, preceteris autem uxorem tuam. Oxo
> nij 22. April. Anno
> 1553.
>
> Tuus ex animo
> Petrus Martyr.
>
> HISTORIA DE EX-
> HVMATIONE CATHA-
> RINAE NVPER VXORIS DOCTIS-
> simi Theologi D. Petri Martyris, ac eius-
> dem ad honestam sepulturam re-
> stitutione Oxonij facta iij.
> Idus Ianuarij.
> ANNO M. D. LXI.
> Cc 4 Iaco-

A page from Canon Calfhill's account, written in 1562, of the exhumation of the bones of Catherine Dammartin, wife of Peter Vermigli, who died on 15 February 1553.

Her first parliament concerned itself with the repeal of all Edward's religious changes: once again, the church came under the authority of the pope, Latin was reintroduced, as were all the daily services, and the new Prayer Book was scrapped. Her second parliament took things back even further, undoing all the work of her father.[35] During the summer of 1556 Cardinal Pole instigated a Visitation of Oxford to ensure that Protestant books and English Bibles were destroyed, and that Catholic teaching was foremost.[36] While some physical changes were irreversible, rood screens made a reappearance, and in some churches craftsmen were employed to carve and paint new statues. The trappings of Catholicism were reinstated at cathedrals across the country, and there is no reason to assume that things were any different in Oxford. It is possible that there was an attempt to restore

Frideswide's shrine at the instigation of Cardinal Pole, perhaps in connection with the exhumation of the bones of Vermigli's wife, who had died on 15 February 1553.[37] On the orders of Pole, because her bones were so close to St Frideswide's – and might therefore pollute the holy relics – Catherine's body was exhumed and placed on, or reburied in, the deanery dung-heap, where they remained until the accession of Elizabeth, when they were reinterred in the cathedral, together with the relics of Frideswide.[38]

Some things did remain under Mary, including the cathedral schools that had been created. Christ Church's school was small, being just for the choristers, with no grammar school for the boys to continue their education. It was as important to teach Catholic tradition as it had been to instil reforming ideas; to most boys in the schools this was new. For their teachers and clergy, and the country at large, the chopping and changing must have been confusing.

But Mary's reign was even shorter than that of Edward. She died in 1558, leaving England waiting for still more bewilderment under Elizabeth.

* * * * *

At the end of Mary's reign several dioceses, including Oxford, were without a bishop. King had died on 4 December 1557, to be buried in a splendid Gothic tomb in the cathedral, and although Thomas Goldwell, the bishop of St Asaph, had been nominated to take King's place, no successor had been appointed by the time of Elizabeth's accession.[39] Elizabeth called Hugh Curwen back to England after a tempestuous period as archbishop of Dublin to take the see in 1567, but he was extremely ill, never took up his place and died the following year. Then, possibly to divert the bishop's income to her own use, the new queen decided to leave things as they were. For most of her reign, except for the period 1589–92, when John Underhill, the former rector of Lincoln College, held the see almost entirely *in absentia*, the bishop's throne in the cathedral remained empty.[40] Instead, the management of the diocese was seconded to the archdeacon, John Kennall, who was a canon of Christ Church from 1559 to 1591 and received his income from the endowment.[41]

Elizabeth came to the throne in November 1558, and slowly the exiles began to return. Jewel, on his arrival back in England, wrote that he was astonished at Mary's success in overturning the Protestant church in such a short period of time, and was distressed that only two like-minded men were resident in Oxford.[42] But Elizabeth immediately instigated a programme of restoration and replacement on a scale that was actually more sweeping than Mary's had been. In spite of resistance from the Catholic bishops, Elizabeth and her parliament passed the Acts of Supremacy and Uniformity in the spring of 1559, and commissioners were sent to Oxford to conduct another reforming Visitation.[43] A couple of college heads – at Balliol and Lincoln – jumped before they were pushed, but four more were ousted by the Visitors, including Christ Church's Richard Marshall, who was probably not much missed even by the Catholic members.[44] Marshall's place was taken first by George Carew. Carew, from Devon, had Protestant sympathies – during the 1530s he had been a chaplain to Henry VIII, and then later to Edward VI – but his first loyalty was to the Crown. Although Mary had been cautious of him at the start of her reign, he won her over and survived as a clergyman, with livings and other church offices almost entirely in the south-west, throughout Mary's reign and into Elizabeth's. It was Carew who conducted Elizabeth's coronation Mass, leaving out the elevation of the Host on the orders of the queen, something no bishop was yet prepared to do. He was a safe pair of hands to oversee the beginning of the newly re-reformed Christ Church, but resigned the position in 1561 after being appointed to St George's, Windsor, as dean and registrar of the Order of the Garter.[45] Elizabeth installed Thomas Sampson in the deanery.

Sampson had been a reformer and spent 1554 to 1558 on the Continent. On his return he expressed some concern about the nature of Elizabeth's Protestant church; he did not like the royal supremacy or bishops or even vestments. So when the opportunity came to offer him a clerical position that was not a bishopric, he was the perfect choice. It was Sampson, rather than Carew, who removed the last traces of Catholicism from the cathedral, including statues, paintings, tabernacles and Mass books.[46] But Sampson, along with Laurence Humphrey at Magdalen College, continued to refuse to wear vestments, and paid the price. In 1565 he was arrested and deprived of the deanery, the first cleric in the new church to be dismissed for nonconformity.[47]

The Visitors to Oxford in 1559 were Thomas Bentham, who had been in exile under Mary, William Masters, another clergyman, and Stephen Nevinson, whose family had been close associates of Thomas Cranmer. Having been an academic, he was now to follow a career in ecclesiastical administration.[48]

In 1559 Elizabeth regained supremacy over the church, restored the English Prayer Book and reappointed the clergy who had been deprived under her sister. At least, she restored those who wanted to return to Edwardian Protestantism. Many did not, and in the three years after the Acts of Supremacy and Uniformity were passed the archbishop of York, all thirteen bishops who were still in office, twelve deans and over a hundred church dignitaries and canons were removed. Still more resigned. The change-over actually involved more men than in 1553 and 1554.[49]

At Christ Church, apart from the dean, Canon Richard Bruarne had to resign his regius chair – possibly because of a homosexual relationship with a pupil, Roger Marbeck – but he appears to have held on to his canonry until his death in 1565.[50] Interestingly, it was Marbeck who was appointed in his place.[51] Marbeck's appointment as canon was, perhaps, to be expected, but his survival at Christ Church seems remarkable. He had been educated at Eton College, possibly even taught by Bruarne, who held a fellowship there from 1548, and was elected to a Studentship at Christ Church in 1552. He took his BA and MA during Mary's reign, and although never ordained, he was given various clerical positions, including a prebendary at Hereford Cathedral and, in 1565, Bruarne's canonry at Christ Church. He was also appointed public orator – his Latin was elegant – with a significant salary, and elected provost of Oriel College. When Queen Elizabeth visited Oxford in 1566, it was Marbeck who gave the welcoming speeches to the queen, with which she was evidently impressed. But Marbeck blotted his copy-book, marrying the daughter of one of the city aldermen. Anne Williams was not just a Catholic but 'a notorious whore'. Marbeck resigned all his positions except his Christ Church canonry, and began to study medicine. He was appointed fellow and registrar of the College of Physicians, conducting his duties there and at Christ Church with diligence. In 1596, towards the end of his life, he accompanied Admiral Howard to Spain and wrote an account of the sack of Cadiz and the Spanish navy.[52]

William Tresham was unsurprisingly removed, to be replaced by James Calfhill. Calfhill had probably not left England during Mary's reign but had instead retired to the country. On his return to Oxford in 1561 as a canon and sub-dean, it was he who organised the reburial of the remains of Catherine Vermigli. While preparing a suitable site in the cathedral, he came across some bones in two silken bags and deduced them to be those of Frideswide. In order to protect the saint against future violation, he reburied the two women together and wrote an account of the event.[53]

Thomas Day survived in the third stall until 1567, when he was replaced by Thomas Thornton, tutor to Sir Philip Sidney. Alexander Belsyre, the fourth canon, had become the first president of St John's College, founded in 1555, but had retained his canonry. In 1559 he was deprived of both positions, from St John's for embezzlement and from Christ Church for refusing to acknowledge the queen's supremacy.[54] His successor was Thomas Kent, who had been a canon before 1553, but he died in 1561. Herbert Westphaling, who received the stall and the Lady Margaret professorship of divinity, was a reformer, and was one of the men who petitioned for the appointment of Sampson as dean.

Canon of the fifth stall was Henry Siddall, who had flitted backwards and forwards in his religious convictions as suited the times. Christ Church's Chapter Clerk in the mid-eighteenth century, James Gilpin, wrote of Siddall that 'all Ed 6ths reign he was a Protestant, in Q. Mary's a Papist & in Q Elizabeths a Protestant again'. Gilpin acknowledged, however, that Siddall was a very good Treasurer during the period of great scarcity of corn, and within three years he had pulled the college out of debt. Siddall remained a canon until 1572.

James Courthopp, in the sixth canonry, had defended the Catholic cause against Ridley during the 1554 disputation but had also been a good friend to the Protestant Jewel. He died in 1557, and William Chedsey, firmly Catholic, took his place as canon and as president of Corpus Christi College. He was deprived by the Visitors in 1559, and Robert Bankes, who had been deprived of the eighth stall under Mary, was brought back. The last two canonries were occupied by Thomas Bernard, who had been deprived and then returned, and by John Kennall, soon to be archdeacon.[55]

The canons all had their own lodgings, several of them in the Great Quadrangle, which had probably been designed to house Wolsey's senior college officers. The quad became, in effect, the cathedral close, mirroring arrangements at other cathedrals. After the deanery, the next-best house was the one next door, followed by the lodging on the north side of the great gate (now partly the Porters' Lodge). The third- and fourth-best were the residences in front of the church and the Priory House. The remaining four were in Chaplains' Quad, the south-west corner of the Great Quadrangle and then the lodgings in Peckwater and Canterbury Quads.[56]

The residences were supposed, at least according to a 1546 decree by Henry VIII, to be allocated by seniority rather than by canonry, or stall. This caused complications from the very beginning. In theory, by a decree confirmed in 1593, when a canon died or moved on to pastures new, the man who had served the longest would move from his residence to a better one. If the canon decided that he would rather stay put, then the next canon down was offered the house. While this may have worked when the canons were unmarried, moving from one house to another was potentially very unpopular with men who were married with families (the clergy had been allowed to marry again after Elizabeth's accession). So it was not long before residences began to be passed to one's successor in the canonical stall without any sense of the 'ancient order for antiquities'. Debates over the allocation of lodgings continued from the sixteenth century all the way to the twentieth.[57]

By the time of Elizabeth's first visit to Christ Church, in September 1566, therefore, the Dean and Chapter were staunchly Protestant. The Dean was Thomas Godwin, a particular favourite of the queen – tall, handsome and clever. He had been educated at Magdalen College and was appointed headmaster of the grammar school in Brackley in 1549. On Mary's accession,

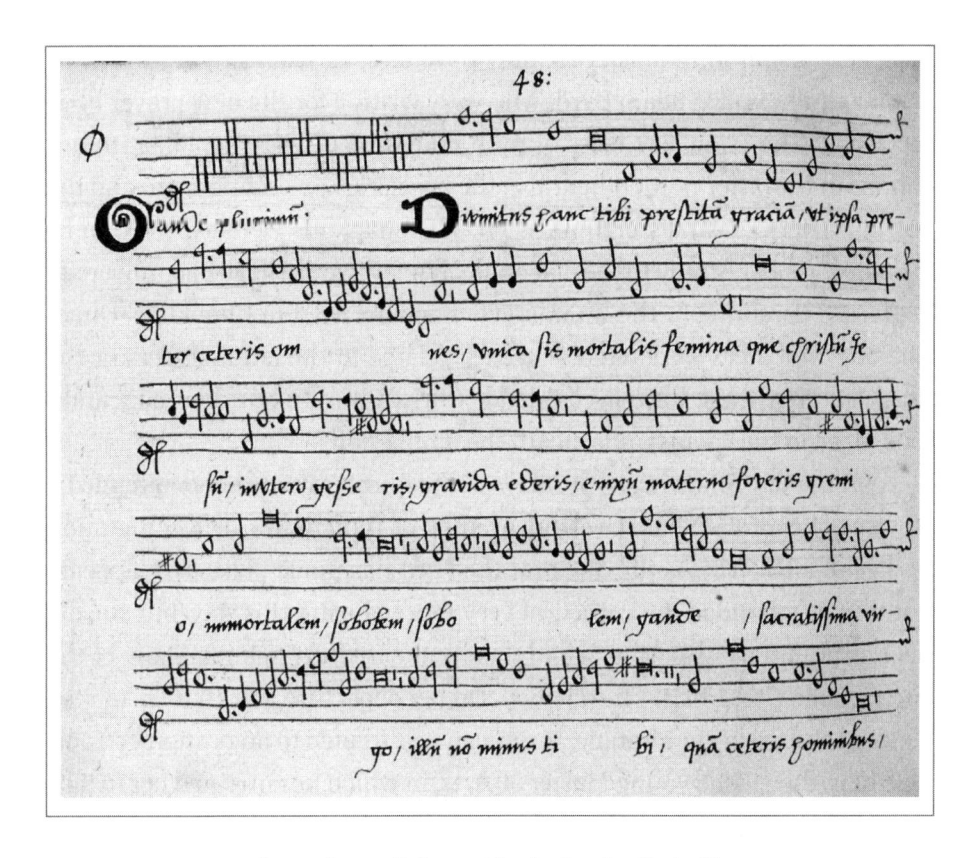

*A page from a Tudor part book, showing the treble
part of John Taverner's* Gaude plurimum.

rather than go into exile, he resigned his mastership and decided to study medicine, keeping his head down. In 1558, however, he was introduced to the queen, and his career was assured. Godwin's medical qualification may have come in handy during the royal visit; during the splendid plays that were put on for her visit part of the stage – a wall and some steps – collapsed, killing three men and injuring more.[58] On her first night in Christ Church, the queen attended services in the cathedral; psalms were sung, accompanied by various musical instruments, and the dean delivered speeches in Latin. Elizabeth, like her father, enjoyed traditional church music, which was permitted by the 1559 injunctions as long as it was modest. The choir, probably now in rows instead of gathered around a single book, as would have been usual in monasteries, may have already been singing works by Thomas Tallis and William Byrd, who were writing for the new prayer book services.[59] The choir at Christ Church consisted of the chaplains (minor canons in the other new cathedrals), the lay clerks, or singing men, and the boy choristers – usually eight of each. The chaplains were expected to be ordained, probably only to the diaconate, but few would have had university degrees.[60] Presumably, the unmarried chaplains lived in Chaplains' Quad. The boy choristers were often, it seems, related to the adult singers or the organist. They must have lived outside Christ Church, but their education took place in the rooms underneath the dining hall.[61]

On the day following, a Sunday, all the queen's counsellors attended a service to hear Dr William Overton, a canon of Winchester, deliver a sermon on Psalm 118, 'This is the day that the Lord has made'. Elizabeth appears not to have attended the cathedral very much during this stay, but she did hear disputations in St Mary's and then in the Divinity School. Many of the participants were Christ Church men. On her departure, after a week of residence in the Great Quadrangle, the queen was treated to an oration by Tobie Matthew, then just a young Master of Arts, in which he entreated her to take care of the college, which 'her father established, her brother adorned, and her sister augmented'.[62] Elizabeth approved of the young man, and it was not long before he began to climb the clerical ladder. Ten years later Matthew was appointed dean of Christ Church, and thirty years after that he was made archbishop of York.[63]

The early years of Elizabeth's reign are badly recorded in the archive. The long series of disbursement books, apart from a single one covering a portion of 1548, do not begin until 1577, and the Chapter Books are more concerned with the administration of the college, and the annual election of Students, than with the running of the cathedral. In the 1570s orders were laid down to regulate all aspects of Christ Church life, including rules governing attendance at services and the study of the catechism by the students, chaplains and almsmen.[64] Many of the decrees of the Elizabethan era were made around 1577, just after Tobie Matthew had been installed as dean. It was not uncommon, any more than it is now, for a new broom

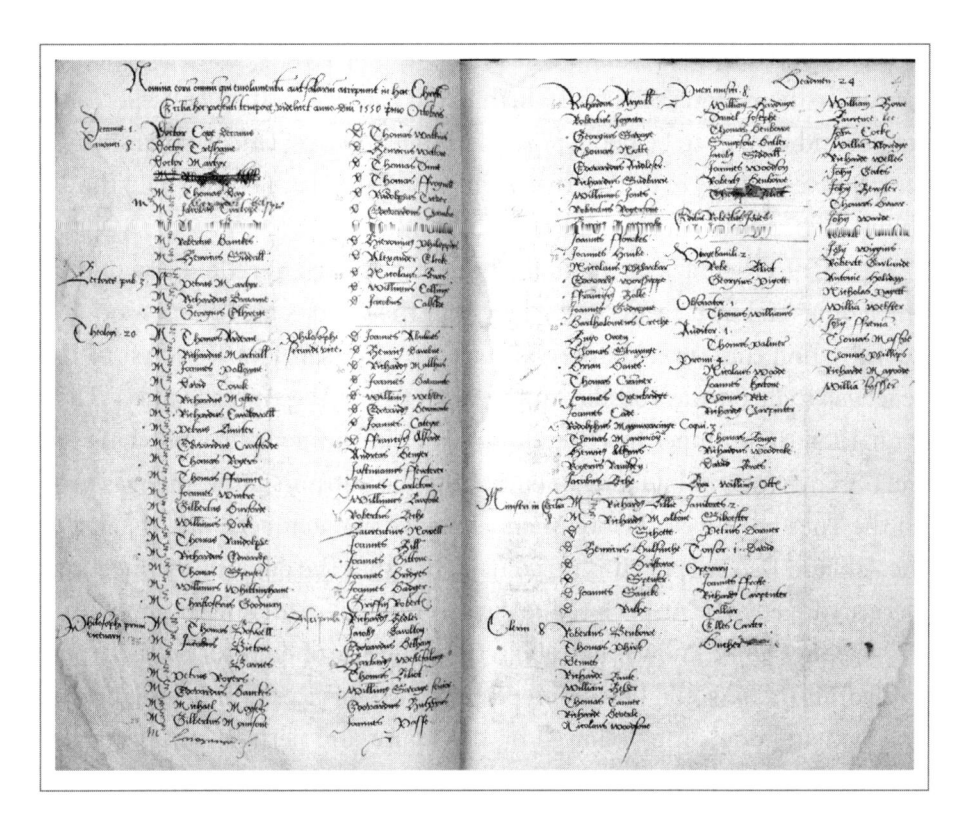

A list, dated 1 October 1550, from the first Chapter Book, recording the members of Christ Church who were paid from the endowment, beginning with Dean Cox and the eight canons and concluding with the college and cathedral staff, and the almsmen.

to sweep diligently into the corners, but Matthew was a rising – if not fully risen – star in the Elizabethan firmament, a man who worked vigorously for the moderate Protestant cause, backing the Chancellor, the Earl of Leicester, in his stand against excessive Puritanism as much as against Catholicism.[65] He laid down rules about the number of sermons Christ Church men were to preach in the parishes where they held the incumbency, about Bible reading and about decency and conformity to dress codes.[66] Candles were bought in abundance, and the bells were evidently rung frequently; the accounts are full of payments for bell ropes and baldricks. In 1582 seven psalm books were purchased for the choir, along with a new Great Bible, costing 20 shillings, to replace the original, which was 'torne and broken'.[67] Almost exactly a year later the canons sent back the bible to Garbrand, the bookseller, as it was 'found by use' to be badly printed in many places. One wonders why it took twelve months to discover this, but Garbrand was fair and paid the 15 shillings difference between the old Bible and the new.[68]

In 1590 the days for regular Chapter meetings were laid down: only one a quarter, but it seems very likely that the canons met much more frequently than that, over dinner, perhaps, or after services. The first of the year was to be on the Tuesday in the week before the Annunciation (Lady Day), then the summer meeting on the Tuesday immediately following the Act (or Encaenia) in late June or early July; the autumn gathering was to be on the Tuesday a week before Michaelmas (25 September), and the last at the Audit in December.[69] It is no coincidence that the dates of the meetings were arranged to be just before the days of rent payment and lease renewal.

Neither do we know much about the structure of daily services. In most cathedrals there would have been perhaps two services of morning prayer, one said and one sung, followed by the litany and perhaps ante-communion (half the service, without the communion itself), also in the morning. Evening prayer would have been conducted in the afternoon, before it was dark. On Sundays the same sequence may have been supplemented with full communion every week or just once a month. Sermons, delivered by the canons in turn, would have been heard on Sundays without communion.[70] There may have been separate services at Christ Church for the students too.

In some cathedrals lay people were discouraged from attending services until Archbishop Parker ruled that the public should be allowed to worship as long as they conformed to the newly established forms.[71] How far the congregation at Christ Church ever included people from outside the academic community is hard to say. In some ways the required attendance of young, unordained men and members of the canons' families, including their wives and children, may have made it more welcoming to lay folk, but the odd site of Oxford's cathedral, tucked privately within the bounds of the college walls, may equally have made it an offputting place to visit.[72]

The old cathedral, at Oseney, was being ransacked for materials for building. Henry VIII had given permission for the Dean and Chapter to use any lead, timber and stone from the abbey site, but it was an easy target for local people to raid for their own repairs.[73] So in 1582 the Chapter decided to move as much as it could manage from Oseney to Christ Church. It must have been a mammoth task, and the accounts report that carters were paid in one session alone for the removal of fifty-seven loads of freestone, and four of timber.

Some of this was used to build a west wall to replace the wooden planks that had closed off the end of the priory church after the fall of Wolsey. On 19 July 1582 William Pickhaver – who seems to have been the Dean and Chapter's 'go-to' carpenter at this period – was paid 3s. 4d. for four days' work bracketing on the scaffolding and for helping to take down the 'old board wall'. He also assisted the masons with the centring for the window. It took about eighteen months to build, and incorporated a huge new west window which looked out only on to the east side of the Great Quadrangle and can have been of little use as a source of light. While the builders were doing one job, the Chapter took advantage and made sure that full use was made of their skills. New stalls were made so that the canons could sit comfortably to listen to sermons, seats were repaired in the Lady Chapel and half-done work at the entry to the choir was finished off. Paving was laid in the church and the cloister.[74] One driver for this sudden rush of work may have been the imminent diplomatic visit of Prince Alasco (or Laski) of Siradia in Poland. It seems, however, that visiting the cathedral was not high on the prince's agenda; he did hear two or three sermons during his stay, but evidently preferred the fireworks in the Great Quadrangle, which he watched from his window on his first night, and the plays and tremendous pageantry on the following two.[75] Elizabeth's second visit to Christ Church was in late September 1592. This time, on the Sunday, she did come to the cathedral to hear the sermon given by Dean James.[76] Perhaps the cathedral was more comfortable this time round, with its new wall and window, and brand-new furniture.

Cathedrals, now the largest ecclesiastical bodies in the country, were useful for patronage and to extend royal control. Bishoprics were royal

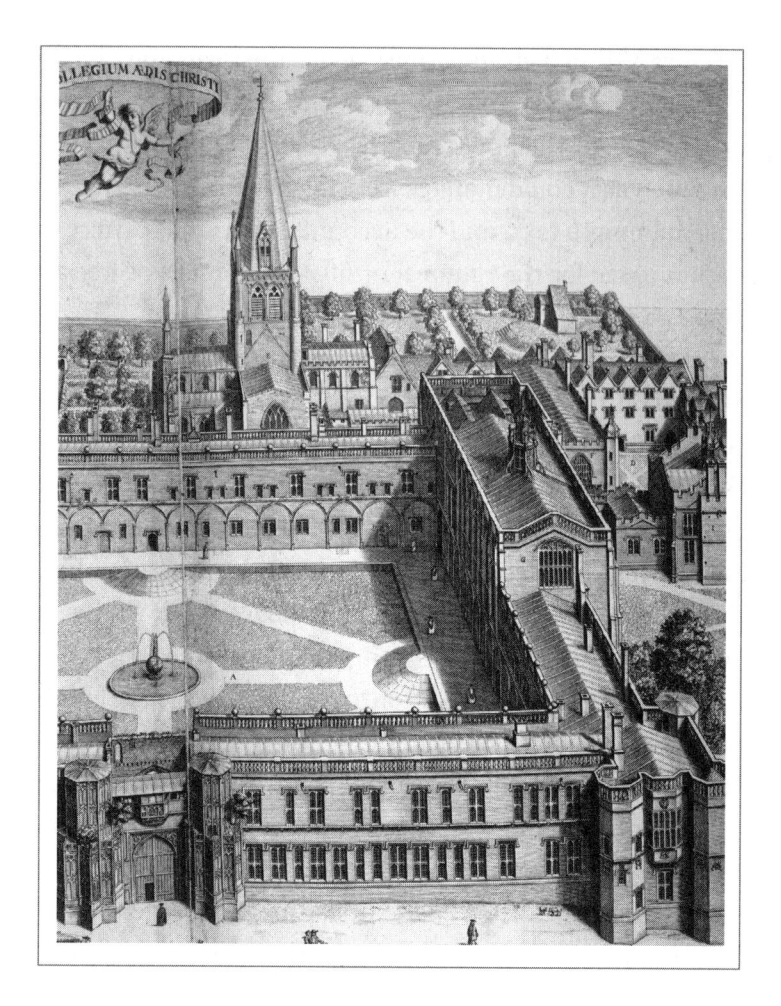

A detail from an engraving of Christ Church by David Loggan from the 1670s, showing the cathedral and the surviving priory buildings behind the Great Quadrangle.

appointments, but Oxford barely saw a bishop for most of the Elizabethan period. Cathedrals also served a purpose in education and poor relief in the absence of monasteries, although on a much-reduced scale. It was in the later sixteenth century that the word 'cathedral' began to be used on its own for the first time. They were still, however, unpopular in some quarters; more reforming Protestants wanted to see them abolished, and there was a suggestion that they could be a source of revenue to see the country through the war with Spain.[77] Christ Church was in a safer position than any other, with its dual function as college chapel as well as city cathedral acting, not for the last time, as a protective shield. Because it was a college chapel, Oxford Cathedral was not used for secular purposes such as a library, court-house, grand burial chamber or social centre, all functions fulfilled by other diocesan seats across the country.[78] Neither did it suffer a lack of income, supported as it was by the endowment granted by Henry VIII and augmented by Mary. But on this occasion all cathedrals survived, along with church courts and canon law, parochial patronage and traditional church music.

7

Revolution and restoration: the seventeenth century

Very soon after the appointment of John King as dean, King James I visited Christ Church in 1605. The monarch entered the cathedral and was escorted to the communion table under a purple canopy carried by six doctors of divinity, and two treble cornets were purchased for the occasion, at a cost of 53s., to accompany the choir and other musicians. Special verses were commissioned, in Latin for James and in English for his queen.[1]

Dean King was a reliable pair of hands, with impeccable Christ Church credentials. He was nephew of the first bishop of Oxford, Robert King, who had funded his education at Westminster and then at Christ Church from 1577. After graduation and ordination he was appointed chaplain to John Piers, who had been dean of Christ Church from 1570 to 1576. King was later given significant church positions in London, and became renowned as a preacher. Chosen by Archbishop Whitgift to give the first Sunday sermon at court after the death of Elizabeth, he soon found favour with the new monarch and with Queen Anne. He was popular with the Students of Christ Church, who petitioned for and supported King's installation as dean. Only a month later he was chosen as one of the chaplains to preach at the Hampton Court Conference of 1604, an event that was to secure the religious settlement of Elizabeth's reign.

In the last twenty years or so of the sixteenth century there had been some moves in favour of a return to a more traditional way of worship.

Archbishop Whitgift worked hard to maintain and enforce the Elizabethan settlement in the face of the Spanish Catholic threat. He was of the opinion that unity of religion was essential, and the defeat of the Spanish Armada in 1588 'proved' that this moderate Protestant way was right.[2] In the 1590s Richard Hooker, a canon of Salisbury Cathedral, began to write his eight volume *Laws of Ecclesiastical Polity*, a work that aimed to defend the ceremonies of the church and the Elizabethan prayer book. The Arminians, as they came to be known, encouraged reverence, particularly towards the communion table, as well as observance of liturgical seasons and festivals.[3]

There was some consternation and hope on both sides of the Protestant divide in 1603 with the accession of James I; the Catholics thought that James, having been born to the Catholic 'martyr' Mary, Queen of Scots, might be sympathetic to them, and the bishops were concerned that he might not uphold the Elizabethan settlement.[4] Would there be yet another upheaval in the religious life of the nation? The more radical Puritan faction jumped in quickly and presented James with a petition while he was still travelling down from Scotland to London in April 1603. This, which became known as the Millenary Petition, stated that the signatories wished to be relieved from the 'common burden of human rites and ceremonies'. Among other demands, they wanted the abolition of the sign of the cross at baptism, the ceremony of confirmation, surplices, the ring in marriage, genuflection and the reading of the Apocrypha in lessons.[5] James proposed a debate over which he himself would preside and in which he would participate – both referee and player. The Hampton Court Conference took place over three days in January 1604.[6]

The round-table conference was attended by both bishops and Puritan leaders. John Rainolds, the president of Corpus Christi College, was one of the more radical attendees. Christ Church was represented by the dean, Thomas Ravis, and Tobie Matthew, once dean but now archbishop of York, was also a leading light. The king evidently delighted in the debates but was firm; he trod a middle path, both anti-Catholic and anti-Presbyterian. As long as he was monarch, there would be bishops. Small adjustments were made to the Prayer Book, the catechism was extended and bishops were now required to ensure that their parish priests were properly educated. But the principal outcome of the conference was the commissioning of a new version of the Bible.[7]

The proposal came from John Rainolds, and a large body of around fifty revisers was established. It was to be based on the Bishops' Bible of 1568, which was less anti-episcopal than its popular predecessor, the Geneva Bible, but also less accessible. The bishops, particularly Richard Bancroft, bishop of London, were less than happy about this superseding of a text that had been approved by themselves, and Bancroft, having been overruled by the king (who saw that a Bible authorised by him would establish the idea of a national church) determined that he would set the terms of reference. It was Bancroft who chose the translators and gave them their instructions, which were conservative and not welcomed by the more Puritanical among them. He insisted that 'old ecclesiastical' words be retained – such as 'church' over 'congregation' and 'baptise' over 'wash' – and that any words that could be interpreted in more than one way were translated using the forms employed by the ancient fathers and by the tradition of the church.[8]

The chosen men were split into six groups: two in Westminster, two in Oxford and two in Cambridge. The regius professors of Greek and Hebrew from both universities were naturally included. Each group worked on an allocated section of the Bible and would then hand around their texts to the other groups for criticism and approval. The final version would be settled by the leaders of each group.[9]

The Oxford groups, which met at Merton and Corpus Christi colleges, were headed by John Harding, the president of Magdalen College and regius professor of Hebrew, whose team dealt with the Old Testament prophets, and by Thomas Ravis, who had charge of the Gospels, the Acts of the Apostles and Revelation.[10] Under Ravis were other Christ Church men, including Richard Edes, once canon of Christ Church but now dean of Worcester Cathedral, Canon Leonard Hutten and John Perrin, later to be appointed regius professor of Greek. John Harmar, who had previously been Greek professor and had produced the first book printed in Greek at Oxford (an edition of six sermons of John Chrysostom), was also one of the scholars. One of the two overall supervisors, and author of the preface to the Authorised Version, was Miles Smith, a canon at Exeter, who had been a chaplain at Christ Church for four years.[11] The preface explained that a middle route had been steered between Puritan and Roman, and the new version, which was published in 1611 – although never officially 'Authorised' – soon replaced the Bishops' Bible. The cathedral must have acquired one soon after publication, but the accounts record that a 'churche bible of the new translacione' was paid for by the Auditor, Philip King, in 1616.[12]

James I, then, rather than bringing yet more upheaval, began his reign as a peacemaker following the middle course of Elizabeth. Christ Church was at the forefront of religious life in the nation; all of its deans from 1558 had been senior Puritans with the ear of the monarch. Its members may well have been extremely proud of the deans and canons who had worked on the new Bible laid on the lectern. And just before the visit of James I to Oxford a bishop was installed – a novelty as, apart from a couple of years during Elizabeth's reign, the diocese had gone without for its first fifty years. John Bridges had established his credentials while dean of Salisbury by producing, in 1587, a mammoth work entitled *Defence of the Government Established in the Church of England*. The book set down a scriptural basis for the episcopacy but rather over-egged the pudding and became the butt of jokes and much criticism. He was appointed to the see of Oxford at the age of sixty-eight, perhaps as an acknowledgement of his long service as chaplain to Elizabeth and now newly to James.[13] He was resident in the diocese but did little. He died at Marsh Baldon in 1618, to be followed by John Howson, a completely different kettle of fish.

Bishop Howson had been a Student at Christ Church, and after appointments to canonries at both Hereford and Exeter he was appointed as a canon of Christ Church in 1601 and the next year to the vice-chancellorship of the University. He and William Laud, then a senior fellow at St John's College, were both summoned to the royal court to answer for their criticisms of the Geneva Bible's anti-episcopal annotations, and both were cleared. A few years later the king invited Howson to publish his sermons, which clearly steered a middle road between Catholicism and Presbyterianism, and he was soon appointed to the bishopric. He was alarmed at the state of the diocese and worked diligently to restore the teaching of the catechism, the use of the prayer book and confirmation as a rite.[14] He was concerned, among much else, to root out nonconformist practices, to ensure that parish churches were properly equipped for Laudian, High Church services and to confirm that schoolmasters were teaching their charges the correct grammar – that is, the grammar set out by Henry VIII – and to behave correctly in church.[15] Howson's relationship with the cathedral is not documented, except for the provision, by the college joiner, of a new 'wainscot pew' for the bishop in 1620.[16] As bishop and as an alumnus of Christ Church he ought to have been welcome to teach and preach in his diocesan seat. However, Bishop Richard Corbett, Howson's successor to the see, had been not just a Student but also dean before he was bishop, and even he was required to ask permission of Dean Duppa before he was permitted to ordain and confirm. Duppa insisted that this was a mere courtesy and that any reasonable request would not be refused, but Corbett was irritated and announced that he would perform his duties elsewhere.[17] The relationship between bishop and Chapter was never easy, made harder by the physical location of the cathedral within the curtilage of the college.

But these were internal and minor irritations. More widely, James's even keel was at risk. Perhaps the most famous of the Arminians, William Laud, had been given his first serious step on the clerical ladder in 1608, when he was made chaplain to Richard Neile, the bishop of Durham.[18] The position brought him to the notice of the court, and in 1610 Laud was elected to the presidency of St John's College amid some controversy but with the support of James I.[19] He began to climb the ladder, being appointed to the deanery of Gloucester, where his preference for the trappings of religious ceremony would be noticed. He and his patron Neile made changes in their cathedrals which were expected to be exemplars for their parish churches. By one side the two bishops were applauded for restoring reverence and focus to church services, but by the other they were seen as crypto-Catholics. Priests were to wear copes, bowing to the communion table was expected and men should remove their hats. One of the most controversial issues was still the position of the communion table. The new code of canon law passed in 1604 stipulated that it should be 'within the church or chancel', but wherever the priest could best be heard. Laud wanted it to be at the east end, with its short ends to the north and south, prominent with a fine covering and ornamented. There should be railings around it, and, now that the requirement for it to be portable had been removed, it could again be of stone or marble.[20]

A few changes were made in Christ Church during the 1620s, the most expensive and perhaps most Laudian being the provision of a new double organ and case in 1624, made by Thomas Dallam, probably the greatest organ-builder of the time. The organ itself cost £260, and there were additional expenses of its carriage to Oxford, the organ-builder's time and the making and decorating of the ringing loft above it, and of the staircase to the ringing loft.[21] At the same time, new paving was laid in the church, some leadwork was repaired, and 'posts' were painted. Seven yards of damask were purchased (at 9 shillings a yard) to make a cloth for the communion table, and a new Bible was purchased for 40 shillings.[22] Intriguingly, in 1614, the Chapter also paid for five hundred copies of the psalms as translated by the sixteenth-century Swiss reformer Leo Judas.[23]

In Oxford, Corbett was only briefly bishop; he was translated to Norwich in 1632, and replaced in Oxford by John Bancroft, nephew of Richard and a friend of Laud. He made sure that the archbishop's reforms were carried out in the churches within his diocese.[24] Having collated to himself the vicarage of Cuddesdon, just south-east of Oxford, Bancroft built the bishop's palace there; prior to this there had been no formal residence for the bishop of Oxford. Both parish and palace were to be held by the bishops of Oxford in perpetuity.[25] However, the first palace would not survive for long.[26]

Over the course of his reign, James began to move more towards Arminianism, and Corbett leaned towards conservative Protestantism more surely than any of the earlier deans.[27] Bishop Corbett and his successor in the deanery, Brian Duppa, whether or not there was any personal antipathy between them, were both friends with or at least aligned with William Laud. Both men enjoyed the patronage of George Villiers, Duke of Buckingham and the royal favourite, and Duppa was tutor and spiritual adviser to Prince Charles. It was Duppa who, perhaps to coincide with the appointment of

The doorcase of the seventeenth-century Cuddesdon Palace is the only surviving piece of the house, which was destroyed by fire in 1958. It was given to Christ Church for safe-keeping in the 1960s and was placed at the door between Killcanon and Blue Boar Quad.

Laud as Chancellor of the University in 1630, rearranged the interior of the cathedral, installing screens to separate the chapels from the transepts and commissioning a new set of windows from the brothers, Abraham and Bernard van Linge.[28]

Little is known about the alterations, as the disbursement books for the 1630s are missing, but there are a few accounts noted in the back of a receipt book from 1631. Marble steps, perhaps up to a newly elevated communion table, were installed, and a new stone floor was laid throughout by the master mason Nicholas Stone, replacing many grave slabs, some of which were alleged to have been used for drains in the Great Quadrangle in later years. The interior, including the timber roofs, was whitewashed.[29]

Revolution and restoration: the seventeenth century

Brian Duppa undertook the first major refurbishment of the cathedral after its foundation. Part of his work included the inserting of screens – with Renaissance doors and Gothic panelling – underneath the arches between the transepts and the chapels. The circulation of pilgrims to the shrine no longer being part of the church's purpose, the screens served to close off the chapels and create quiet, enclosed spaces. The screens survived until Scott's restoration.

Columns and rails for new windows were supplied, and the choir was wainscoted, creating the box pews which were much later described as 'third-class railway carriages'.[30] The van Linge windows are described in a long poem, published in 1656, and included images from the New Testament such as the Nativity, the Last Supper, the Crucifixion, the burial of Christ and Pentecost. The Old Testament was represented with pictures of the Fall of Man, the parting of the Red Sea, Abraham and the sacrifice of Isaac, Noah's Ark, Elijah's ascent into heaven, the burning of Sodom and Gomorrah, and two of Jonah.[31] New silverware was made for the cathedral, including an engraved silver ewer and basin weighing 111½ ounces, and a new verge.[32]

The box stalls rose about 11 feet from the floor of the chancel and, with the galleries added for the choristers, effectively blocked off any view of the chancel from either side. In the nineteenth century they were unflatteringly described as resembling 'third-class railway carriages'.

There was friction in many cathedral cities between the Chapter and the civic authorities, manifested in disputes over seating or order in processionals.[33] In Oxford, apart from the aloofness from the bishop, any touchiness may have been more between Chapter and University. Certainly, in 1617, the University complained that the way into the cathedral was inconvenient and that it was rather unbecoming for the senior academics to have to process up and down steps and through a tiny door on the south side, quite apart from the difficulties involved in manoeuvring coffins in and out. Proposals – unfulfilled – were put forward to make a new door in the west end, anticipating George Gilbert Scott's 'tunnel', which was knocked through the east side of Tom Quad in the 1870s.[34] At least this would have given a grander entrance, but once inside, especially after the construction of the screens across the chancel and the north and south chapel aisles, the cathedral would hardly have been conducive to comfort or grandeur. College services all took place in the choir, with everyone squashed in between the Jacobean pews; the public, if they came at all, were isolated in the nave or the dark chapels either side of the choir; and any University services took place just in the nave.[35] It must have been evident to all, even in the mid-seventeenth century, that Christ Church was not functioning as either diocesan cathedral or civic church.

In 1634, metropolitical Visitations were commissioned by Archbishops Laud and Neile to enquire into the condition of buildings, the residence – or non-residence – of the clergy, the leasing of property, the conduct of worship and the preaching of sermons.[36] Although there is no indication in the Chapter minutes that the commissioners came to Oxford, there is some evidence that Laud's men did arrive at the cathedral door. However, Laud was Chancellor of the University, and Laud and Duppa supported each other in their various appointments, so perhaps the commissioners found little to trouble them. Christ Church's buildings were in good condition, and Duppa was in the process of ensuring that they met Laud's expectations; the clergy were largely resident; the property was bringing in the income that was expected; and worship and sermons were governed as much by the demands of the University as by the church. If injunctions were issued, then no record of them survives.

At the height of his Personal Rule, Charles I and his wife, Henrietta Maria, visited Oxford, and attended private and public services in the cathedral, as well as being royally entertained with plays in the Hall.[37] He would have seen the beautiful new windows and possibly approved Duppa's new box pews and the stone screens which separated off the chapels of the north and south transepts from the remainder of the church, with the organ screen closing off the east end of the cathedral completely. Little did he expect that, within only a few years, he would be resident in Christ Church fighting for his beliefs and his throne.

But Archbishop and Chancellor Laud was making himself increasingly

A late eighteenth-century image of the nave looking east, showing the organ on its screen under the chancel arch, which, with the Duppa screens separating the chapels from the transepts, effectively excluded any congregation from services. Only University sermons were delivered in the nave.

unpopular, not least by his allegiance to Charles I. In 1640 new canon laws put the communion table back at the east end, surrounded it with rails and determined that this would be the place for the conduct of communion. It must have appeared a retrograde step to the more Puritanical in spite of the assurances that this had, in fact, been part of the Elizabethan settlement.[38] With the recall of Parliament in 1640, Laud's fate was assured. He knew that he would be the fall guy and made preparations accordingly. In 1641 he was impeached and, when judicial process failed, he fell victim to a Bill of Attainder.[39]

Cathedrals were immediately in the firing line at Westminster, not least for their substantial incomes, which must have looked tempting both to the greedy and to those who wished to use them for more charitable and useful purposes. In May and June 1641 debates were held in the House of Commons which allowed the case to be presented for and against the existence of cathedrals. On the merit side, supported by the Universities, who had their own MPs, cathedrals were a force for good in the community, maintaining sermons and schools, benefiting the local economy, providing employment for younger sons and paying their taxes. The demerit side suggested that deans and Chapters were not fulfilling their duties of residence, teaching and hospitality; they were not maintaining roads or caring for the poor; and they encouraged music, especially organs, which were papist. On 15 June the Commons resolved to abolish deans and Chapters.[40]

The validity of these criticisms varies from cathedral to cathedral. Christ Church certainly educated, although the grammar school was just for the boys of the choir; it also gave to the poor – the almshouse was maintained for twenty-four poor men (more than in any other cathedral), and other charitable giving at home and away is recorded throughout the disbursement and Chapter books.[41] The accounts also show that a regular contribution was made for roads and bridges, and Christ Church certainly offered employment – in the grounds, the kitchen and for domestic servants – and spent widely in both city and county.

On the outbreak of the Civil War, the negative ideas were reinforced by resentment that the cathedrals supported the king financially, and between 1642 and 1645 the Commons and the people began to attack cathedrals on all fronts. Laud's cathedral at Canterbury suffered violence and damage, along with Chichester, Rochester and Winchester. In August 1643 Parliament sanctioned this destruction with an ordinance that required the demolition and removal of anything that smacked of superstition. Once again, the communion tables were to be moved down the church, and there were to be no crosses, crucifixes or images. It hardly seems likely that many churches would yet have had the chance to put the table and rails back after the 1640 canon law was passed. There is little evidence, if any, that the communion table at Christ Church was moved up and down the chancel at the whim of prevailing thought. As the organ was very central in the cathedral, it would have been difficult to do.[42]

> ## King Charles's hay
>
> During the nineteenth century William Francis, the dean's verger, went up into the choir vault with a London architect (possibly George Gilbert Scott) to work out how the pendants of the vault were attached. The men discovered that there was a considerable quantity of hay stored there. The assumption, particularly as a local botanist identified the hay as of a type of grass no longer grown, was that it was stock laid in for Charles I's horses during the king's residence in the Civil War. The story has stuck, but it does seem extremely unlikely that anyone would have gone to the trouble of taking sacks of hay up into the cathedral roof when Christ Church had stables and outbuildings in abundance.

When war broke out in 1642, Christ Church was called into service. In August, Royalist troops began to arrive in Oxford, and for two or three weeks into September Christ Church scholars were joined by those of other colleges in drill practice in the Great Quadrangle and in building defences, and the king appealed to the University for financial support. The colleges responded, and more than £10,000 was raised in a week. The Parliamentary forces were not far away – in Banbury and Aylesbury – and in the confusion over the allegiance of Town and Gown, the Royalist troops left, leaving Oxford open. Colonel Goodwin, for Parliament, arrived in the city on 10 September. The colleges were disarmed, and any attempt to get plate or coin out of Oxford was foiled. Dean Samuel Fell had tried to ensure that his and Christ Church's property was safe, and had smuggled some across to a house in St Ebbe's, but it was discovered, and guards were put on the gates to ensure there was no further attempt to thwart Parliament. But only a month later Goodwin's soldiers were called away from Oxford to join the Earl of Essex. Oxford had not been garrisoned. The Battle of Edgehill, in Warwickshire, on 23 October, was indecisive, and both armies began to work their way towards London, with the king entering undefended Oxford a few days later.[43] He made Oxford his base and Christ Church his residence for the next four years. Charles resided in the Deanery; his 'parliament' met

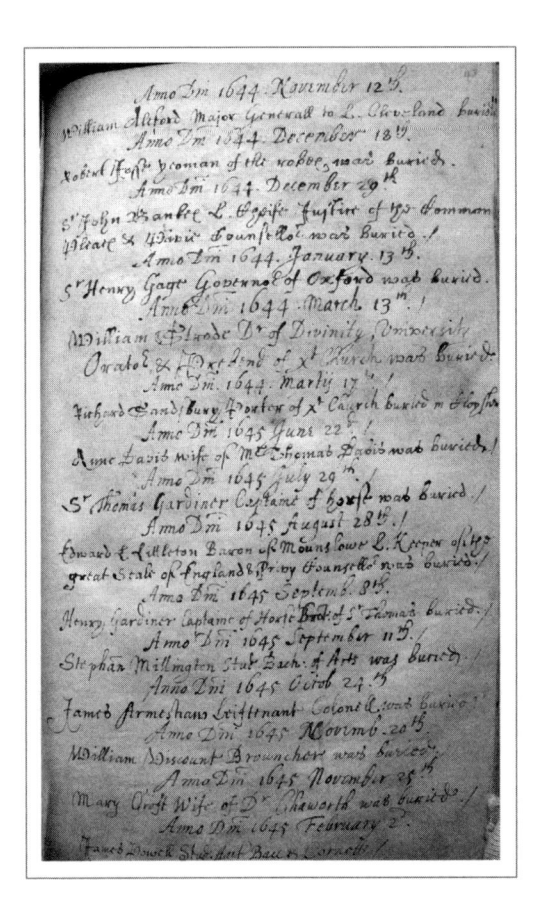

Revolution and restoration: the seventeenth century

The cathedral register of baptisms, marriages and burials is one of the few documents that give evidence of the court, college, army and cathedral all trying to operate together during the years of Charles I's residence. This page records the burials of everyone from the Christ Church porter to the Keeper of the Great Seal.

in the Hall; the Privy Council gathered in the south-west canonry; and the cathedral conducted the baptisms, weddings and funerals of members of the court and military.

At the Maundy service on 30 March 1643 the Lord Almoner, Walter Curle, bishop of Winchester, performed the *pedilavium* (washing of the feet), as was customary. The king may have presented the Maundy money, but he was not a regular attender at the ceremony. Monarchs often ducked out of the duty if plague was rife and, judging by the cathedral register of burials,

The pulpit is Jacobean, and made from oak by William Bennett, a local joiner. It is hexagonal and stands on a base or stem adorned with caryatids. The canopy is topped by a pelican, symbolic of the sacrifice of Christ on the Cross, which seems to have wandered around the cathedral. It is said to have been carved for an organ in about 1608 by John Bolton, and then moved to the bishop's throne until 1899, when it was put back on the pulpit.

Oxford was not a healthy place to be in 1643.[44] When attending services in the cathedral, Charles sat in the vice-chancellor's stall, made in 1614 by William Bennett, perhaps commissioned by or for William Goodwin, dean and vice-chancellor, whose epitaph records him as 'the good dean'.[45] And the sermons he heard would have been preached from the pulpit, created by the same Bennett.

In 1643 Parliament sequestered all the estates of Chapters that had contributed to the king's war effort. In 1645 the Prayer Book was forbidden and replaced by the Directory, and in 1646 bishops were abolished, although it was not until after the execution of Charles I in January 1649

> ## Cavalier monuments
>
> The eight monuments to men of Charles I's court and army were gathered together in the Lucy Chapel in the 1870s. More were buried in the cathedral, as can be seen in the cathedral register, but have no memorial.
>
> Sir Henry Gage and Major General John Smith were professional soldiers; Viscounts Grandison and Brouncker were courtier soldiers; William Pennyman was a Christ Church alumnus, a Member of Parliament and Governor of Oxford in 1643; Sir Peter Wyche was an ambassador and Comptroller of the King's Household; John Bankes was Lord Chief Justice, and his wife held Corfe Castle for the king with her daughters and a very small garrison; Edward Littleton was Keeper of the Great Seal.

that cathedrals were abolished as institutions and their finances diverted. Only moneys for schools, almshouses and highways were retained, and the clergy were stripped of their houses and incomes.

But even this did not satisfy the more radical Puritans. In 1651 the demolition and reuse of cathedral fabric was proposed. Lichfield was chosen as the first to go, and the lead was stripped from its roof. Canterbury was to be next, but in the end cathedral buildings survived, albeit in varying states of repair, and often with fixtures and fittings that, by their Laudian or High Church nature, perhaps should have been removed. Many were used for secular purposes such as prisons, stables, workshops, billets and warehouses. Those that did remain available for worship became civic churches.[46]

Meanwhile, Christ Church was surviving the worst. Universities were exempt from the seizures of land and property, and Christ Church's dual nature protected the cathedral from most of the excesses. There had been another exchange of personnel with the Visitation of 1647, when sixty-one Christ Church men – from college and cathedral – were expelled. Some of the old soldiers and sailors in the almshouse were removed if they had served in the Royalist forces, and preference was given to those who had supported Parliament, such as Matthew Brown, appointed in October 1650, who had served under Major General Skippon and received such a severe wound,

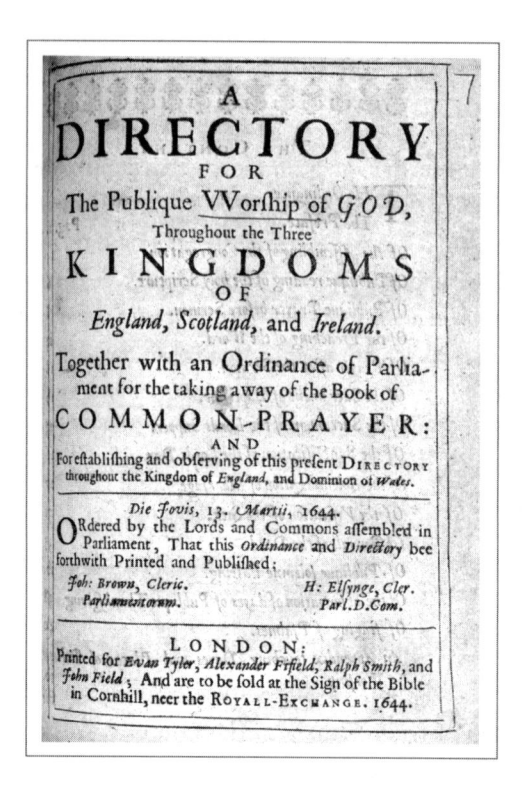

> A
> # DIRECTORY
> FOR
> The Publique Worship of GOD,
> Throughout the Three
> # KINGDOMS
> OF
> *England, Scotland,* and *Ireland.*
>
> Together with an Ordinance of Parliament for the taking away of the Book of
> ## COMMON-PRAYER:
> AND
> For establishing and observing of this present DIRECTORY throughout the Kingdom of *England,* and Dominion of *Wales.*
>
> *Die Jovis,* 13. *Martii,* 1644.
> Ordered by the Lords and Commons assembled in Parliament, That this *Ordinance* and *Directory* bee forthwith Printed and Published;
>
> *Joh: Brown, Cleric.*   *H: Elsynge, Cler.*
> *Parliamentorum.*   *Parl.D.Com.*
>
> LONDON:
> Printed for *Evan Tyler, Alexander Fifield, Ralph Smith,* and *John Field*; And are to be sold at the Sign of the Bible in Cornhill, neer the ROYALL-EXCHANGE. 1644.

The Directory for Public Worship replaced the Book of Common Prayer during the Commonwealth period.

perhaps at Naseby or at the siege of Oxford, that he was unable to continue his army career.[47]

The bishop, Robert Skinner, who had probably been with the king at Christ Church or in nearby Cuddesdon through much of the previous four years, lost his livings in 1646, and retired to his parish of Launton, near Bicester, where, according to his own writings, he worked tirelessly but carefully to maintain the Anglican prayer book service, conducting confirmations and ordinations.[48] Along with every other church and cathedral, Christ Church adopted the new service book, which 'directed' worship, as the name suggests, rather than supplying the whole service. Cathedral services were to be just on Sundays, and communion was now to be taken regularly and seated around a table.[49]

One of the other aspects of church life that disturbed the more radical

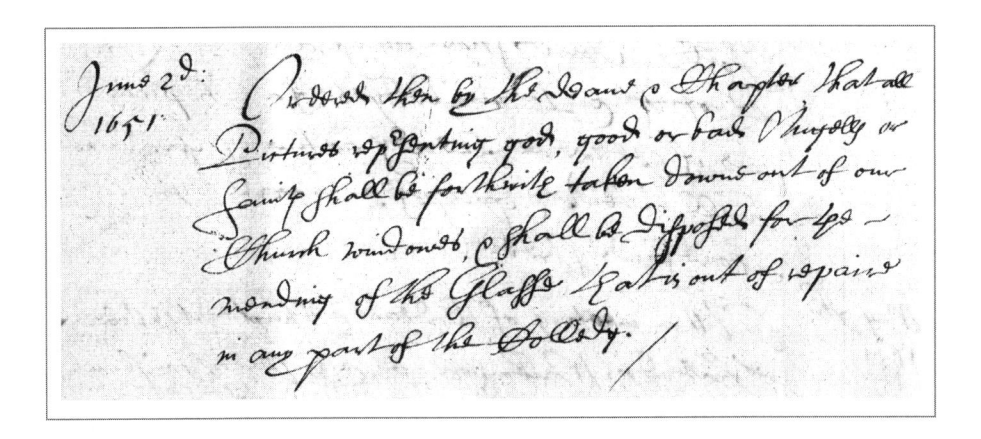

Chapter decree of 2 June 1651 ordering the removal of the stained- and painted-glass windows from the cathedral.

Puritans was music, particularly the presence of organs. From the earliest surviving disbursement books there are records of payments for the pricking out of musical texts, for psalm books and for service books. Then, in 1608, Thomas Dallam was paid £20 for a new organ and a carpenter called Keys made 'the case abought the Organs'. A carver and a gilder evidently beautified the joinery.[50] A much more expensive double-organ had been purchased, as we have seen, in 1624, and together with its screen it occupied the space under the chancel arch. But the organs were ordered to be removed in July 1649.[51]

The biggest loss to the fabric was the van Linge windows. On 2 June 1651 a decree was issued that 'all Pictures representing god, good or bad Angells or Saints shall be forthwith taken downe out of our Church windows, and shall be disposed for the mending of the Glasse that is out of repaire in any part of the Colledg.' Installed barely twenty years earlier, one of the greatest schemes of Flemish painted glass in the country was reduced to fragments, aided by the furious feet of the Puritan canon, Henry Wilkinson. The image of Jonah watching and waiting angrily for the destruction of Nineveh survived intact; Jonah's human frailities and the lessons to be learned from them saved the window. Jonah was very definitely neither God, angel nor saint.[52]

The new regime at Christ Church after 1649 is well documented in the Chapter book for the period. In fact, a new book seems to have been begun to mark a fresh beginning, starting with a meeting dated Thursday, 20 March 1649. Only five men were in attendance, including, at the head of the table, the new dean, Edward Reynolds, imposed by Parliament after the removal of Samuel Fell. Seated with him were four of the eight canons: the sub-dean, John Wall, along with Christopher Rogers, John Mills and Henry Cornish. These men were Presbyterian, rather than Independent, in leaning. Anthony Wood described the Presbyterians, rather disparagingly, as 'very severe in their course of life, manners or conversation, and habit or apparel'.[53] John Wall had been a canon since 1632 and had been deprived of his position in March 1648. He was the only member of the pre-Commonwealth Chapter to be reinstated by the Visitors.[54] Rogers, Mills and Cornish were all intruded by the Visitors: Mills had been Judge Advocate of the Parliamentary army but was deprived of the canonry in 1651; Rogers had been one part of the Visitation; and Cornish was renowned as a nonconformist preacher. The canons not in attendance at the meeting were: Henry Wilkinson, zealous Puritan and soon to be appointed Lady Margaret professor of divinity; Ralph Button, public orator and canon, although not ordained; Edward Pococke, oriental scholar and regius professor of Hebrew; and Henry Langley, who had been appointed University examiner for fellowships and scholarships.[55]

Their business was limited to two resolutions: to take special care to ensure that the stipends of vicars and curates in impropriated parishes be augmented, and to grant a Mrs Franklyn a licence of alienation as she had incurred high costs in building repairs after a fire.[56] The meeting is signed off by Samuel Bedford, the auditor. It signified the way that Christ Church's business would be conducted throughout the Interregnum: with almost no change at all. If anything, the management of the endowment was more efficient than it had been before. The Chapter book actually recorded meetings – seemingly much more regular than before – rather than just the election lists and installation of deans and canons that had made up the bulk of the first book.[57]

Reynolds had made a promising start in Parliamentary Oxford. He had been sent to Oxford to prepare the University for reform immediately after the departure of the king in 1646, and then was made a Visitor in 1647. It was Reynolds, no doubt, who had to deal with Dean Samuel Fell, a staunch Royalist who defied the Visitors at every possible opportunity.[58] The sixty-one Christ Church men who were expelled included all the canons and forty-six Students. Even the almsmen were investigated; all those who had served in the Royalist army were expelled and replaced by Parliamentarians.[59] On 12 April 1648 Reynolds was appointed vice-chancellor and dean of Christ Church, as well as receiving his Doctorate of Divinity. As dean, Reynolds began to put Christ Church's house into Presbyterian order. The organs had already been removed, but on 6 May 1650 he issued several decrees, one of which was concerned with the times of daily cathedral prayers. Reynolds noted that prayers had originally been scheduled at 10 a.m. and 3 p.m., but these had ceased; instead he instigated a full hour of prayer beginning at 5 a.m. and then again at 5 p.m. Academic disputations were to fit in around prayers. The services, including those on Sundays, were to be conducted by the chaplains.[60] As always, the academic and the ecclesiastical get muddled: all members of Christ Church were expected to attend daily prayers, both morning and evening, and senior members were to ensure that the young men of college dressed soberly and appropriately. Swearing was to be punished with a fine.[61] But, in spite of his work for Parliament, Reynolds refused to take the Engagement – the oath of loyalty to the government without king or parliament – and was deprived of his positions.[62] In his place came John Owen, an Independent. Owen was a local man, born in Stadhampton, with a father who he described as nonconformist. He was educated at Queen's College and ordained by Bishop Bancroft. In 1648 he was invited to preach to the army besieging Colchester and then to the House of Commons, where he came to the attention of the leading army officers and of Oliver Cromwell. He travelled to Ireland and Scotland with Cromwell, and on his return to London in early 1651 he was appointed dean of Christ Church, attending his first meeting on 9 May.[63]

Owen continued running cathedral and college in much the same way as Reynolds had done. His first tasks were to employ a new chaplain,

The Commonwealth Dean, John Owen, was appointed after Edward Reynolds refused to take the Engagement, and held the post until 1658. This image was engraved by George Vertue and published in 1721.

at the request of the Committee for the Reformation of the University, and to appoint Henry Wilkinson sub-dean. Chaplains who held MAs were also given the task of preaching in the college's churches in the immediate vicinity of Oxford.[64] Ralph Button was nominated as his proxy for those occasions when the dean was not in Oxford or otherwise occupied with duties for Cromwell.[65] Wilkinson and Button were, perhaps, the two most radical among the canons. Owen was a busy man: over the course of his deanery he sat on committees and commissions, gave sermons, wrote books and was appointed vice-chancellor. In 1654 he and his brother William were appointed to the Oxford commission for the ejection of ignorant and scandalous clergy and schoolmasters, and it is in this role that, although he was a true Puritan, Owen's moderation is evident. He intervened on behalf of

Edward Pococke, who had retired to his living of Childrey, in Berkshire, after being ousted from his canonry and professorship, where he had continued to use the Book of Common Prayer instead of the new Directory. Owen also turned a blind eye to similar house services conducted by John Fell just down the road in Thomas Willis's house in Merton Street. It was only when Robert South tried to use the Book of Common Prayer within Christ Church that he put his foot down.[66]

Owen was increasingly busy until the death of Oliver Cromwell in September 1658, so it is hardly surprising that the only minutes signed by him are those nominating his proxies. There is actually a gap between 4 March 1659 and 20 February 1660 when no minutes are recorded at all. The dean was tied up with the succession of Richard Cromwell and the chaos that descended with military rule, General Monck's attempts to restore the Rump Parliament, and the threat of yet more civil war. The canons were continuing to manage business without consistent record-keeping by the Registrar, or Chapter Clerk, John Willis.[67] The final notice of the Commonwealth period, dated 24 March 1660, announced the return of Edward Reynolds after Parliament's removal of Owen from the deanery.[68] Bell-ringers were paid for two days' work in the loft celebrating the return of the king, and a large bonfire was lit in the quad.[69]

Reynolds was a moderate, and actively promoted an episcopacy that would be acceptable to both Anglicans and Presbyterians, as well as assisting with the drafting of the Worcester House Declaration in October 1660, which granted 'liberty to tender consciences' and indulgence in some ceremonial matters.[70] Cathedral posts were promised to the most learned and pious *presbyters* of the dioceses. Charles's choice of word was deliberate.[71] The restoration of the Church of England at the heart of the country, as an inseparable and integral part of the government and lives of all the people, was expected and accepted, but the grandees of the Anglican community were less impressed by the enthusiasm for toleration held by both Charles II and his brother.[72]

Reynolds held the deanery for only a few short months before being appointed bishop of Norwich. He was replaced by George Morley, who had

The cathedral organs

In 1979, after all sorts of difficulties, a new organ, by Rieger of Austria, was installed and dedicated. It had been part of the dream of Dean Cuthbert Simpson, who had left a bequest to Christ Church in 1659 to provide for the choir. The new instrument was fitted into a screen and case that had previously been moved and altered on numerous occasions over the centuries.

We know that there was an organ at Christ Church, and at Cardinal College before that. John Taverner, the celebrated composer and organist, was appointed in 1526 to play and to prepare the choir for the grand opening ceremonies for Wolsey's new college. From that time forward, college accounts record the stipends of an organist and a choir master – very often the same man.

From the earliest surviving disbursement books there are records of payments for the pricking out of musical texts, for psalm books and service books. Then, in 1608, Thomas Dallam was paid £20 to make and supply a new organ, and a carpenter called Keys made 'the case aboughat the Organs'. A carver and a gilder evidently beautified the joinery.

Thomas Dallam was the organ-maker of choice in the early seventeenth century. His first major commission was for Queen Elizabeth, who had asked him to make and deliver an organ to the Sultan in Constantinople. He went on to build organs for St George's, Windsor; Norwich Cathedral; King's College, Cambridge; St John's, Oxford; Eton College; and the Scottish Chapel Royal. The next reference to an organ in the accounts is the purchase of a new and expensive double organ and case in 1624, also by Dallam. The organ was expensive and, with the associated costs of transport and decoration, and the expense of the making and decorating of the ringing loft above it and the staircase to the ringing loft, the total equates to between £45,000 and £50,000 in modern terms. The entry in the disbursement book seems to have been largely overlooked in earlier accounts of the cathedral's fixtures and fittings. From the 1630s the organ stood on its screen under the chancel arch. But, after the defeat and execution of Charles I in 1649, the organs were ordered to be removed, not to be seen again until after the Restoration in 1660, when it seems that one of the old ones was reinstated. It was another twenty years before Bernard Smith, known as 'Father Smith', was commissioned to build something more fitting. Smith was organ-maker to the king and worked across the country installing new instruments, and building the organ cases, in colleges, cathedrals, royal chapels and fashionable London churches.

In 1856, during Billing's work on the cathedral, the organ and its screen were moved to the south chancel arch and then, just a few years later, in 1884, they were moved to their present position at the west end of the nave.

Every newly arrived organist requested alterations to the organ, and over the centuries its case and pipes were cleaned and re-gilded on numerous occasions. Today Father Smith's 1680s case still survives in part, standing on part of the screen from the 1630s, with additions by George Gilbert Scott, and now containing the 1979 organ.

ODNB; Wood, *Life and Times*, i (1891), 347, 356, 358; Hiscock (1946), 216; CCA D&C viii.c.1/8; CCA xii.b.52; CCA D&C i.b.3, 1v; CCA xii.b.69, fol. 7

been a canon until the evictions in 1647. Morley's arrival, and the Restoration generally, was greeted with much celebration – bell-ringing, bonfires, a cavalcade and an escort of eighty horsemen – and yet another shifting of personnel in cathedral, college and almshouse. All but one of the canons, John Wall, were replaced.[73] Decrees were issued to take Christ Church back to the 1640s.[74] Like Reynolds, Morley was involved in the Worcester House Declaration and the subsequent Savoy Conference which reviewed the Book of Common Prayer, representing the Episcopalian side. Also like Reynolds, he was dean only for four months, before he was made bishop of Worcester. John Fell, who, with his friends Richard Allestree and John Dolben – now both canons – had maintained prayer book worship in Oxford throughout the Interregnum and had largely managed Christ Church while Morley was occupied elsewhere, was appointed the new dean. The spirit of Fell's father, Samuel, who had died of a broken heart the day after the execution of Charles I, ran deep within John, who had matriculated as a Student at Christ Church when he was only twelve. Restoration and refurbishment were high on the agenda. Another restoration was that of the bishop, Robert Skinner, who had also been deprived of his seat in 1647. He was appointed to the University Commission and set about vigorously purging both university and diocese, and ordaining large numbers of new clergymen to fill vacant places.[75] Surplices reappeared in the cathedral, the organ was restored and sung services recommenced.[76] The reappearance of surplices was not universally popular, however: Wood records that some were stolen from the cathedral and pushed down into the cesspit under the privy behind Peck 6 staircase.

Latin prayers for the college were re-established at 8.30 p.m. every evening, and communion services – with a preceding collation by the dean or one of the canons – reinstated on a monthly basis.[77] The Book of Common Prayer was used publicly again. Eighteen new prayer books were purchased in 1660, followed by more carried up from London in January 1662. The following September the vice-chancellor was paid for five further copies.[78] A damask cloth was purchased for the communion table, along with a wafer box, two new verges, mats to kneel on and ropes to rehang the candelabra.[79]

In other cathedrals the return of furnishings to the Laudian arrangement was probably more obvious than it was at Christ Church, where it is unlikely that much had changed beyond the ornamentation. Everyone was squashed into the choir for services, except for the odd member of the public who might have bravely entered the cathedral, or on those occasions when the University visited for a formal sermon. There would have been no room to move the communion table backwards and forwards as fashion and politics dictated.

In September 1663 Charles II visited. He followed in the footsteps of his predecessors from the eleventh century and, in the choir, touched for the king's evil. A touch from a divinely appointed monarch was long believed to cure scrofula, a swelling in the lymph nodes of the neck.[80] A decade later he intervened in a dispute between Christ Church and the University about the location of University sermons.[81] The University was thoroughly put out that Fell wanted sermons by canons of Christ Church to be given in the cathedral rather than in St Mary's. It was very inconvenient, as the cathedral was further away; it was difficult to hear anything, particularly in the north transept; the seats were uncomfortable; and the bell couldn't be heard from any distance away. That it was difficult to hear anything may have been a justifiable argument, and the seats probably were a bit hard – cushions were a novelty that seem not to have appeared for many years – but inconvenient? And surely the peal of cathedral bells, in a city without traffic, should have been audible for considerable distances? The king gave his judgement with the wisdom of Solomon. When the sermon was being delivered by a canon in his capacity as canon, the service would be in the cathedral; at any other time it should be at St Mary's.[82]

Fell's time in the deanery was marked by improvements to the physical environment of the cathedral and college. As soon as he was appointed, he set about building two new canons' residences on the north side of the Great Quadrangle. The space had been little more than a building site since the fall of Wolsey and the cessation of construction of the Cardinal's chapel. Samuel Fell had begun work, but the Civil War had intervened, and the supplies that had been brought in were soon commandeered for the building of the city's defences. In February 1662 there had been fierce gales, and much damage had been done to the roofs of all the buildings in the Quad, so there was work aplenty to be getting on with. The pond was dug in the centre of the Quad, the Broad Walk created, Fell's Building constructed and Chaplains' Quad repaired to accommodate new undergraduates, and Killcanon was built as another residence. Tom Tower went up over the great gate, and the eponymous bell was recast and moved there from the cathedral tower.[83] The cathedral church itself appears to have remained unaltered, although the dean did commission a beautiful set of communion plate to replace that taken to fund the Royalist cause.[84]

The archive is not rich in material concerning Fell's relationship with the cathedral. There were obviously some difficulties with some of the chaplains: Richard Berry was evidently a hot-blooded young man who was caught 'cooling his passion' with an apple-seller and then attempted suicide when he was separated from her; and two others were found to be interfering with the choristers.[85] Latin prayers were reintroduced at 8.30 p.m., perhaps in the hope that members would be caught inside by the 9 p.m. curfew before the service finished.

Robert Skinner was elected bishop of Worcester in 1663, and the Chapter books contain copies of the election papers for his successors William Paul and, shortly afterwards, Walter Blandford.[86] Paul had secured the bishopric through the influence of Gilbert Sheldon, archbishop of Canterbury and the former warden of Paul's college, All Souls. Paul was wealthy, and it seems that Sheldon was hoping he would invest in the rebuilding of Cuddesdon Palace, but it was not to be. Paul died in 1665. Blandford had begun his life in Oxford as a servitor at Christ Church, but by the end of the Civil War he was beginning to accumulate positions in church and university. He was elected to the bishopric of Oxford in 1665 but stayed for only six years. Through his connections to the Earl of Clarendon, he moved to Worcester in 1671. Blandford was not at the beginning of his clerical career, and so it appears that Oxford remained either a stepping-stone to bigger things or just a nominal position held alongside other, no doubt better-remunerated, offices.[87] Those who immediately followed Blandford were more of the same: Nathaniel Crew was a court favourite and high achiever who asked for and was given the palatine see of Durham in 1675, whereas Henry Compton was just beginning his career, having been encouraged by Fell to be ordained, and was then made canon and sub-dean with astonishing speed. Within eight years of his ordination Compton was made bishop of Oxford and rector of Witney, and the following year he moved to the see of London.[88] Perhaps it was these constant changes which prompted Archbishop Sheldon, shortly before his death, to recommend John Fell, whose attributes and achievements were already well known, for the see. Fell was to be the only man to hold both deanery and bishopric simultaneously, and applied himself to his diocesan duties as assiduously as he carried out his college, cathedral and University functions.[89]

Charles II died in 1685 and Fell in 1686.[90] For some years there had been concerns over the potential succession of Charles's brother, James, to the throne, and there was, for a short while, a leaning among nonconformists towards James, Duke of Monmouth, Charles's illegitimate son.[91] James II, like his brother before him, wanted toleration and, in his Declaration of Indulgence of April 1687, suspended all punishment for non-attendance and not receiving the sacrament. Archbishop Sancroft and his supporters were horrified; this would destroy the ancient influence of the church on the life of every man and woman in the country. The ultimately successful petition of the Seven Bishops, which declared that the monarch's declaration was illegal, was a nail in James's coffin but was also a sign that the old link between the crown and the church was under strain.[92] The king had a chance, after the defeat of Monmouth's rebellion, to retain popular support, but, like his father before him, he attempted to turn the country back towards Catholicism. He planned to put Catholics into cathedral posts and, on the death of John Fell, appointed the unordained John Massey to the deanery and other Catholics to positions at Magdalen College. It was an open attack on the Church of England and on parliamentary authority. But Christ Church was stuck; its loyalty to the crown – the Visitor – was observed.[93]

Massey's installation took place in the cathedral. None of the canons was willing to conduct the service, but it would seem that Henry Aldrich, the sub-dean, reluctantly took on the unhappy task. Massey was processed from the Divinity Chapel to his seat, where the first patent was read. This was followed by the royal dispensation from coming to prayers, receiving the sacrament, taking of oaths and all other duties as dean. The younger scholars found it all rather funny, but the senior men were grave as the farcical ceremony continued. At the end, probably as soon as they could escape, members of college, cathedral and University left the church, leaving Massey with just Obadiah Walker, the Catholic head of University College and once Massey's tutor, for company.[94]

The bishop during these turbulent two years was Samuel Parker. Parker was Anglican and Royalist through and through, convinced that both the Church of England and the monarch were divinely appointed. Although he was not a Catholic, his adherence to the crown brought him favour, and he found himself caught up in the religious and political controversies at Magdalen. When the college refused the king's Catholic nominee for president, James proposed Parker. Parker was ill and asked to be admitted by proxy. The fellows of Magdalen refused again, and installed their own candidate. The commission for ecclesiastical causes imposed Parker by force, and the infirm bishop took up his place as president for five months before his death in March 1688, probably brought on by a stress-related stroke. Parker and his successor, Timothy Hall, were two of the few bishops who had agreed with the Declaration of Indulgence of 1687. The canons of Christ Church were not best pleased with the appointment of Hall; he was very under-qualified, with little more than a BA from Pembroke College and a few minor church appointments, and they refused to install him. The University refused to grant him a doctorate too. Somehow, probably clutching his royal *mandamus*, Hall held on to the bishopric until his death in 1690.[95]

Both Walker and Massey set up Catholic oratories in their colleges.[96] Massey's was in the old refectory of Canterbury College. He appointed a Jesuit chaplain and seems to have made little impact on Christ Church at all. Anything with even a hint of Catholicism that was published by Walker and his acolytes was countered by Aldrich and his colleagues; graduate students refused to be ordained by Massey; and numbers of admissions to the college dropped markedly. James II visited in 1687, attending services both in the oratory and in the cathedral, where he touched for the king's evil, but the relationship between monarch and University deteriorated. When William of Orange came ashore at Brixham on 5 November 1688, there was almost universal delight. Massey left Oxford under cover of darkness on 30 November, and James fled the country in December and was deemed to have abdicated.[97]

Christ Church breathed a corporate sigh of relief. In Massey's place came the polymath and *bon viveur* Henry Aldrich. Aldrich had been at Christ Church since 1662, first as an undergraduate and then as tutor and canon. As sub-dean, he had largely run the college in the last years of John Fell's deanery, and it had been anticipated that he would be the natural successor to Fell.[98] He was a musician, a collector of books and prints, a practical architect, a mathematician and a logician. At his installation the traditional homage to the previous dean was left out of proceedings; rather, the documents proclaimed Aldrich to follow Fell as the Chapter had hoped just two short but terrible years earlier.[99]

Aldrich's installation as dean was followed shortly by the appointment of yet another new bishop, John Hough. Hough had been caught up in the battle at Magdalen College when the college fought the monarch for a non-Catholic president: he had been the fellows' choice.[100] In 1690 Hough achieved a double victory over Parker, being granted not just the diocese but also the presidency of Magdalen College. Like most of his predecessors, Hough's impact on the diocese and cathedral was minimal. Within nine years he was translated to Lichfield.[101]

Along with the rest of the nation and its church, Christ Church had seen a century of turmoil. There had been twelve deans, serving thirteen terms of office, and fourteen bishops, and it was time for a period of consolidation and then renewal. The collegiate side of the foundation certainly achieved that throughout the eighteenth century, with deans who restored and rebuilt both the physical site and the educational reputation. How far the cathedral flourished in the same period is another matter altogether.

8

Torpidity and tranquillity: the eighteenth century

The eighteenth century was a quiet period; the Victorians later viewed it as a period of stagnation, detachment and pomposity in the Anglican church. It has also been commonly held that the University was largely moribund throughout the period. But the seventeenth century, which had started with such promise, had seen nothing but turbulence, from the Personal Rule of Charles I through to the departure of James II in 1688. With England beginning to change dramatically, on the cusp of both agricultural and industrial revolutions, the church and the state were concerned about social unrest. There was a desire for stability and the established order.[1] Queen Anne was determined to end the turmoil and to balance the Tory and Whig powers of her government.[2]

Christ Church, as an educational establishment, along with University College, bucked the slump, and the eighteenth-century deans, building on the work of John Fell, put the college on an ever-rising academic trajectory. But did the cathedral follow suit?

Most, if not all, of the deans and canons were pluralists. At the top of the tree, several of the eighteenth-century deans – Smalridge, Boulter, Bradshaw, Conybeare and Bagot – held the impoverished bishopric of Bristol in conjunction with the deanery. William Markham was simultaneously dean and bishop of Chester. And, uniquely to Christ Church, several canonries were attached to professorships.[3]

The funding of the dean and canons at Christ Church – as at the other Henrician foundations – was rather different from that in other cathedrals. In the old cathedrals profits from specific properties were attached to individual prebendaries or canonries. At Christ Church, with its unique double foundation of college and cathedral, the endowment was attached to the whole body, and the sum of the profits from that endowment was used to fund the stipends of all 'foundationers', whether dean, canons, Students, choristers or senior staff. Dividends and windfalls – from timber sales or mining profits or entry fines, for example – were shared among the dean and canons to supplement their incomes.[4] The canons could also hold vicarages, for which they were obliged to fund curates, and many came from well-to-do backgrounds, often with personal incomes.[5] They were well housed and well paid. If they had interests in a specific area of the country, they often took responsibility for managing Christ Church's local estates on visits home. They were knowledgeable in worldly affairs and, judging by the Chapter minutes, when not overseeing the education of the undergraduates they took much time to ensure the uninterrupted flow of rents and profits into the coffers. The Dean and Chapter met regularly, in the Chapter House or the audit house, to run both college and cathedral.[6]

Henry Aldrich was a Tory, and firmly supported Archbishop Sancroft in his dislike of religious toleration. He was appointed to a commission in 1689 that was tasked with revising the liturgy to allow moderate nonconformists to be brought into the Anglican fold while still penalising those whose views were more extreme. This was known as 'comprehension', and Aldrich found it too hard to swallow – omitting ceremonies just to allow a broader church was not something he favoured, so he walked away from the discussions. A safe pair of hands, though, Aldrich was appointed as prolocutor to convocation in 1702, with the express wish of Queen Anne that he work towards moderation, not least damping down the more extreme views of one of his erstwhile Christ Church colleagues, Francis Atterbury.[7]

Atterbury, with the initial patronage of Robert Harley, an active and rising Whig politician, was appointed to the deanery after Aldrich's death. It took nearly a year from the first suggestion to actual installation, and in some

The memorial to Dean Henry Aldrich, who died in 1710, was set up in 1732 and includes a winged and wreathed skull representing mortality, immortality and the resurrection of a person of virtue and renown.

ways he seems an odd choice. As a tutor in the 1690s, Atterbury evidently hated the place. He had wanted to move on to bigger, more political, things, and his short period as dean of Christ Church was hardly successful. He made himself unpopular with his Chapter, not least because he ignored all traditions of both college and cathedral, and attempted to manage all affairs by himself without any representation to the canons.[8] It would seem that Atterbury was rarely in Oxford and, just as when Massey departed, Christ Church breathed a sigh of relief when the dean was installed as bishop of Rochester in 1713.

After the death of Aldrich, Christ Church suffered a series of short-tenured deans until the 1730s, with three dying in office and one, Boulter, moving to the bishopric of Armagh. George Smalridge benefited from following Atterbury into the deanery; he would have been hard pushed to fail.[9] Under his deanery, and those of his immediate successors (Boulter, Bradshaw, Conybeare and then Gregory), the system of education was overhauled. At the same time the college began to draw back from University and national politics, becoming less Tory and more Whig, while remaining a fashionable and high-achieving place to study.

It was under Bradshaw, in the 1720s, that two undergraduates became increasingly concerned about the general slackness of religious observance. There is some suggestion that there was a weekly communion service in the cathedral – not something that necessarily took place in every college – but Charles Wesley wrote home in January 1729 bemoaning the irreligiosity of Christ Church men: 'Christ Church is certainly the worst place in the world to begin a revolution in; a man stands a very fair chance of being laughed out of his religion at his first setting out, in a place where 'tis scandalous to have any at all.'[10]

Judging by the Chapter minutes of the period, it seems that Charles Wesley, and his brother John, had a point; the Dean and Chapter were continually dealing with impious behaviour among the students. But there seems to have been little happening in the cathedral to encourage piety. A set of William Croft's anthems was purchased for the choir in 1724, but apart from this there is barely a single minute recording any activity in the church. Those entries that do exist concern college activity rather than that of a cathedral: the Challoner divinity lectures were revived in 1751, and in 1761 a new termly lecture in the catechism – to be read in the Latin Chapel – was introduced for all undergraduates and BAs. In 1783 Bishop Butler was refused permission to prepare his ordinands in the Chapter House, much as his predecessor, Richard Corbett, had been a century and a half earlier. The Dean and Chapter were irritated to be asked for something that the bishop no doubt felt was his right, and the Chapter's refusal was received with both annoyance and a terse comment to the effect that the bishop had been elected to the see by the Chapter, at the recommendation of the king, and the Chapter ought to be discredited for their refusal.[11]

The only real upset in the cathedral during the eighteenth century was

Torpidity and tranquillity: the eighteenth century

Engraving by W. H. Gibbs of Charles Wesley, who, with his brothers John and Samuel, began the Methodist movement.

the dismissal of Thomas Lamprey, one of the chaplains. In 1737, having been a chaplain and responsible for the conduct of many of the cathedral's services since 1714, Lamprey was given notice to leave because he was married. He must have been rather shocked: he had been married for seven years, and lived openly with his wife and children. But he was not to be cowed. Lamprey took his case to the Lord High Chancellor, as representative of the monarch as Visitor. All the canons swore that a chaplain's place was void on marriage, but there was ample evidence that chaplains had been married before. The lack of statutes potentially proved a slight stumbling block, with the Chapter barrister suggesting that it might be awkward to prove one way or another. However, governance by custom rather than statute, as was Christ Church's way, worked once again in the favour of the Dean and Chapter; if Students were expected to resign their positions on marriage, then so should chaplains. The case was dismissed, and Lamprey had to pack his bags.[12]

As Christ Church rattled through deans for the first half of the eighteenth century, there was much more continuity in the diocese. William Talbot had been appointed in 1699, a Whig in a Tory cathedral. Although renowned as a good preacher, he was a wealthy, worldly man with contacts, and appears to have had little to do with his diocese. In 1714 he was made dean of the Chapel Royal, and the following year bishop of Salisbury. In 1722 he was translated to Durham. John Potter was a very different type of cleric; he was a Yorkshireman, a nonconformist until his conversion to Anglicanism, a servitor at University College and a classical scholar. Soon after his ordination, he was appointed chaplain to Thomas Tenison, the archbishop of Canterbury, and his career trajectory was assured. In 1708 his talents brought him the regius professorship of divinity and a canonry at Christ Church. Potter had reluctantly held the position of sub-dean under Atterbury and was expected to succeed Smalridge in 1719. He refused both the Christ Church deanery and, a few years later, the bishopric of Bath and Wells, perhaps holding out for a bigger prize. In 1737 he was rewarded, perhaps through the patronage of Queen Caroline, with the arch-see of Canterbury.[13] Potter was a good Christ Church man, taking on a task that no one else had wanted. He married while he was a canon – although apparently not in the cathedral – and his wife bore him ten children, of whom two were baptised in the cathedral and one buried there, but he seems to have had little impact as bishop.[14] Thomas Secker, like Howson before him, was a diligent and authoritarian bishop in his diocese, making several Visitations in spite of holding the bishopric of Bristol, a prebendary at Durham and the vicarage of the fashionable parish of St James's in Piccadilly. He resided at Cuddesdon during the summer months and spent considerable sums on the house, its gardens and the parish church.[15]

Throughout the eighteenth century cathedrals across the country were adapting their buildings for the current fashion for regular communion and sermons, preferably held in the choir. Some were rebuilding and extending; others opted to take the service to the nave if large numbers of the public came to listen.[16] But little happened at Christ Church. Apart from a new window that had been installed at the east end in 1696 showing the Nativity, the eighteenth century was marked just by basic maintenance and the purchase of a few luxury items. Three new bells, paid for by the benefaction of a Mr Morgan and made by the master bell-founder Abraham Rudhall of Gloucester, were installed in 1741, which appears to have entailed a complete reconstruction of the bell-frame; the Latin Chapel roof was repaired in 1748; the cloister was whitewashed in 1759 and the cathedral in 1794; the organ was repaired and its pipes re-gilded. For college members, new velvet cushions were provided for the canons and noblemen (with cloth for the commoners).[17] Otherwise, the only additions to the church were new memorials, which only served to emphasise that this was a collegiate chapel rather than the diocesan seat.[18] The only nod to a diocesan function was a request by the Chapter in 1785 that the Treasurer provide a marble font with a silver-gilt basin.[19] Even if the font had been made, which it evidently was not, most baptisms in the cathedral were of the infants of canons.[20]

Among all the deans of the eighteenth century, it is surprising that Henry Aldrich, whose interest in architecture was practical and modern, and who was probably responsible for the design of All Saints Church on the High Street and repairs to St Mary's, did nothing to the cathedral.[21] He was certainly interested in services and in the music, singing in the choir as well as writing new pieces and re-setting pieces by the great Tudor church musicians.[22] Perhaps he was too busy elsewhere; after all, it was Aldrich who planned Peckwater Quad and the New Library, two major projects that were to transform the physical nature of the college.[23]

It is also surprising that the cathedral remained relatively untouched in view of a burgeoning interest throughout the seventeenth and eighteenth centuries in the history of cathedrals.[24] Anthony Wood wrote his account of the churches and monastic establishments in Oxford in the middle of the seventeenth century, and at roughly the same time William Dugdale published an account, with illustrations, of all the country's monasteries and cathedrals. In the 1720s Daniel Defoe commented that Christ Church Cathedral 'was lofty, but by no means deserves particular attention' and Celia Fiennes

• THE KING'S CATHEDRAL •

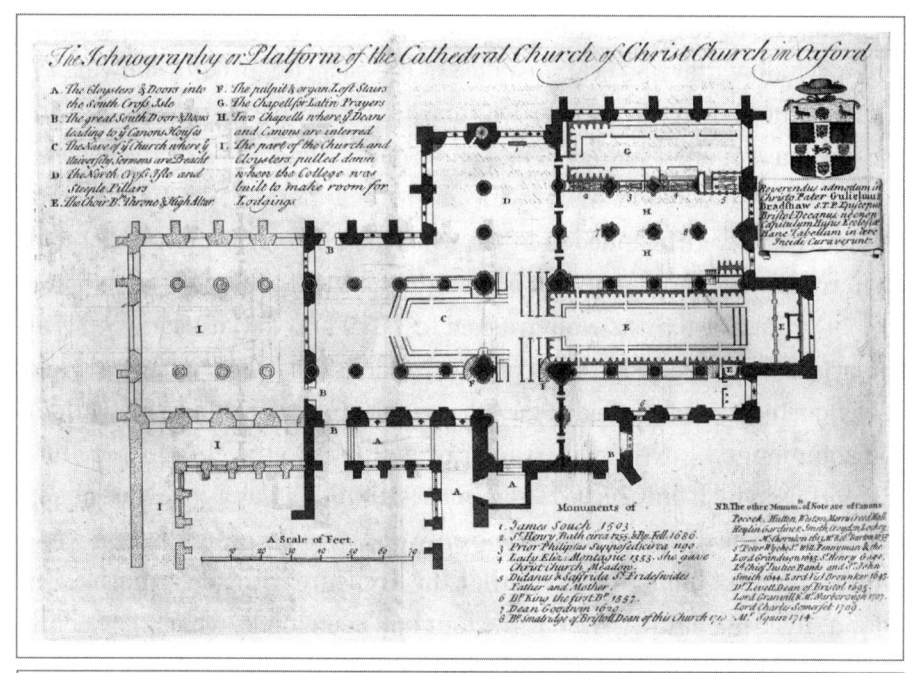

Two plates from Browne Willis's account of the cathedral from 1730, showing the ground-plan and the north prospect, which gives the impression that the cathedral is standing in a field.

merely remarked that Christ Church was large.[25] In the second quarter of the eighteenth century Browne Willis, who had been an undergraduate at Christ Church from 1700 to 1704, worked on his account of all the cathedral churches of England and Wales. Perhaps because he was an alumnus, Willis was less scathing than Defoe: he admitted that the cathedral was 'truly no elegant structure' and small, at least when compared with Oseney, but it was 'neatly wainscoted with oak'. The choir was paved with black and white marble and the remainder of the church newly laid with freestone. Gravestones that had been in the choir were moved out to the choir aisles, principally on the north. All but two had lost their brasses. There was an excellent organ, and the cathedral was generally kept in excellent repair.[26]

Unlike other cathedrals, there were no histories dedicated just to Christ Church. The Dean and Chapter did, however, have some sense of the importance of their historical records, even if they were not overly concerned with the history of the building: in 1772 Henry Keene was charged with converting the north side of the medieval cloister into an archive. For the first time the college and cathedral muniments were to be housed in one place.[27] The sash windows of the new muniment room, designed to fit within the late medieval tracery of the cloister walk, were an odd compromise between the classical and the Gothick.

In some ways, this mix-and-match style was all the rage, at least in the middle years of the eighteenth century, which were marked by the rise of Romanticism and the beginnings of a revival of 'Gothick' architecture. Lacock Abbey, in Wiltshire, was given a Gothic makeover in the 1750s, followed shortly by Horace Walpole's confection of Strawberry Hill. Both houses, though, retained classical elements and proportions, with just the application of medieval motifs. By the end of the century, however, the notion that the classical and the Gothic could be mixed had fallen out of favour, and when the west tower of Hereford Cathedral collapsed in 1785, it was James Wyatt, working in his favoured medieval style, who was called in to undertake the rebuilding. His work at Hereford, and at other cathedrals, was criticised for a lack of understanding of medieval architecture; he reorganised and 'tidied' interiors, which horrified men such as the draughtsman

The estimate from Henry Keene for the conversion of the north cloister walk into a muniment room, dated 1772.

John Carter, a Fellow of the Society of Antiquaries, who developed a deep and technical knowledge, and drew elevations and measured plans and sections for the society's Cathedral series. The two men did not see eye to eye.[28] But substantial changes at Christ Church would have to wait.

By the end of the century Charles Wesley's observations on services at Christ Church were still perfectly valid. John Byng, Viscount Torrington, recorded in his diaries that he attended 'evening prayers at X. Church, which was miserably performed. Our Church is terribly upon the decline, which as a gentleman and a Churchman, I grieve for; some management, or teaching, we should have for our money. Every minister of a sectary comforts himself with a deanery, whilst the slumb'ring Dean or the sporting Curate equally disgrace our Church!!' [29] Byng's views were held more widely; the richness and the torpor of the Anglican church would soon be questioned at high levels.

9

Reform and renewal: the nineteenth century

The early years of the nineteenth century saw increasing demand for parliamentary and university reform. Paralleling this was an increasingly loud call for something to be done about the church. John Wade's *Black Book* investigated and attacked the Establishment across the board, but began with the church, exposing its riches.[1] The lassitude and torpidity of cathedrals, which had prevailed since the Glorious Revolution, was challenged. Gentlemen travellers, such as William Cobbett – following in the footsteps of Daniel Defoe, Celia Fiennes and John Byng – saw wealth and worldliness partnered with tiny congregations. The bishops did nothing to improve the public image of the Anglican church when twenty-one of the twenty-six voted against the Reform Bill in the House of Lords in 1831. Once the Act was finally passed the following year, Earl Grey and his successor as Prime Minister, Robert Peel, established an ecclesiastical commission.[2] Peel's brother-in-law Lord Henley wrote a 'Plan of Church Reform' which suggested placing the appointment of bishops into the hands of a commission, paying bishops, in effect, a salary and ending movement between dioceses except to take an archbishopric. Again, the money saved would go towards new parishes and to help poor clergy.[3]

Whereas the great Reform Act had addressed the rotten boroughs, Peel's proposals for the church were intended to reposition the established church as an integral part of society while also promoting its core values and interests. The proposals included rooting out all unnecessary clergy – those without a cure of souls, such as non-residentiary canonries – and redistributing the wealth released by this to augment poor livings and establish new parishes in growing urban areas. It was not a universally popular move, and one of its chief opponents was Bishop William van Mildert at Durham. Van Mildert had been equally vociferous against the Reform Act and so, when the Ecclesiastical Commission was made permanent in 1836, his name was not included in the list of commissioners.[4]

Van Mildert died in 1836, and events moved on apace, supported by Archbishop Howley and Charles Blomfield, the bishop of London. Blomfield reported to the House of Lords that St Paul's Cathedral had a dean and three residentiary canons with incomes somewhere between £10,000 and £12,000 a year in total, and another twenty-nine clergy whose positions were sinecures. Just a short distance to the east, though, there were areas with one church and one clergyman for every eight or ten thousand people. The first report of the Commission (1835) dealt only with episcopal boundaries and incomes, but the second dealt extensively with capitular bodies (those headed by a Chapter) and their revenues. Christ Church was found to have the third-highest surplus of all cathedral foundations, after Durham and Westminster, of over £14,000.[5] Bristol, so often held alongside Christ Church, was worth only £3,000 per annum. Christ Church fought back, using its dual nature, pleading in a petition to the Lords that its canonries were different from those in other cathedrals and requesting that they all be 'retained for the encouragement of sound theological learning, which is essential to the welfare of the Church, for the general benefit of the University with which their Body is so intimately connected'.[6] Six months later, in December 1836, having seen the determination of the Lords and the Ecclesiastical Commissioners to reform cathedral canonries, the Dean and Chapter sent in a second petition. In it, they pointed out that Christ Church was the patron of a considerable number of augmented livings which would continue to benefit if the Commissioners permitted Christ Church to hold on to the profits of any suppressed canonries. It was allowed to hang on to its canonries, but one was attached to the archdeaconry and two more to

> ## The new diocese
>
> The 1840 Act increased the size of Oxford diocese with the addition of Berkshire and a small part of Wiltshire. St George's, Windsor, having been part of Salisbury diocese, now fell within Oxford, but the office of Chancellor, once held by the bishop of Oxford, was removed after Thomas Banks Strong was rather too outspoken during the abdication crisis of 1936. The Chancellorship is now held by one of the Knights Companion.
>
> The Ecclesiastical Commissioners wanted to add Buckinghamshire (from Lincoln) too, but Bishop Bagot felt that the county would make the diocese unmanageable. Bagot was translated to Bath and Wells in 1845, and the Commissioners took the opportunity to make the change. From being one of the smallest dioceses in the country, Oxford was now one of the largest.
>
> Warner (1924), 241; ODNB

the professorships of pastoral theology and ecclesiastical history. It was also accepted that the number of canonries would eventually be reduced from eight to six.[7]

And so the Cathedrals Act, as it was widely known, was passed in 1840, restricting the number of canons and vicars choral at all cathedrals, and fixing their stipends. Clause 7 of the Act specifically stated that, except in the matter of the annexation of the new professorships to canonries, nothing in the Act 'shall in any Manner affect or apply to the Cathedral Church of Christ in Oxford'.[8] The profits from suspended canonries, except at Christ Church, were to be handed over to the Ecclesiastical Commissioners, along with the separate estates of cathedral dignitaries. Somewhere in the region of £300,000 was released.[9] One Christ Church man who saw the value of these reforms was Edward Bouverie Pusey. He thought that in considering their duties and responsibilities, perhaps initially to fight the reforms, clergy would not only have impressed on others the importance of their roles but would also have learned a new appreciation of their offices.

The Dean of Christ Church through this period of national reform was

Reform and renewal: the nineteenth century

This bust of Edward Bouverie Pusey – theologian, regius professor of Hebrew and one of the leaders of the Oxford Movement – stands in the Chapel of Remembrance. The cross on the altar in the Lucy Chapel once belonged to him. There is also a floor slab in the nave commemorating Pusey, his wife and two daughters. Pusey's son, Philip, is buried in the garth.

Thomas Gaisford, who, although he had tutored Robert Peel, was anything but a reformer. Although he sat on the Ecclesiastical Commission, he held the living of Westwell (in Christ Church's gift) from 1815 to 1847, canonries at Llandaff and St Paul's from 1823 until his death in 1855, a further canonry at Worcester from 1825 to 1829 and the 'golden stall' at Durham, followed by the deanery at Christ Church from 1831. He was also regius professor of Greek from 1812 until his death. No one was required to give up their offices; 'surplus' canonries were suppressed only when the last holder died or moved on.

A sketch by Henry Liddell of his predecessor as dean, Thomas Gaisford. Liddell was renowned for doodling during meetings.

* * * * *

Throughout much of the eighteenth century, as we have seen, little was done to any cathedral buildings until after the rebuilding at Hereford in the 1780s and 1790s. By the middle years of the nineteenth century, just as their incomes were being reduced as a result of the Cathedrals Act, many of the country's cathedrals were in a poor physical state.[10] The Chapter at Christ Church had not been entirely neglectful, but, with only a couple of exceptions, work had definitely been essential repairs rather than planned restoration.[11]

Stepping in to advise cathedrals on their restoration programmes was the newly founded Cambridge Camden Society, established by undergraduates in 1839, which advocated a return to medieval Gothic architecture both in existing churches and in new buildings. The architectural changes advocated by the Society went hand in hand with a desire to return to a form of worship more centred on the symbolic and sacramental elements.[12] The Society issued a handbook, *A Few Words to Church Builders*, in 1839 and then in 1841 began a journal called *The Ecclesiologist*. Christ Church was

Details from Edward Burne-Jones's St Frideswide window in the Latin Chapel, showing the saint hiding from Prince Algar in a hut (at top) and administering healing to women (above).

The window at the east end of the Latin Chapel was created by Edward Burne-Jones. The scenes tell the legend of St Frideswide, beginning with her education by St Cecilia and St Catherine, and ending with the saint's death.

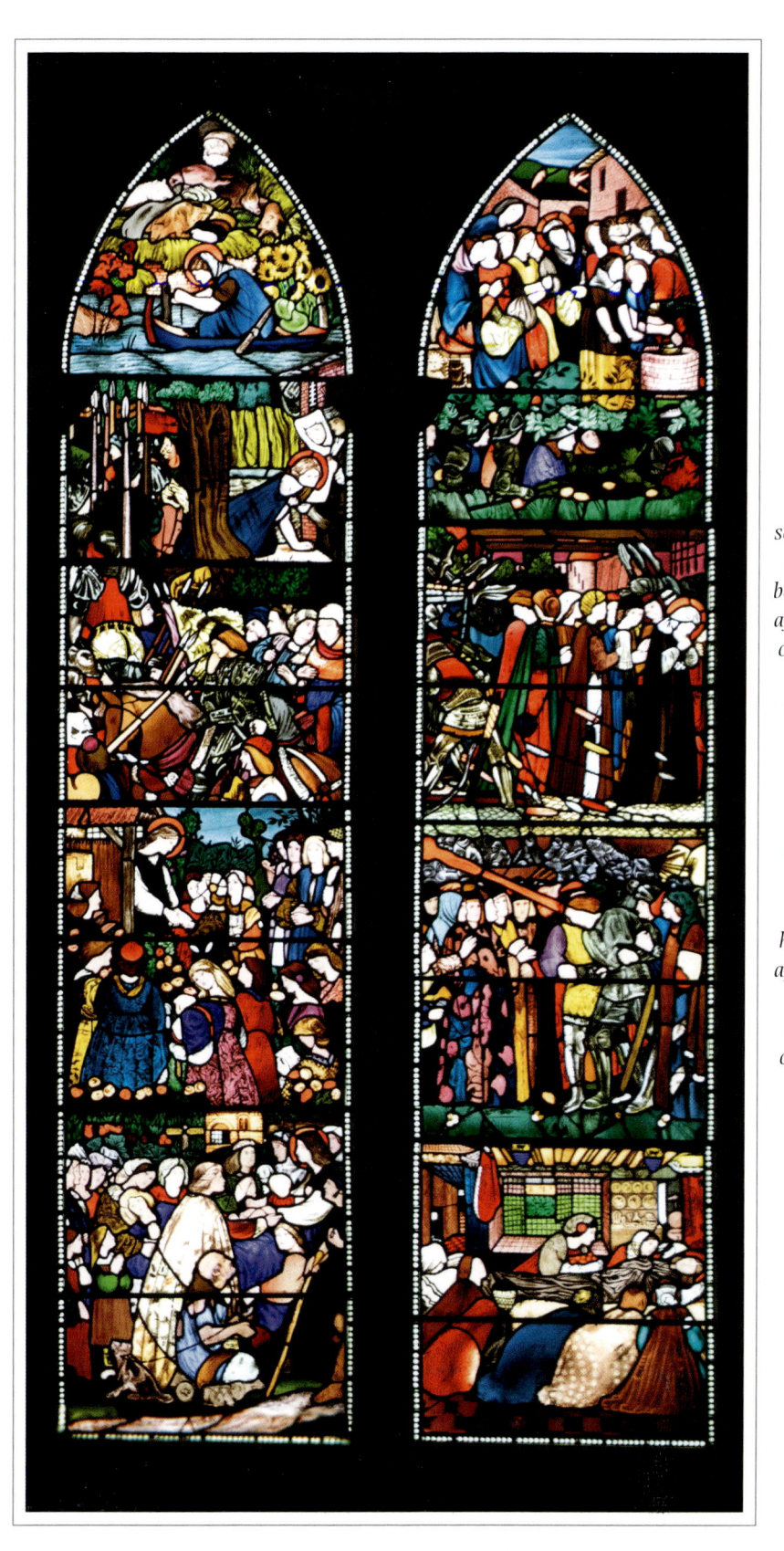

The final picture shows, in the background, what appears to be a flushing toilet, something which had only very recently become commonplace after the introduction of mains drainage at the time when the window was made. The top of the window, in the tracery above the story (shown in the top photograph on page 6 of the plates; not visible here), perhaps more appropriately depicts the trees of life and a ship of souls conveyed by angels.

Left: The Romanesque Chapter House doorway, showing clearly how the levels have been changed in the cloister and also the effects of burning, probably from the fire of 1190.

Below: Large monastic churches of the Norman period were generally built in three layers: a main arcade at ground level, then a triforium (arches in front of the aisle roofs) and then a clerestory to let light in. At Christ Church, which is only 40 feet high (low when compared with the 70 feet of Durham Cathedral), the triforium is enclosed within the arches of the arcade resting on giant piers to give an impression of height. The beautifully carved capitals of the lower arches are only on the aisle side of the giant piers, in order to give them an uninterrupted face.

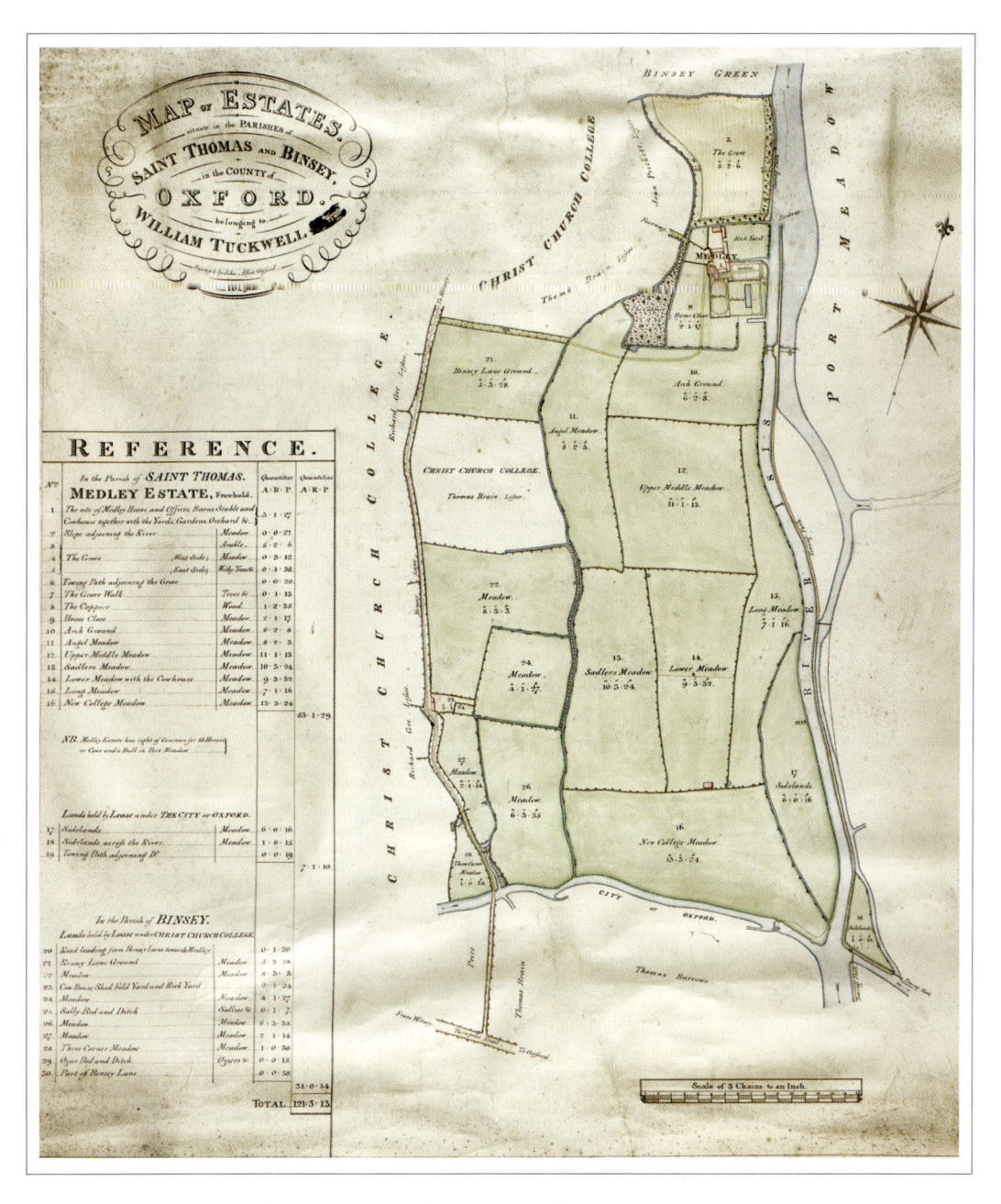

Map of estates situated in the parishes of St Thomas and Binsey in the county of Oxford, farmed by William Tuckwell. The Medley estate (plots 1 to 16 on the map) was given to the priory around 1138 by the burgesses of Oxford in exchange for stalls in good positions at the annual Fair.

The shrine platform, of which only fragments remain, dates from the second translation of the saint in 1289. The reliquary, which would have been covered in precious stones and made of gold or silver, was lost at the Reformation. Parts of the shrine were found in a well during George Gilbert Scott's extension to the nave, and other pieces then recovered from elsewhere in the fabric. It was reconstructed using wood to fill in the gaps and placed in the Lady Chapel. In the 1960s it was moved to the Latin Chapel to stand in the position thought most likely to be the site of the shrine after the 1289 translation. It was reconstructed again in 2002.

Lady Chapels became increasingly popular in the thirteenth century, and were often placed beyond the high altar at the east end of the church. Either this was not possible at St Frideswide's or there was a desire to build as close to the shrine of the saint as possible. The Lady Chapel at Christ Church is an example of Early English Gothic and has clusters of shafts in its piers, with deep mouldings and stiff-leaf carving on the capitals.

The central boss of the Chapter House ceiling shows Christ in Majesty surrounded by St Peter, St Paul, St John the Evangelist and St Matthew, painted c.1260.

Elizabeth Montacute (or Montagu) was the daughter of Peter de Montfort. She married Baron William Montagu and her eldest son, also William, a close companion of Edward III, was made Earl Salisbury in 1337; he died in 1344. Elizabeth died in 1354. Her tomb was evidently designed to be seen from all sides, and it is likely that it was moved from the centre of the decorated bay to its present position under the arch by Dean Brian Duppa in the 1630s.

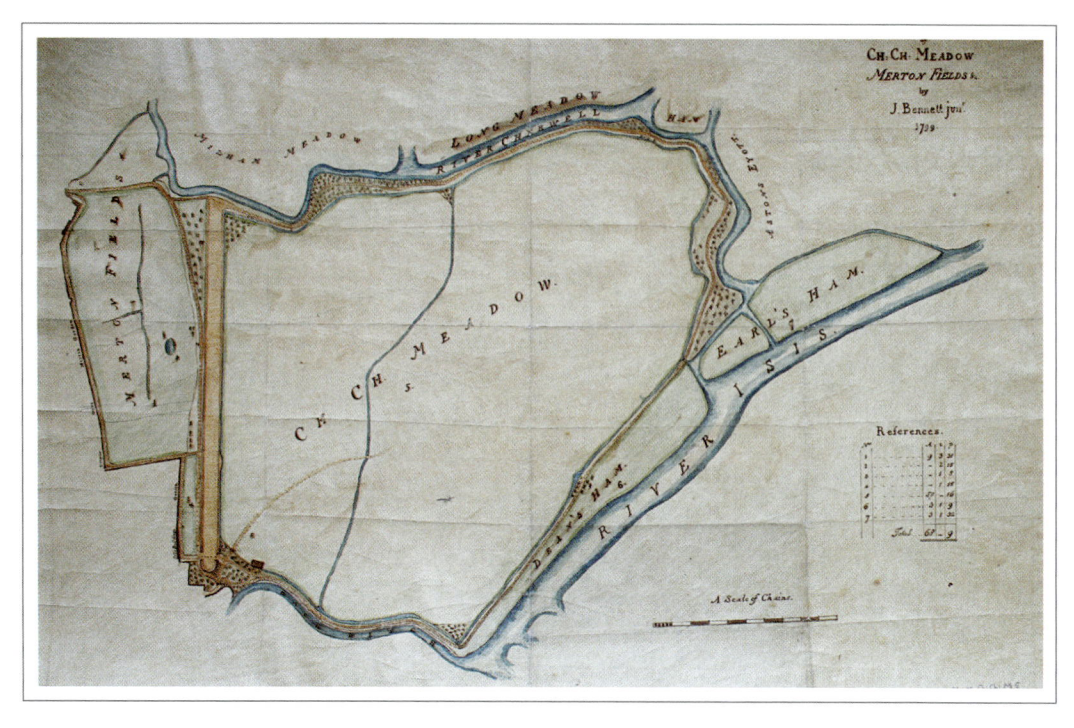

J. Bennett's map of Christ Church Meadow in 1799. Lady Montacute gave 46 acres for the maintenance of her chantry. The Shire Lake – the stream across the centre of the meadow – marked the line of the county boundary between Oxfordshire and Berkshire until 1974.

The Becket window in the Lucy Chapel, a rare survivor, contains the oldest glass in the cathedral, made in about 1320. The reticulated tracery is rare in its design, which begins much lower down the window than was conventional.

The St Catherine window in the Latin Chapel. Catherine was tortured on a spiked wheel after refusing to marry the pagan emperor Maxentius. She is the patron saint of young girls, students, nurses and craftsmen associated with wheels. A second Catherine window is at the east end of the south choir aisle (the Chapel of Remembrance). It was designed by Burne-Jones and erected to the memory of Edith Liddell (one of the daughters of Dean Liddell), who died on 26 June 1876 and is buried in the garth.

The construction date of the fifteenth-century Perpendicular 'watching loft' is rather late for it to have been used for this purpose (two hundred years after the second translation of Frideswide's relics). It is more likely to have been a chantry chapel for Sir Robert Danvers, Justice of the Common Pleas, whose wife is buried beneath. The site, close to the shrine, would have been chosen at around the same time as the saint's re-sanctification at St Paul's in 1480. The loft was repaired and conserved in 2009.

The beautiful choir roof consists of an arrangement of lierne ribs across the vault, terminating in pierced pendants. Its date is disputed; long thought to have been constructed by William Orchard in the very late fifteenth century, it is now considered to be from a century earlier.

Above: Bishop King's tomb, originally in the chancel and then set into the wall of the south choir aisle before a final move to stand between the aisle and the Lucy Chapel. It is of Purbeck marble and medieval in style, unlike the seventeenth-century Rococo memorials surrounding it.

Left: A late eighteenth- or early nineteenth-century watercolour of the north transept, showing clearly the Duppa screens, the aborted early sixteenth-century alterations to the clerestory and the split capitals of the triforium.

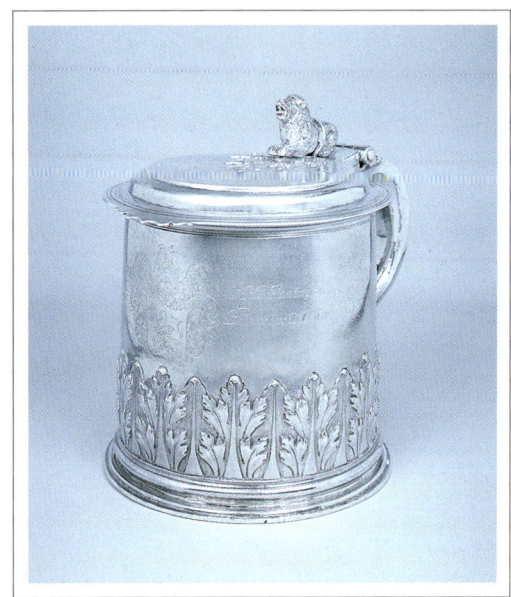

Items of the chapel set given to Christ Church by John Fell after the Restoration to replace the set 'loaned' to Charles I. The silver-gilt pieces are hallmarked between 1660 and 1662.

The St Michael window, by Clayton and Bell, was installed in the north transept in 1875, in memory of the 8th Marquess of Lothian. Its design, with only one scene, is unusual and may be derived from the medieval glass at Fairford in Gloucestershire. The window had contained van Linge glass – along with a depiction of Jonah, one of the few sections to survive the Commonwealth – and showed the entry of Christ into Jerusalem. Bizarrely inserted within it was the Becket scene later restored to the Lucy Chapel by Scott.

This picture by Robert Buss (engraved by Day and Haghe) shows the chancel before Billing and then Scott started work with the Duppa stalls, concealing much of the Norman masonry. The undergraduates are squashed unceremoniously into cross pews, with the senior members looking down on them from the stalls. The window at the east end is the late seventeenth-century Price window showing the Nativity.

Designed by Burne-Jones, and unusually signed by him, this window was installed in the Lady Chapel in 1872/3 in memory of an undergraduate, Frederick Vyner, who was captured and killed by Greek brigands in 1870. The figures in the window represent Samuel, David, John the Evangelist and Timothy. The windows were painted by Charles Fairfax-Murray.

The Virtues window in the south nave aisle, also by Burne-Jones, is dedicated to the memory of Edward Denison, an alumnus of Christ Church who was a pioneer of missions to the East End of London. He died young, and Dean Liddell took on the mantle, chairing the Christ Church Mission in Poplar. His daughter, Alice, carved the door for a new church in the parish dedicated to St Frideswide. The church was destroyed in the Blitz, but the door was saved and is now at St Frideswide's Church in Osney.

The wheel window was created by George Gilbert Scott, based on evidence that he found in the masonry of the east wall, and funded by one of the Students, Henry Liddon. It shows Christ in Majesty, in the centre, surrounded by ten angels.

described in an article in the 1847 edition. The author, while in some ways fair to a small priory church that had greatness thrust upon it, did not intend to flatter at all:

> shorn of proper proportions and subject to every kind of barbarous usage, it has been on the one hand elevated in theory to a rank to which its architectural character did not entitle it, and has been thus made the subject of much unfair criticism; on the other its rank has been by many practically forgotten by its absorption into the college buildings, and consequently is all but unknown to many visitors and even some residents in the University.

However, in spite of its being largely Romanesque rather than in *The Ecclesiologist*'s favoured Decorated style, the author of the report acknowledged the cleverness of the design of the triforium (see colour plates), which gives the appearance of height in an actually low elevation.[13] He looked rather fondly on the small blocked arches in the east end of the chapels, hoping rather than believing that they belonged to the original Saxon church, bemoaned the blocking of the tower lantern by the choir loft, made no bones about his dislike of the east window of the chancel and was horrified by the verger's cottage built into the south transept. Perhaps unsurprisingly, the only part of the church that did meet with approval was the Latin Chapel.[14]

The Ecclesiologist was critical not just of the perceived damage to the cathedral fabric but also of its relationship, or lack of it, with the diocese:

> the result of its unhappy connexion with the Royal College has been that the true character of the chapter has been quite obliterated; the church has sunk to a college-chapel, from whose festival worship the laity are excluded, and which is probably the only cathedral in Christendom where there is never a sermon preached, or a communion offered, for the benefit of the people of the diocese.

The author continued: 'the insufficiency of room for the congregation at the sermons is a crying and a growing evil; and if the custom of preaching in the cathedral is to be continued, as is on many grounds plainly desirable, it is surely an imperative duty on its governors, for this reason alone, to restore the church to its fair proportions.'[15] Even the Dean and Chapter, writing to the Ecclesiastical Commissioners in 1854, maintained that the cathedral was 'nothing more than a college chapel' and a cathedral only in 'the legal acceptation of the term'.[16]

There had been a suggestion in 1842, in a letter from a Mr H. Coddington, presumably to the Dean, that Wolsey's work be swept away, the nave extended back to its original length and a new west front be erected. But Christ Church was evidently not quite ready for restoration on that scale. Dr Bull, the Treasurer, greeted the proposal with some disdain, calling it an 'extraordinary scheme' and commenting that Coddington had been 'a strange man in his day'.[17] There were plans afoot, too, for a new window at the east end to commemorate the tercentenary of Christ Church in 1846. This would replace the late seventeenth-century Nativity scene (designed by Thornhill, executed by William Price and funded by Peter Birch), which had already reduced the five-light arrangement to only three.[18]

But it was not until the arrival of the energetic and determined Dean Henry Liddell, appointed in 1855, that any real work was done to bring the cathedral up to scratch, both physically and liturgically. Liddell appears to have been interested in everything, rather as the earlier 'builder-dean' Henry Aldrich had been. His primary academic work was the production of a Greek–English lexicon, with his friend and colleague Robert Scott, but he was also an aficionado of architecture and art. He and John Ruskin were mutually appreciative in their early years at Christ Church in the 1830s and at the beginning of Liddell's deanery; the Gothic Meadow Buildings of 1863 may have been the result of a collaboration between the two men.[19]

Liddell's first task in the cathedral was to make the place more comfortable and accessible, and more conducive to worship, and he was intimately involved in the work.[20] The report in *The Ecclesiologist* in 1847 succinctly laid down the principal difficulty that has dogged Christ Church for centuries:

> The restoration of this church, should its guardians ever awake to a sense of its beauty and its degradation, would be a work of great difficulty. The two present uses of the cathedral are clearly inconsistent: the members of the overgrown college cannot be accommodated in

the choir with even common reverence and decency; if more room were provided by extending the stalls to a sufficient distance westward, the already insufficient space for the audience in the nave would be reduced almost to nothing; while to unite the two, and preach the Sermon in the choir, would be manifestly against ritual propriety [...] If S. Frideswide's is to perform with decency any one of its functions as cathedral, college-chapel, and University-church, a sweeping reform cannot be avoided. The nave must, at whatever cost, at whatever sacrifice, be restored to its proper dimensions, and the teachers of Theology no longer dwell on the ruins of the church they should protect. If the whole body of the College must be accommodated in the cathedral, that body must, at whatever sacrifice of collegiate splendour, be reduced to the members of the Foundation.[21]

This notion was, of course, unacceptable. Numbers of students were rising rapidly, and any suggestion that there be a reduction in college size would have been thrown out. Commoners had been part and parcel of the college almost from day one.[22] But something had to be done: the undergraduates were squashed on to benches in the chancel right up against the sanctuary rail, east of the organ, which stood on its screen under the chancel arch; the choir were precariously situated on a platform above the organ, with the bell-ringers still further up in the tower; and the senior members, noblemen and gentlemen commoners occupied Duppa's seventeenth-century stalls, which were so tall as effectively to exclude any members of the public from viewing any part of a service, let alone participate in it.[23] Before Liddell's time, according to Henry Thompson, his biographer, the function of the church as a diocesan cathedral had barely been recognised, and the bishop, on his rare visits, 'would slink into his seat from the side aisle as though he were almost an interloper'.[24]

The architect John Billing was commissioned in 1856 to oversee the work, which was undertaken by two local tradesmen, John and William Fisher. The contract was signed on 11 July and the work was to take no longer than eight weeks, at a cost of £620.[25] There was concern about destroying Duppa's work completely, so all the changes were made using the old timbers, with nothing new added at all. All the old woodwork was to be

> ## Burials
>
> By 1843 every churchyard in Oxford was full, and the need for new cemeteries had become urgent. There was also an issue of hygiene; overcrowded burial sites were potentially dangerous for the health of the city, and internal burials were increasingly frowned upon. Christ Church gave nearly five acres in St Thomas's to provide space for internments from the parishes of St Thomas, St Aldate, St Ebbe, St Peter in the Bailey, St Martin and St Michael. Areas would be assigned to each parish, with a separate space for burials from Christ Church. Oseney cemetery would be conveyed to the Commissioners for Building New Churches and duly consecrated. The garth, nestled outside between the south transept and the south choir aisle, was reserved for the burials of deans and those dying in college.
>
> Orme (2017) 203–4; CCA D&C i.b.10, 97 and 158; CCA MS Estates 140, fol. 140; CCA MS Estates 143, fols 158 and 354

dismantled, cleaned, marked and carefully stacked. Old stalls, possibly Wolseian, were placed in the Latin Chapel. Even the positions and layout of the floor joists and sleepers were carefully noted so that they could be replaced exactly. Care was also taken to protect the marble floor during the works.

The foremost task was the opening up of the chancel to the rest of the church. A major issue for *The Ecclesiologist* was the presence of the pulpitum between the chancel and the nave; opening up the nave appealed to the Victorian love of theatre.[26] Christ Church did not have a pulpitum as such, but the organ on its screen occupied the chancel arch, blocking the view from the nave to the sanctuary. Billing moved the organ around by ninety degrees so that it stood under the arch to the south transept, which gave a view from the west end to the new tercentenary window by the brothers Gérente at the east. The stalls for members of the college were extended westwards so there was no longer any need for the unsightly cross-benches. The choristers were brought down from their eyrie and could now stand safely on the floor in the crossing, and the non-college congregation were given new seats in the north transept.

Once the visual problems had been to some extent resolved, or at least improved, Billing turned to repairs and to comfort. The masons were required to repair the piers in the choir and tower, which had been considerably cut about in the 1630s to ease the installation of the stalls, with best Bath stone, taking care to match the existing mouldings. The half-columns to the three tower piers were to be completed to match the north-west pier. Perhaps most important, though, to the congregations, whether college or cathedral, was the new warm-air heating apparatus.[27] Cathedrals across the country were trying to make their congregations warmer and more comfortable, to encourage people to attend late evening services.[28] A new furnace vault was dug, which involved some 'underbuilding' of the nearby buttresses, and then the ground for flues was dug and the flues constructed, keeping masons and bricklayers busy from August to October – the schedule was sensibly arranged to avoid term-time and major festivals. Only a little carpentry spilled over into November. The work under the floor necessitated the lifting of memorial slabs and the protection of coffins. In August 1856 a stone coffin with a richly sculptured lid was discovered in the north choir aisle. The coffin contained a pewter chalice and paten, which suggested that the occupant had been an abbot or prior.[29] There was also considerable excitement when a large chamber, nearly nine feet deep and over seven feet wide, was discovered between the west piers of the choir. It was quickly labelled as a reliquary chamber, but its original use remains a mystery.[30] Once Billing's work was completed, the local newspaper waxed lyrical about the now visible and enhanced beauties of the cathedral.[31] The general public began to attend services in numbers previously unknown, and there were new demands on its space.[32]

Not long after Billing's invoice had been settled, a few more alterations were made, not the least of which was the installation in 1859 of the St Frideswide window in the Latin Chapel, which tells in graphic-novel style the legend of Frideswide.[33] John Bull, the Treasurer, had died on 21 February 1856 and had bequeathed £500 for two new painted windows, on the condition that they were erected within three years. Edward Burne-Jones, a friend of Ruskin and William Morris, was commissioned as designer for the windows, which were manufactured by James Powell & Sons of the

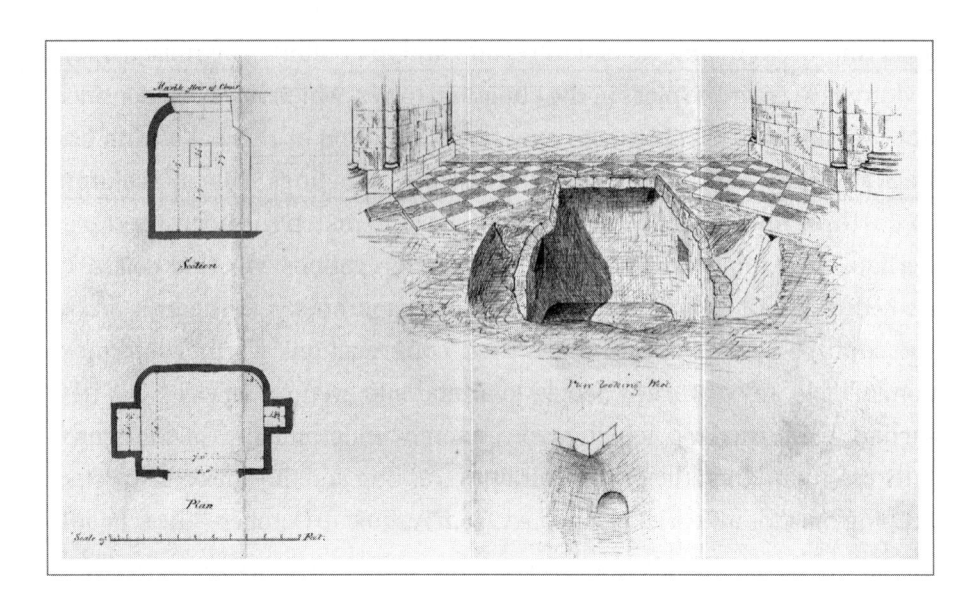

While working in 1856 to install a heating system into the cathedral, John Billing uncovered a large chamber between the pillars of the east tower arch (where the organ had stood until this date). Its purpose is unknown, but it is possible that it was a safe hiding place for the relics of St Frideswide or, possibly for the priory's and University's money chests. After the discovery, the chamber was filled with bones and broken gravestones disturbed during the building work.

Whitefriars Glassworks. This was a relatively new firm, established in 1834, by James Powell, a wine merchant. The company's rise to prominence in the mid- and late nineteenth century saw them working with all the major Arts & Crafts names of the day.

Odd and intrusive balustrades that had been erected in the clerestory in the seventeenth century were removed at some point in the first half of the nineteenth, but no further changes took place for several years. Liddell had been taken ill, and the construction of Meadow Buildings must have been a preoccupation. However, the principal reason for delay in continuing the restoration of the cathedral – Henry Thompson, Liddell's biographer and Christ Church historian, says that Billing's work was always intended to be just a stopgap – was the major overhaul of Christ Church's constitution in the 1850s and 1860s.[34]

On 2 June 1866 George Gilbert Scott laid before the Chapter two designs for the fitting out of the cathedral. The suggestions, along with a plan, were discussed at some length.[35] Did Liddell ask him for the proposals? It seems unlikely, as Christ Church was at that time still in the last stages of settling its statutes, something finally achieved in August 1867. The rough costings for the work were sent to the college by an Arthur B. Thompson ten days later, at Scott's request as he was away in the north of the country. The tasks that he thought necessary were in fact little more than a reordering of the seating in the cathedral and a new altar and reredos. The higher estimate was for £8,680, while the lower was for £5,680.[36] Unsurprisingly, the plans were not taken forward immediately, but, very soon after the Christ Church Oxford Act was passed, a surveyor, John West Hugall, was contracted to fulfil one of the requirements of the statute – that there should be a decennial survey of the fabric to ensure its maintenance and 'sustenation'.

Hugall's survey was submitted in only six weeks, and evidently recommended work on the cathedral.[37] A Committee for the Restoration of the Cathedral was established on 11 March 1868, with representatives from both Chapter and the newly created Governing Body.[38] The committee was chaired by the dean, with Thomas Chamberlain, Archdeacon Charles Clerke, Edward Bouverie Pusey and Richard Jelf from the Chapter and, on the Governing Body side, Robert Faussett (the Treasurer), Charles Sandford, Henry Thompson and Dean Liddell's right-hand man, Thomas Vere Bayne. By this time, the zeal of the Cambridge Camden Society was being moderated by societies such as the Oxford Architectural Society. The destruction of features that did not fit with the medieval was now rather frowned upon, so the choice of Scott as architect, whose ideas had always been less narrow than those of the early proponents of the Gothic Revival, was probably a considered one, even though it appears that he either put himself forward for the job or was approached directly and privately by Dean Liddell.

Interestingly, the Chapter members of the committee actually showed little interest in the task ahead. Archdeacon Clerke was prepared to go where Liddell followed; Pusey resigned because of ill-health in 1872; Jelf died in 1871; and Thomas Chamberlain was busy with his parochial affairs in St Thomas's. Only William Bright, who took Jelf's place, showed any enthusiasm. Vere Bayne and Faussett, however, were not only keen but were a formidable duo. Vere Bayne was a born administrator and committee man, while Faussett was a skilled accountant, seeing Christ Church through the turbulence of the agricultural depression and its fall-out. Both men had their own architectural ideas too. Vere Bayne wanted to return Christ Church to Wolsey's plan, to the point of creating what he believed Wolsey would have done had he not fallen from grace. Faussett liked Jacobean both at home and at work. Henry Thompson, a mild man who cared deeply for his college and its fabric, later acknowledged the untiring attention that the dean had lavished on the restoration.[39]

By early 1869 the Committee and the Governing Body were ready to take the restoration to the next stage. The Governing Body made an initial donation from corporate funds of £1,000, which was matched by the Chapter, but there was soon disagreement over the launch of an appeal to old members, with the canons being particularly against the idea. At a committee meeting on 16 March, Vere Bayne, ever practical and sensible, suggested that it would be wise, before any fundraising was attempted, to get proper plans and estimates for all the different aspects of the anticipated works. There were five main areas for discussion: the woodwork of the choir, nave and transepts, including moving the organ; the east end; the great window of the north transept and the windows – as many as thirteen – in the aisles; the south transept, possibly to include the re-creation of a south aisle (if there had ever been one), the muniment room and the south porch; and the re-extension of the nave into the Great Quadrangle with a new west window. The Governing Body, which of course included the professorial canons, was also required to decide whether or not to have a competition to find an architect or just to appoint someone.[40]

This last issue was probably already decided, even though the committee recommended that Gilbert Scott, John West Hugall and Thomas Deane should all be approached. The letters to the three men were evidently sent; Scott responded on 12 April that, while he was grateful for the letter inviting him to tender for the project, he would withdraw, as he disliked the idea of any competition for work on a sacred building. There is considerable pique in the letter, which suggests that he had been promised the contract or at least given the impression that the job was his. On 15 April, after discussion in the Governing Body, a hurried and mollifying reply was sent to Scott by the dean, asking him to set to preparing plans and estimates but to be mindful of cost: 'they do not wish any part of the work to be shabbily done, but they think [...] that as little as possible should be expended in ornamentation. They would prefer grave, solid work.' Liddell asked for an additional proposal to be taken into account: the restoration of the pitched roofs of the church, the lines of which are still visible on the tower. Scott accepted the commission by return of post.[41]

By the end of May, Scott wrote to the dean advising him that his report was well advanced. He had apparently asked for some cleaning to be done, no doubt to aid his survey, and was concerned that the mason was being a little too zealous in removing plaster and whitewash from either side of the Chapter House door and asked him to be restricted to just gentle washing in order to avoid damage to the 'ancient tooling'. Just a few days later, Scott's full survey arrived in Liddell's post. It was a full document, two-thirds of which was concerned with the history of the fabric, and the remainder with a condition survey and the briefest of estimates. There was an element of regret that the priory church had been rebuilt, at the end of the twelfth century, in a Romanesque style rather than the new Decorated style, which was beginning to sweep across Europe. But Scott recognised that the work at St Frideswide's showed 'the perfecting of the round-arched style into a high and refined form of art'.[42]

Structurally, Scott said, the main walls were sound, but in his next paragraph he suggested that there was considerable stone decay in some parts. He was concerned that any stone 'which retains ancient work in an intelligible state should be carefully preserved'. Only those that were decayed to the point of shapelessness or that were needed for structural reasons should be renewed. Stone as close to the original – perhaps Taynton – should be sourced. Internally, there should be little more than a gentle brushing to remove whitewash, taking care not to damage original toolmarks or any wall-painting that might survive. These were just repairs, Scott said.

WEST ELEVATION.

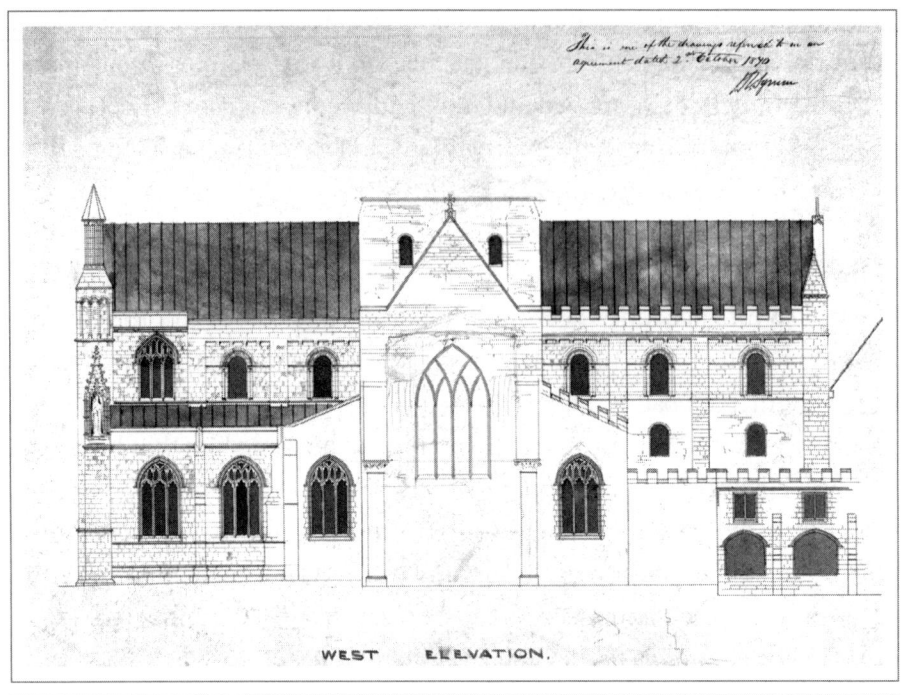

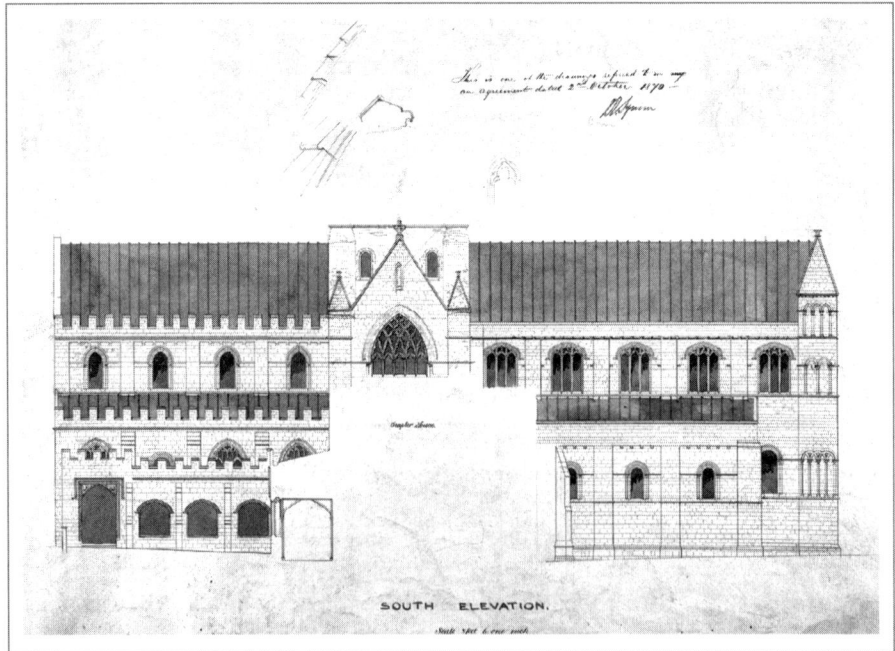

SOUTH ELEVATION.

Elevations of the cathedral showing George Gilbert Scott's designs, signed by Symm, the builder. Two are annotated with pencil sketches by Scott.

Reform and renewal: the nineteenth century

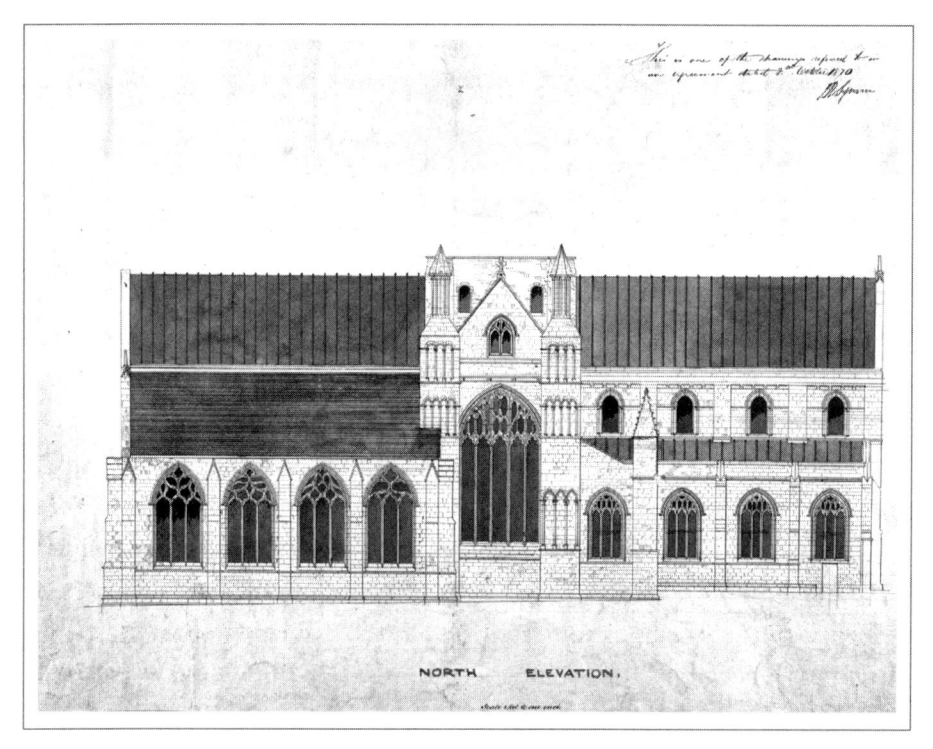

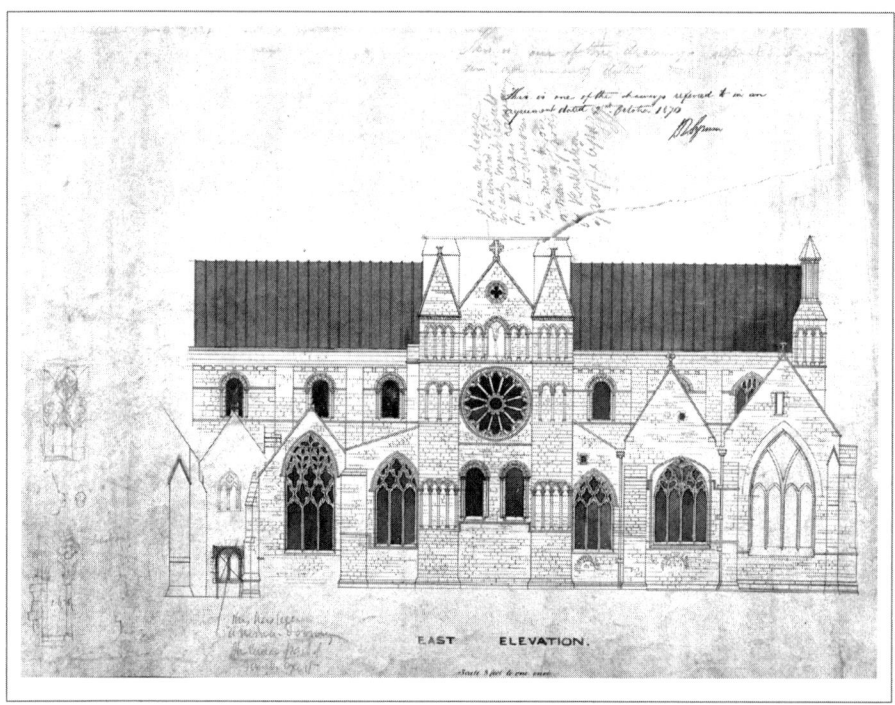

NORTH ELEVATION.

EAST ELEVATION.

Moving on to restoration, Scott revealed his concerns, which so contrasted with those of the early Ecclesiologists: 'every stage in the history of a sacred edifice has its value, and possesses an interest of its own, so that the obliteration of the work of any one period is like tearing out a leaf in the visible history of the structure.' Even so, he referred to more modern changes as 'mere mutilations'. He evidently disapproved thoroughly of the alterations to all the windows that had taken place in the seventeenth century to allow for the installation of the van Linge glass, and wanted to restore them if it was possible to work out their designs. The loss of much of the tracery in most of the windows distressed him considerably.

Other matters involved the restoration of the south transept, which for some time had been used as a house for the verger, and of the cloister. Scott was more ambivalent about putting back the high roofs, and suggested that this could be done as just an external feature, leaving the later fifteenth- or sixteenth-century ceilings untouched.[43] On the extension of the nave into the Great Quadrangle, the architect felt that, while this would be desirable for the church as cathedral, it would be less so for church as college chapel, a dilemma that also raised its head when he discussed interior fixtures and fittings. He would attempt to reduce the clash of requirements as far as was possible by retaining the college chapel feel while making the enclosing screens so unobtrusive that the rest of the cathedral could be used effectively for large cathedral occasions and by the 'ordinary' congregation.

Only the last fourteen lines, in small print, of Scott's fifteen-page report relate to actual costs: £12,000 for the repairs and restoration of the fabric; £7,000 for internal refittings; £2,700 for new stone vaulting in the naves and transepts; £2,500 to add external pitched roofs, covered in lead; £300 to open up the tower lantern; £800 for the restoration of the cloister; and £12,000 to restore the nave to its original length. New glass and painted decoration were not costed.[44] Compared with Scott's other cathedral projects, this was modest, but he took it no less seriously than he did his larger commissions.[45]

All through June 1869, and then once term began again in the autumn, discussions took place between Scott, Liddell, the Restoration

Committee and the Governing Body. One letter from Scott talked about the historical evidence for the original length of the nave and whether it had western towers, and another about the evidence for the original windows.[46] In November, approval was given by the Governing Body for an appeal to the old members, and a letter was drawn up that outlined all of Scott's estimate but indicated that, in the first instance, the Governing Body was only considering the fabric repairs, internal refitting and the restoration of the cloister at a cost of nearly £20,000.[47] The Queen, as Visitor, gave £100, and the Chapter responded willingly, nearly all of them donating £250. Most of the old members also responded positively with gifts of £5 or £10, some as much as £100. The Earl of Glasgow contributed £500, matching the dean in his generosity.[48] However, as is so often the case, the appeal was not universally popular: some members, particularly those who were vicars in poor parishes across the country, wrote back to comment that their own churches were falling into ruins around their ears, and to suggest that Christ Church should be contributing to the repair of these rather than beautifying and altering their own chapel. The vicar of Batheaston, in Somerset, was particularly scathing: 'I must confess [...] that any zeal in the cause is very low, in consequence of the rough and peremptory refusal of the College to give me a farthing's help when two years ago we spent close upon £2,000 on our church here. And I have still more work in hand in order to finish.'[49] These comments were a little unjust, if understandable: the Dean and Chapter had always helped out their incumbents, and their churches, since the foundation. Some were quite specific about the use of their donations: John Barclay Thompson, for example, was not particularly concerned with the restoration of the cathedral per se, but rather wanted his gift to be used for the 'comfort, convenience, and dignity of the Senior Students in their chapel'.[50] Others objected to the employment of Gilbert Scott: he was just too ubiquitous and far too influential. And at least one, Granville Leveson Gower, at the time Secretary of State for Foreign Affairs, was against the destruction of part of the quad to recreate a new west end: 'What we know of Ch.Ch. is Wolsey', he said, 'and to destroy part of his Quad to extend the cathedral into it thereby marring his design would in my opinion be a great mistake,

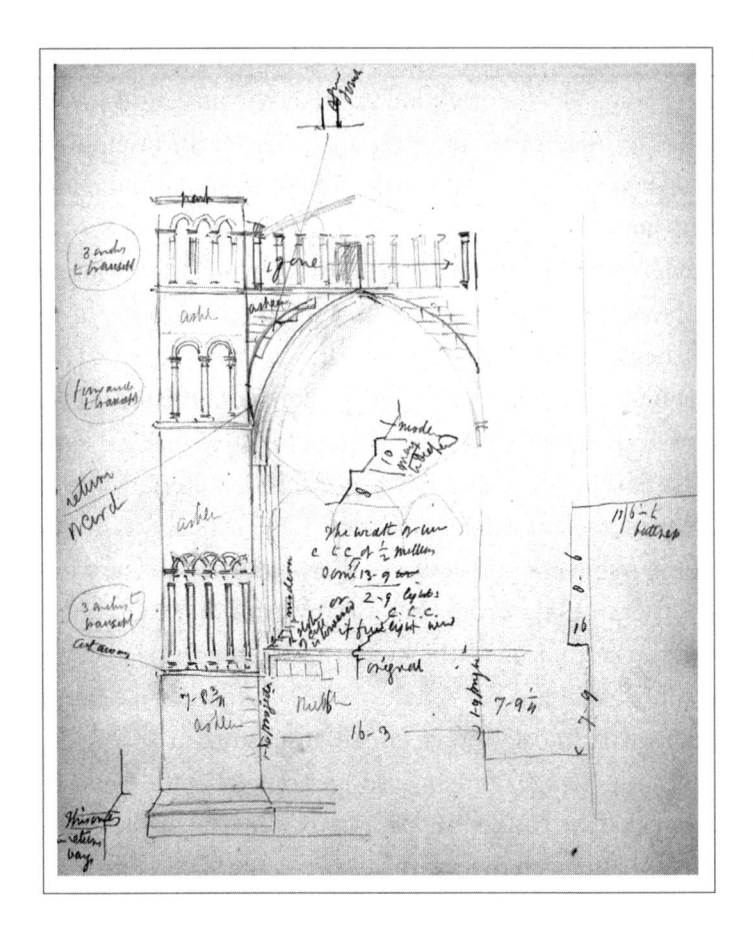

Scott's rough sketch of his thoughts for the east end of the cathedral, including measurements for either two or three windows below the wheel.

and I fervently hope you will run short of money for that part of the work.'

Work began in 1870 with a local company, Symm & Co., contracted to do the work under the supervision of Thomas Leigh as Clerk of Works.[51] Invoices were soon pouring in from masons, organ builders, carpenters, ironmongers and heating engineers. Scott's original plan for the east end was to restore the Decorated window that had been altered in the very late seventeenth century to take James Thornhill's depiction of the Nativity, but during his survey the architect was certain that he had found evidence of a round window. In the end, under Scott's direction, Symm's reconstructed the whole of the east end, incorporating the wheel window and round-headed 'Romanesque' windows below, based on a scheme at Laon cathedral.[52] The tracery of most of the other windows, reduced and altered to allow the installation of the van Linge glass in the 1630s, was renewed. Only the Jonah window was retained, at the request of several members.[53]

Throughout the restoration, and in the years immediately following it, new windows were commissioned and installed, some to the designs of Burne-Jones, in the Lady Chapel, the north choir aisle, the south choir aisle (which would later become the Military Chapel), the south transept and the huge St Michael window in the north transept.

One essential task, certainly in Scott's eyes, and one that had been raised by *The Ecclesiologist* back in 1847, was the restoration of the south transept, part of which had been walled off, possibly in the eighteenth century.[54] The writer of the 1847 article was outraged:

> it will hardly be credited by those whose eyes have not witnessed the sacrilege, that a portion of the church is actually desecrated. In so vast a college the hire of a single room cannot be dispensed with, but the House of God must be defiled; a bay of the south transept and one of the adjoining chapels are blocked off to form a residence for the verger. On this subject we can hardly trust ourselves to speak. Where are our hopes of reform, when such an example is set by the guardians of what should be a model-church for England?[55]

Scott ripped out the eyesore, replacing it with the present sacristy, built following some of the original twelfth-century features that were rediscovered.[56] Archdeacon Clerke, who had given £100 for the creation of a proper vestry in this position, withdrew his money, feeling that Scott's solution was rather mean.[57]

Scott also opened up the tower, revealing again the arcade which had been hidden by the ringing platform. The bells, which Scott said were placing a dangerous strain on the tower, were removed and placed in a rather ugly, and supposedly temporary, shed (nicknamed, by Charles Dodgson, the 'meat-safe') over the Hall stairs.[58]

Other items that were removed included the despised Duppa screens, which blocked off the chapels on either side of the choir, and what remained of the choir stalls after Billing's work just fifteen years earlier. The new stalls, of walnut, were constructed in Symm's yard, and the wrought-iron work – modelled on that around the tomb of Queen Eleanor of Castile at Westminster Abbey – was manufactured by Francis Skidmore of Coventry, with whom Scott worked closely on many projects, including the Albert Memorial.[59] The open-ness of the ironwork was Scott's compromise between college chapel and diocesan cathedral.[60] The paving was made and laid by Clayton and Bell, primarily window designers and manufacturers, who also collaborated with Scott on the Albert Memorial in London. The inspiration was the floor of Siena Cathedral.[61]

In January 1872, when much of the work funded by the old members had been achieved, a fresh appeal was sent out to the diocese asking for assistance with the extension of the nave, the restoration of the pitched roofs (in spite of Scott's apparent abandonment of the idea), tidying up 'external incumbrances' from the south side of the choir with a view to providing

---

Bishop Wilberforce

During the first half of the nineteenth century, appointments to the bishopric had been rather short-lived. Some had been good, particularly Lloyd and Bagot: the former a popular teacher and theologian, and the latter a very practical churchman. However, in 1845, just before the arrival of Henry Liddell as dean, Samuel Wilberforce was appointed. He was energetic in the diocese, travelling constantly, taking ordination and mission particularly seriously, setting up a new theological college and clerical retreat at the rebuilt episcopal palace at Cuddesdon and increasing the number of livings in the patronage of the bishop. For the first time in Christ Church's history, episcopal Visitations of the cathedral took place regularly.

Wilberforce has become famous for his response to Darwin's *On the Origin of Species*. He was translated to Winchester in 1869, and died in 1873 after falling from his horse. The new bishop's throne was dedicated to his memory.

ODNB

additional access to the cathedral, the provision of the bishop's throne and a new reredos. The Dean, Canons and Students were quick to reassure the diocese that fabric repairs would be funded by Christ Church, with all subscriptions to the fund being used for restoration.[62] The pitch was clever; perhaps with the exception of the restoration of the high roofs, the request was for items that were likely to appeal directly to the members of the diocese.

The extension of the nave and the proposal to knock through the canonry to the Great Quadrangle were controversial.[63] The fact that Wolsey had knocked down several bays in order to build the quad is grist to the argument that all of the priory church would have been demolished. From 1525 the only public entrance into the church was through the south door. It was not only inconvenient, as had been pointed out as far back as 1617, but it was not grand or suitable for processionals, or even just suitable for the diocesan cathedral. In the eighteenth century any dignity the entrance might have had would have been ruined by the construction of the Muniment Room in the north cloister walk. By the summer of 1872 the Chapter and Governing Body must have realised that the £12,000 that Scott had estimated for a full restoration of the west end was not going to be raised, and so they compromised, again. On 5 July, Symm tendered for the project with an estimate of £1,492. The Dean and Governing Body must have quibbled a bit for, just twelve days later, Mr Symm wrote back with a revised quotation of £928.[64] The work was to include creating the new entrance, carving the oak ceiling and making the new entrance doors. The ironmongery for the doors – hinges, lock, iron bands etc. – was made by Skidmore.[65] Scott's design was for a simple bay in a plain Romanesque style to fill the gap between the sixteenth-century west wall and the back of the east side of the Great Quadrangle, and then a 'tunnel' entrance knocked through the canon's residence, with a double arch making use of Wolsey's unfinished cloister masonry. It was not universally popular either within the college or outside. One elderly tutor refused to remove his hat until he had reached a certain point within the cathedral, on the grounds that he was still 'in Dr Mozley's dining-room'. Plans for a gable or tower over the entrance were soon abandoned.[66]

The design of the altar for the east end became a battleground. In

A letter from Scott to Dean Liddell discussing the number of bays that Wolsey may have demolished in order to build the Great Quadrangle.

June 1872 Canon William Bright, a member of the Restoration Committee, expressed his approval of Scott's design – ornamented, with dignity and character – and offered the full cost of £156. The Treasurer, Faussett, and the dean were less than keen on the ornamentation and had pared the plans back until the altar was barely recognisable. Bright was anxious and regretful that his offer had been brushed aside; he described the dean's proposal as 'shabby and unworthy, just where shabbiness and unworthiness are least tolerable'.[67] The final result was another compromise: an altar table with elaborate legs, described as resembling a 'strange, many-legged insect', but with just a simple inlaid cross rather than the marble top that was Bright's preference.[68]

One of the final items – apart from the reredos, which was not installed until 1882 – to be placed in the newly refurbished cathedral was the bishop's

Reform and renewal: the nineteenth century

Drawing by F. P. Barraud (1824–1900) of the nave and chancel about ten years after Scott's restoration. The bishop's throne, dedicated to Wilberforce, is visible just outside the sanctuary on the right.

throne. The cost had been estimated at £1,000 but the pot was still short of £85 at the end of 1875. A proposal was made to the Restoration Committee that £50 be contributed from the Restoration Fund, but this was not approved. However, the carving and erection of the immense structure, designed by the firm of Farmer and Brindley in Italian walnut to match the new stalls, and which was to stand on the south side of the chancel, just outside the sanctuary, continued. By the following June a report to Committee indicated that work was well advanced.[69] For the first time the bishop's place in the cathedral was truly acknowledged, even if the funding of the throne had been left largely to the members of the diocese.[70]

A summary account of expenditure on the restoration, dated 26 September 1873, shows what an immense project this was. Although the nave and chancel are rightly seen as the main thrust of Scott's efforts, the account reveals how much of the cathedral was touched in some way, from the major works at the east end and alterations to the underfloor heating to delicate work on stone mouldings, monuments and wooden carvings.[71]

Scott's work did not stop with the cathedral. He moved on to restore the cloister, removing the excrescence that was the eighteenth-century muniment room and, in the process, uncovering considerable evidence of the twelfth-century south transept. And he raised the cloister ceiling where it had previously cut the Norman doorway, so that the Romanesque carving could be seen in its full glory.[72]

Scott's work represented the last major works done on the cathedral until recent times. Soon after the completion of the cathedral and cloister restoration Thomas Bodley was employed to do something about the sad state of the Chapter House. At some point in its history – in the seventeenth century, according to Henry Thompson – the Chapter House had been divided into two rooms and the floor of the inner portion, where Chapter business and dinners were conducted, raised by a few feet to accommodate the Chapter's wine. This was swept aside and the room restored to its original proportions. Its size was appreciated immediately when a celebratory party was held for the senior Students on St Frideswide's Day, 1880.[73]

Major restoration concluded, there were other smaller, but important, tasks carried out on the furnishings and fittings over the remainder of the nineteenth century. The font, ordered in 1785, had never been manufactured, so Thomas Bodley had come up with a design which met with the approval of Chapter. On 16 June 1881 it was announced that a font of rosso antico – a fine-grained pink or red marble – and white Mansfield stone would be made, which was duly installed in the Lucy Chapel on 30 March 1882. The first baby to benefit was the daughter of the Warden of Keble College, E. S. Talbot, on 13 May.[74] In the same year the elaborate reredos was placed in the sanctuary at the east end, which entailed the shifting around of old furnishings: the old reredos was moved to the Latin Chapel, and all the old woodwork there removed.[75] In stripping out the panelling from the chapel, once it had ceased to be used as a lecture facility for the regius professor, the

Easter sepulchre on the north side was rediscovered, where the Host would have been deposited on Good Friday.[76]

There was, however, one very important work carried out during Liddell's time in the Deanery. In 1870, during Scott's labours, fragments of the twelfth century shrine base were discovered in a drinking water well behind the south-east canon's lodgings as the nave was being extended westwards. Once these pieces had been found, the search was on for further stones, and soon sufficient pieces of the hard crystalline limestone were found to manage a reconstruction in 1889, which was placed between the Lady Chapel and the north choir aisle.[77]

By 1891, when Liddell retired, the cathedral was in good shape. Its fabric was restored, and it was worthy to be opened out for the wider diocesan uses that Liddell had been keen to encourage.[78]

* * * * *

Scott's work on the cathedral had been delayed for a few years largely because of the major reform of the constitution of college and cathedral that took place in the 1850s and 1860s. As we have seen, major reform had taken place in the cathedrals, culminating in the Cathedrals Act of 1840. Christ Church had, by and large, avoided the major consequences of this legislation, but there was more to come. Internally, the grumbles of the Students of Christ Church concerning their lack of influence over college affairs, always simmering in the background, were getting louder. They wanted to be recognised as Fellows, with a share of dividends from estates, as they would be in other colleges. And reforms of the examination system in the early part of the nineteenth century, as well as the introduction of new subjects, put additional pressures on the shoulders of the tutors. Externally, the government wanted to look more closely at the 'state, discipline, studies, and revenues' of the universities and colleges and so established the Oxford University Commission in 1850. The commission wanted to reform the governance of the university and re-establish some control over the largely autonomous colleges. Dean Gaisford, a trenchant conservative who disliked reform in any shape or form, refused to answer any of the commissioners' questions, arguing that government interference threatened Oxford and Cambridge as independent bodies.[79]

Most of the proposals of the commission related to teaching, but there was considerable concern over the use of revenues to fund large bodies of Fellows, especially when most of those Fellowships were not open to competition. The University, and the colleges, should be reaching out to poorer students and a wider community. Their statutes should be reformed for modern times. At Christ Church, the commissioners were alarmed to discover that the entire surplus revenue – around £14,000 per annum – was divided between the dean and canons only, with the Students receiving stipends of only £25 to £45, depending on seniority.[80] Both the Students and the royal commissioners thought this was unacceptable. Gaisford, needless to say, argued that as Christ Church had no statutes there was nothing to reform, and that it would be far better to 'admit the anomaly [of Christ Church's constitution] as it exists, than attempt to remove it in part (for it could never be wholly removed), at the great hazard of introducing new elements of doubt, dissatisfaction, and confusion'.[81] Perhaps largely because all but two of the commissioners were Christ Church men, including William Gladstone, the resulting legislation, the 1854 Oxford Act, touched Christ

---

Honorary Canons

In 1860, the Ecclesiastical Commissioners drew up a scheme to allow for up to twenty-four Honorary Canons in each cathedral, partly as compensation for the reduction in the number of residentiary canons. Eight could be appointed in the first year and two more in subsequent years. The men could preside at services in the absence of dean and canons, and could preach.

It took a while for the scheme to settle at Christ Church while issues of seniority, seating and processional arrangements were ironed out. Only one member of Chapter attended the installation service of the first Honorary Canon, on 23 July 1866.

Curthoys (2012), 89, 230

Church relatively lightly. The colleges were obliged to draw up new statutes but, while the Commission on Capitular Bodies was still active, reform at Christ Church was all but impossible.

One major hurdle to reform at Christ Church was removed when Dean Gaisford died on 2 June 1855. He was replaced by Henry Liddell, who had been an active member of the University Commission. By Michaelmas term 1855 the dean and canons were supposed to have drawn up their own scheme for reform, but had failed to do so. The Chapter was unwilling to give up any of its governing powers, and the Students refused to have anything less than full Fellowships, as their colleagues did in other colleges. Money became the over-riding issue, at least in the early days of discussions. In order to pay the Students as full Fellows extra funds would have to be found, and those two canonries which were due to be suppressed after the 1840 Cathedrals Act were the obvious source. An Amending Act was introduced in 1856 which allowed the two canonries unattached to professorships to be abolished and their revenues redirected. Liddell actually proposed that two more should go as well: the canonries attached to the Lady Margaret professorship and to the pastoral theology chair. If he had had his way, the Governing Body of Christ Church would have been reduced to just the dean and four canons. Gladstone said no; the suppression of two was enough to introduce some necessary reform. The commissioners, in discussion with Dean Liddell, drew up the Christ Church Ordinance – the Chapter refused to discuss it, and the Students were not asked to participate. Of the fourteen points of the ordinance, only one had any direct impact on the cathedral – the reduction of the number of chaplains, so that the stipends of the remainder could be increased. The principle that some senior Students should be involved with governance was accepted, and their stipends were substantially increased, but the number who would sit on the new Governing Body was tiny; power remained with the dean and canons.

The fourteen points settled nothing, but Liddell warned the canons not to be belligerent; if the commission felt that they had to impose something on Christ Church, it would be the canons who lost out. The Students began to meet seriously and laid down their own proposals. For the first time it was suggested that the educational side of Christ Church should be completely separated from its cathedral function, with the Chapter taking no part in the governance of the college. The fourteen points were discussed and debated, but when the final ordinance was passed in 1858, it satisfied no one. That the Students had not been raised to the level of Fellows in other colleges still rankled, and in 1864 the dissatisfaction reached the press. Thomas Prout, who was principal agitator on the part of the Students, had a letter published in *The Times* attesting that Christ Church had not been properly investigated, as the Ecclesiastical Commissioners saw it as a college and the University Commissioners saw it as a cathedral. The partial reform of the ordinance had only made matters worse. Prout and seventeen other Students took their demands to Chapter, and at last Chapter agreed to a committee to discuss all the issues with the Students. Prout took advice from Osborne Gordon, an emeritus Student who had left Christ Church for his living in Easthampstead in some despair after the passing of the ordinance. Gordon suggested that Prout go to the Chapter with a proposal that the Chapter, on fixed incomes, should manage the cathedral, and the college should be run by the dean, the sub-dean, the Treasurer and six Senior Students. Unsurprisingly, the Chapter threw the idea out.

There were other matters rumbling that added to the grievances of the Students, not least the domestic administration of the college. The 'Bread and Butter Row' of 1865, ostensibly just a dispute over the cost of daily commons, dragged the governance of Christ Church into the papers again, and was the catalyst that pushed the senior members to sort out the constitution once and for all.[82] The Students prepared a Memorial to go to the Prime Minister, asking for specific reforms or for a Commission of Inquiry. The canons baulked at the thought of another public Commission – and presumably more press coverage – and opted for private arbitrators, or referees, instead. The debates continued for about a year. Just before Christmas 1866 the referees made their award, which included seventeen recommendations to amend the constitution in favour of the Students. On 12 August 1867 royal assent was given to the Christ Church Oxford Act, which, among other reforms, laid down that the dean, canons and Senior Students would form the Governing Body; all powers, possessions and revenues would be vested in the Governing Body; and the dean and canons would retain power over the cathedral, the deanery and the canonical lodgings, with a fixed income for maintenance and management.[83] The only input from the Governing Body concerning the cathedral would be over the times of Sunday services for the college.[84] This last caused some resentment from the Chapter; Pusey said that he 'thought it was agreed that the services in the cathedral belonged to the Chapter and that the Students could not have any voice in them'. Pusey's dismay was probably justified; attendance at Sunday services was not compulsory, and they were poorly attended, so why should the Students have a say in something in which they declined to participate? If they had a voice, 'we should cease to have any authority as to the management of our own cathedral, indeed we should cease to be a cathedral body at all and become a mere college.'[85] The uniqueness of Christ Church was seen to be threatened, not least when over three centuries of tradition were brought to an end with the transfer of the college seal from the Chapter House to the Treasury.

* * * * *

The writer of the article in *The Ecclesiologist* in 1847 expressed his horror at the state of services in the cathedral: 'the church has sunk to a college-chapel, from whose festival worship the laity are excluded, and which is probably the only cathedral in Christendom where there is never a sermon preached or a communion offered for the benefit of the people of the diocese.' He went on to say that the services in other college chapels excelled the few that were held at Christ Church, and so it was hardly surprising that any potential congregation went elsewhere.[86]

The turn of the eighteenth century had been a golden period for music in Oxford, and the city had a rich range of musical activities in which college choirs and individual choristers regularly performed. One of the chaplains, Sampson Estwick, preached in the cathedral for St Cecilia's Day 1696 on the value of cathedral music; one of the singing men, Walter Powell, was reputed to have the best voice in England; and the organists were writing specially for their choirs to try out new styles and to fit music for specific occasions. When Handel visited Oxford in 1733, *Acis and Galatea* was performed in the cathedral as part of a programme of concerts across the city.[87] But things had deteriorated, and in spite of a series of excellent organists, by the time Liddell arrived, cathedral and college services needed attention. All college services included Latin Prayers; on Sundays and Holy Days there were Surplice Prayers, and communion was celebrated once a month after choral matins. There were no college sermons, but divinity lectures were held in the Latin Chapel before breakfast.

The intoning of prayers had been abandoned in Oxford by 1843, except for the State prayers, and the litany was chanted from a low desk in the centre of the choir, as it was in many cathedrals across the country. In spite of all the negative press concerning congregations in cathedrals, Robert Inglis provided the House of Commons with statistics for attendance in the 1840s and reported that Christ Church was often crowded but that, even if this were the case (and perhaps the crowds were just students there by compulsion), the services were reported as being 'the most slovenly and irreverent [...] in any English cathedral'.[88] At one service, early in the century, it was noticed that there was only one lay clerk in the choir and Dean Gaisford was notoriously uninterested in the choir and, possibly, in the cathedral at all.

The cathedral choir school

A choir has been part and parcel of the foundation since Wolsey. The eight choristers, later increased to sixteen by Dean Liddell, were probably all local boys who were educated, fed and paid a small fee by Christ Church in exchange for the performance of their duties. The classroom was the room under the Hall.

In the 1850s the dean gave permission to add fee-paying non-choristers to the school. Slowly numbers grew, and boarders arrived with the opening of a new school building on Brewer Street. In the 1930s the school was formally made a preparatory school.

Lane and Lee (2017)

During his time (1831–55) the choir were poorly behaved and the lay clerks often drawn from among the scouts. Part of the problem may have been pay-related; the Cathedral Commissioners found, in 1854, that the Christ Church lay clerks were the worst-remunerated in the country.[89]

In 1849 Canon Bull composed a memorandum explaining that the choir consisted of only eight men and eight boys (as had been laid down at the foundation) and was smaller than that at other cathedrals. The boys were competent and regular in their attendance, but the men were less so. It was difficult to find men who would or could come on Sundays as well as weekdays, and asking them to find their own substitutes would reduce their already meagre stipends. Bull recommended a better salary for the competent singers to encourage them to come in the evenings. This way the organist – the newly appointed C.W. Corfe – would at least have a core of good men and would be able to prepare a decent anthem as well as a good service.[90] Duty rosters were drawn up so that men only had to attend six of the possible twelve weekday services, but all were expected to come on Sundays.[91] However, Bull's solution evidently was not completely successful, as memoranda flew backwards and forwards concerning the lay clerks and the choir more generally for another six or seven years. In 1853 Bull recounted that the organist and the boy choristers were performing their duties, but that there was still a problem with the attendance of the lay clerks. Under Liddell this would change.[92] Corfe was asking more of the men than they were prepared to do, at least without an increase in pay; all of them were obliged to take additional work outside the cathedral in order to make ends meet, and, unsurprisingly, their employers were not pleased when the men asked for time off to attend services.[93] The Chapter agreed, and doubled the additional gratuity for regular singers, bringing their stipends up from £20 per annum to £30.[94]

Services evidently improved, and Liddell was determined that the cathedral would become much more of a diocesan asset rather than remaining just a large college chapel. When the doors opened after Billing's refurbishment work, on 12 October 1856, *Jackson's Oxford Journal* declared that the cathedral was now worthy of its name and on the same footing as any other

Cathedral clock

David Loggan's engraving of Christ Church from 1673 shows a clock-face on the west wall of the south transept, over the slype. The clock mechanism appears to have been in the cathedral tower, where for many years it must have been important for college and cathedral life until superseded by the construction of Tom Tower, with its prominent bell and clock, in the 1680s. An expert, viewing the old clock mechanism in 1849, said that it bore resemblance to a sixteenth-century timepiece at Hampton Court, but he thought it was more likely to date from just after Christiaan Huygens's invention of the pendulum clock in 1656. The quarter, striking and great wheels (the main gear train, or going train, of a clock mechanism) were of iron, which made it probably earlier than those clocks with brass wheels, the earliest of which was built in 1677.

The clock remained in use, being repaired in 1730 and again in 1737, 1745 and 1824. Perhaps its unreliability, or just its age, caused it to be replaced in 1838 after the famous clockmaker Benjamin Vulliamy had submitted an estimate of £283 for a new cathedral clock, with pulleys and cranks. The Dean and Chapter quibbled over the cost but accepted the estimate in January 1838 and expected completion by the end of September (Vulliamy had said it would take six months). By December the clock was still unfinished and over-budget. By February 1839 the clock – now in use – already needed repair, but this was blamed on the college servant who had responsibility for winding the mechanism. Dean Gaisford asked for the old mechanism to be cleaned and preserved in the tower where it was said to 'deserve the attention of the antiquary'.

Although the clock face on the south transept had definitely been removed before Edmund New made his engraving of Christ Church in 1915, there was still a cathedral clock in 1960, when £125 was spent on refurbishment.

Smyth (1849); CCA GB i.b.8, 472

cathedral with regard to the public. For the first time they would be able to attend its services as the public could in any other cathedral city.[95] Intoning the prayers by the chaplains was reintroduced (with the *Journal* commenting that it was not done well at first, but then no one was used to it). The services were no longer hurried, as they had been when there was no congregation bar the officiating canon and the choir, but were performed well before a growing number of attendees who were, at last, well seated and warm. Even the vergers were civil, something that apparently was novel. At the Commemoration service in 1862 nearly a thousand people were squashed into the church.[96] By this time the choir was back up to scratch and said to be one of the best in Oxford. It performed in choral festivals, which were seen, nationwide, as a means of opening the doors of cathedrals to their diocese and 'bringing home to the scattered portions of [...] a large diocese the value – it might be said the existence – of its cathedral'.[97] Christ Church hosted such festivals in 1863 and 1869, and in November 1873 there was a performance of Bach's Christmas Music at which Christ Church was joined by the choirs of Magdalen and New colleges.[98] In 1874 the choir was one of the participating choirs – alongside those from St George's, Windsor, Eton College and Hereford and Gloucester cathedrals – at the grand reopening of Worcester Cathedral after its major restoration project was completed.[99]

After the retirement of William Corfe in May 1882, it was decreed in Chapter that the organist's choice of anthems should be approved by the Precentor or the Canon in Residence. From the beginning of 1883 weekly service papers were printed.[100]

10

Openness and outreach: modern times

In the second half of the nineteenth century Henry Liddell had led Christ Church through a period of tremendous change, both physically and constitutionally. From 1867, and certainly by the end of Liddell's time in the deanery, the cathedral was to all intents and purposes, and except for its function as college chapel, independent of the academic establishment. It could run its day-to-day affairs with its subvention from the corporate fund and began to open its doors far more widely to the diocese and the city.

Liddell was followed in the deanery first by Francis Paget, a churchman and theologian who had been at Christ Church since his undergraduate days, with only a short period away as a parish priest. He was a reserved man who must have seen the need for a settled period of tranquillity, but was nevertheless active in the foundation of Reading University and was chaplain to Bishop Stubbs until Stubbs's death in 1901, when Paget left Christ Church for the bishopric himself.

The first few years of Thomas Banks Strong's period as dean were relatively quiet too. He was not really an obvious choice to step into Paget's shoes, and most certainly not Liddell's, being quiet, musical, peaceable and single.[1] But he was active in the University, particularly in the extension of Oxford education to the working classes, and a born administrator, a skill that came to the fore on the outbreak of the First World War, when he took

Thomas Banks Strong, Dean 1901–20.

over the commissioning of young students and tutors, enrolling more than 2,000 before the end of the 1914 summer vacation.

Throughout the war the cathedral was the focus of college and city life as perhaps it had never been before. The military presence became increasingly obvious as Christ Church men joined up, coming to services in khaki before they were sent on to fight, and as troops billeted on the House – first soldiers, and then cadets from the Royal Flying Corps – attended services and parades. The colours of the local yeomanry were hung above the sub-dean's stall; organ recitals were given on Saturday afternoons and Sunday evenings to raise money for the Red Cross; and a special commemorative communion service was held once a month.

When the war finally ended, the nation put its mind to commemoration. Military memorials for specific campaigns had become increasingly

An example of the service sheets issued from 1883 until the 1960s, showing a typical week during the First World War, with its intercessory prayers, special parade and commemoration of the fallen.

familiar sights in cathedrals from the 1840s.[2] In 1899 the colours of the 1st Oxfordshire Light Infantry were placed in the cathedral for safe-keeping during the South African wars, to be returned at a special service in 1902 attended by the officers and men, the dean and canons, and the mayor and corporation.[3] Brasses in commemoration of those who had died in the South African wars had later been placed on the wall of the south nave aisle. Soon after the armistice in 1918, while the college was deliberating about and fundraising for a permanent memorial to Christ Church men who had fallen, a plaque was placed in the south choir aisle to the 'Memory of the Officers and Men of the Oxfordshire Yeomanry who fell in France and Flanders'. The two memorial tablets to the fallen of Christ Church – including Students, junior members, cathedral and college staff, and choristers – were designed and carved by MacDonald Gill, and placed on the north wall of the cathedral entrance tunnel and unveiled on Armistice Day, 1921.[4] It took longer – until 1931 – for the whole of the south choir aisle to be set aside as a military chapel, dedicated to the warrior saint, Michael, and to the memory of all the fallen men of the Oxfordshire and Buckinghamshire Light Infantry.[5] The commemorative space began as a much smaller project when the Regimental Committee, under General Sir Bernard Paget, asked if a place could be found in the cathedral for the permanent display of the Roll of Honour, which contained the names of 5,878 men who had fallen.[6] The roll had been inscribed by Irene Bass (later Wellington), a celebrated calligrapher, and was bound by the Clarendon Press and funded by subscription. Soon, however, the idea of a full Regimental Chapel took shape, and the work was put into the hands of Harold Rogers, a local ecclesiastical architect.[7] The scheme was designed around the Burne-Jones window at the east end of the aisle, itself created as a memorial to Edith Liddell, one of the daughters of Dean Liddell. The service of dedication was held on 11 November 1931, with the doors of the cathedral thrown open to more than a thousand invited guests and others who wanted to be part of the occasion.[8]

After all the reforms imposed on cathedrals during the nineteenth

---

The Military Chapel, now referred to as the Chapel of Remembrance, also has a memorial to the Oxfordshire Yeomanry, later the Queen's Own Oxfordshire Hussars, formed in 1798, during the Napoleonic Wars. The queen was Adelaide, consort to William IV.

The Yeomanry was quartered in Meadow Buildings on mobilisation before the First World War. One of the captains was G. T. Hutchinson, Steward of Christ Church.

century, the government started to leave them to run themselves, particularly after 1919, when the Church of England Assembly (Powers) Act was passed.[9] New dioceses were created, and cathedrals built or created from parish churches – twelve in the first quarter of the twentieth century. In 1924 the Church Assembly initiated its own commission, the aims of which were to bring the different types of cathedral administration closer into line. Perhaps more significantly for the older cathedrals, all remaining cathedral endowments were taken under the control of the Ecclesiastical Commissioners. For the first time since the Saxon period, cathedrals were no longer landlords of estates, other than their immediate cathedral closes.[10] Unlike Dean Gaisford in 1855, the dean and canons were helpful in their replies to the commission, a point gratefully noted by the sub-commission charged with dealing with the anomaly that is Christ Church. One or two points in the report raised eyebrows: the Commissioners suggested that the cathedral 'belonged' to the college, and were concerned about the oddness of the dean and bishop walking side by side in procession, but otherwise they were impressed that the Dean and Chapter, in spite of the cathedral's historic use as college chapel, were 'becoming more and more alive to the advance of

The Chapter House paintings

There are tiny fragments of twelfth-century decorative painting either side of the Chapter House door, but most of the work dates to about 1260. The walls are highlighted in red, to simulate masonry, and there is some evidence of red paint in the vault. It is, however, the medallions, painted in a variety of colours, that are the jewels of the Chapter House. The central boss in the eastern bay shows Christ in Majesty and is surrounded by St Peter (on the east), St Paul (west), St John the Evangelist (north) and St Matthew (south).

Only one painting survives in the next bay – of an angel censing the Virgin and Child, on the central boss.

Other paintings have evidently been destroyed perhaps during the Commonwealth period or earlier, at the Reformation.

Diocesan life in our Church, [and] do all that is in their power to make the Cathedral of service in this respect'. Needless to say, Christ Church's unique constitution ensured that the resultant Cathedrals Measure of 1931 largely excluded Christ Church.[11]

However, while cathedrals were looking to their affairs for the Assembly, the Chapter at Christ Church was not idle, and around 1925 it initiated a programme of conservation in both cathedral and Chapter House, focusing on the monuments and memorials, but also continuing Liddell's work in making the cathedral more convenient and comfortable.[12] Henry White had stepped into Strong's shoes as dean in 1920, and proved a bit of a tidier-upper. Throughout his time in the deanery he attended to all sorts of modernisations and repairs across both college and cathedral.[13] The memorials that received specialist attention included those of Robert Burton and Deans Goodwin and Gaisford, and Edward Pusey. The ancient grave slab of Ela, Countess of Warwick, was moved from the Chapter House to the north transept.[14] A conservation report was undertaken on the Nowers tomb and effigy by Clement Skilbeck, who informed the Chapter that only a small portion of the original fourteenth-century effigy remained, with the rest being poorer quality and seventeenth- and possibly even eighteenth-century 'restoration'. He did do some repainting on the area of the tomb below the blazons, but advised that no attempt should be made to recolour the blazons themselves.[15]

During the programme of works the Chapter called in the art historian and wall-painting expert Ernest William Tristram to investigate and conserve Lady Montacute's tomb and its vaulting and the wall-paintings in the Chapter House. For the first time in centuries, the colours and inscriptions in what Tristram called the 'Chapel of the Guardian Angels' were revealed and recorded.[16] Tristram looked carefully at the whole cathedral and discovered and recorded fragments of decorative painting from the twelfth century in the south choir aisle and the Lucy Chapel, from the thirteenth again in the Lucy Chapel, the south choir aisle and in the Lady Chapel, and from the fourteenth in the south choir aisle and the Lady Chapel.

The Latin Chapel was provided with heating and electric light. The

The thirteenth-century grave slab of Ela Longspée, Countess of Warwick, came to Christ Church from Oseney, where the countess had been buried somewhere between 1297 and 1300. Her body was removed to St Mary's in Warwick, which may explain the odd inscription referring to the lady's viscera; perhaps a small part of her remains were kept at Oseney. The stone had been reused as a doorstep to a cottage near the old abbey after its dissolution. When it came to Christ Church is unknown, although it was in the Chapter House in 1924 and the north transept by 1935.

standard lights were designed by Ninian Comper, as were two new kneeling desks for communicants.[17] New frontals and curtains, and rugs, were added to both the main and Latin Chapel altars.

Last, but not least, work was done on some of the windows. Powell and Son were contracted to restore and clean the Burne-Jones Frideswide window and the seventeenth-century Bishop King window. The company also filled parts of the clerestory windows in the north transept with fragments of the van Linge glass which had been found in an attic in Tom Quad. Tiny pieces of fourteenth-century glass, discovered at the same time, were inserted in the re-leaded lower lights of windows in the Lucy Chapel. This

> ## Canonical lodgings
>
> Dean Williams also oversaw discussions about the canons' residences in the 1930s. The Great Quadrangle effectively forms Christ Church's cathedral close with, in the later seventeenth century, five of the canons, and the dean, living there. The allocation of lodgings had never been simple, but it became particularly complicated in 1933, when Kenneth Kirk, the new regius professor of moral and pastoral theology, refused to move into the canonry next to the deanery (now Tom 9) because of its appalling state of repair. It was proposed that Killcanon be sold to the college and the proceeds used to split one of the two north side canonries into two. In 1972 the central east side lodgings were also alienated to the college, and the other north side canonry split in two.
>
> Curthoys (2017), 25, 99

and the windows of the Latin Chapel were cleaned and protected by clear glass on the outside.

In 1933 the whole cathedral was vacuum-cleaned in time for the Cathedral Pilgrimage of 1934, when 1,200 pilgrims visited over the course of a fortnight, donating either 2s. 6d. or a shilling towards relief in 'distressed areas', and then for the 1,200th anniversary of the death of St Frideswide, which was commemorated on 19 October 1935. The whole diocese was invited to attend the special services: there was an 8 a.m. Solemn Eucharist which included the dedication by Archdeacon Shaw of a new altar in the Lady Chapel, which was vested with a finely embroidered frontal.[18] The litany was sung in procession by the clergy, including Honorary Canons, and the choir. The new dean, Alwyn Williams, and his officiating chaplains all wore copes. After a second service at noon there was a celebratory lunch, to which guests from all the archdeaconries in the diocese were invited, followed by a lecture on the life of St Frideswide delivered by the medieval historian Frank Stenton.[19]

Keeping a careful eye on all the work must have been William Francis,

William Francis (1840–1938) was probably Christ Church's longest serving member of staff. In 1859, he applied for a position as Dean Liddell's footman. In 1863, he was made an under-porter and library keeper. One of his duties was to toll the 101 every night at 9.05 p.m., and another was to rise at 5 a.m. every morning during the spring and summer to scythe the grass in Tom Quad. In 1867, Francis was made canons' verger (as well as retaining all his other posts), and later he was appointed dean's verger, the first of only three men to hold the post in the twentieth century. Asked for the secret of his long life and continuing good health, Francis recommended moderation in all things and 'perpetual motion'; by continued activity, he said, there was no time to rust! He retired in 1934, having served Christ Church for more than seventy years.

the dean's verger. Francis had first been employed at Christ Church in 1859 as Dean Liddell's footman, and became a verger in 1867. Astonishingly, he remained in post until 1934, ensuring, no doubt, that the vacuuming was done to his exacting standards and that the cathedral was spick and span before the celebrations of the next two years.[20] He died in January 1938 and was given the rare honour of a memorial plaque in the cloister. Just a year later Dean Williams was offered the bishopric of Durham, and Christ Church entered a new period of turmoil both inside and out.

John Lowe arrived as dean in 1939. He had been a Canadian Rhodes

Scholar at Christ Church in the 1920s and was a true University man, not only taking firsts in both Classics and Theology but also running and rowing for his college. Before his return to Oxford, Lowe had been professor of New Testament Studies at the University of Toronto. He arrived back at Christ Church to find himself quickly facing two major challenges.

The first had been initiated after Dean Williams's move to Durham was announced. On the proposal of Gilbert Ryle and Patrick Gordon Walker, a committee was established to consider whether laymen should be eligible for the headship – not permitted by Christ Church's statutes – and to discover how, if it was decided that this would be the right move, it should be effected.[21] The Chapter was represented on the committee by the sub-dean, Henry Goudge, and by the regius professor of moral and pastoral theology, Leonard Hodgson.[22] From the college were Michael Foster, the philosopher and Senior Censor; Gilbert Ryle, philosopher and the Student who had suggested John Lowe for the deanery; Roy Harrod, economist; J. N. L. Myres, medievalist and archaeologist; Samuel Grant Bailey, lawyer; and Colin Dillwyn, historian. The committee presented a report to the Governing Body in May 1939, just a month after Lowe's installation.[23] Ryle had drawn up statistics – not universally accepted – which showed that in 1939 only four heads of Oxford and Cambridge colleges were in holy orders, whereas in 1900 it had been more than half. Ryle also commented that the number of men in holy orders holding first-class degrees in subjects other than theology had plummeted. So there was a small and diminishing pool of men from whom the dean of Christ Church could be drawn. There was an assumption, unwritten but definitely held, that a dean must be a Christ Church man, and the report made the astonishing statement that 'Of Christ Church men now between 25 and 40 not one is worth consideration as future Dean unless we cease to require Fellowship status.' Hodgson wrote an appendix to the report, questioning Ryle's statements and statistics. Christ Church was different, he argued, and the fact that the number of non-clerical heads of house had declined merely showed that 'clerics have not been appointed to posts for which there was no particular reason why they should be'. At Christ Church, not to appoint a cleric would 'involve a dislocation of the existing structure unparalleled elsewhere'. Hodgson offered a statistic of his own: between 1872 and 1938 the average number of men ordained each year was 567, of whom around a quarter were educated at Oxford. Unless there was a serious decline in the intellectual capacity of those men over time, he suggested, then finding an academic dean should be no harder in 1939 than it was in 1872.

The Committee on the Headship came up with two possible solutions. The first – the 'Presidential' scheme – would retain the dean as actual head of Chapter but only as titular head of Christ Church as a whole. There would be a lay 'president', who would be second-in-command and would have control over the academic establishment. Problems such as control over finances and general policy would need to be resolved, but, because the statutes already allowed the Governing Body to create a presidential role, there would be no need for an Act of Parliament and the changes could be implemented fairly quickly.

The second proposal was more radical and was known as the 'clean cut'. There would be two entirely separate bodies: the Chapter, headed by the dean, and the College, with its own master. The cathedral's lump-sum subvention would be managed by the Ecclesiastical Commissioners, and 'ownership' of the buildings would be reorganised so that the Chapter's property would all be as close to the cathedral as possible.[24] But the cut was not to be complete: the cathedral would still continue to be the college chapel. The committee was quick to point out that this proposal – described in a letter from the dean to Gilbert Ryle as a 'cataclysmic alteration in the legal personality or entity of Christ Church' – would require considerably more work than the presidential scheme; in all likelihood approval would be needed from Parliament, the Church Assembly and the University, and a Royal Commission would probably be required to sort out the details, not the least of which would be the name of the 'new' college; the cathedral would remain Christ Church, but the college would need to be identified separately. The King's College was the obvious suggestion.

At least three members of the committee – Foster, Myres and Grant Bailey – gave a formal recommendation that no action be taken on either

Bishop Kenneth Kirk

Kenneth Kirk was appointed bishop of Oxford in 1937, after the resignation of Thomas Banks Strong. He was concerned that the diocese was too big to be served properly, and so secured the revival of the suffragan bishopric of Reading and the creation of a new suffragan see of Dorchester. With the archdeacon of Buckingham already bishop-suffragan for that county, the needs of the diocese could be managed better. Centrally, Kirk oversaw the finances of the diocese and brought all administration from Cuddesdon to Oxford. He remained bishop until his death in 1954.

ODNB

---

suggestion. At the vote in the Governing Body nine voted for separation but nineteen against.[25]

In 1939 war intervened, the discussions terminated and Lowe faced the second challenge of his deanery. During the First World War, Christ Church had found itself almost a military encampment, with only a few students but perhaps more significant in the city and the diocese as a focus for prayer and commemoration. The cathedral rose again to the occasion with preparations both before the war and during hostilities – not least, the feeding and baptism of refugees from the blitz of Bristol and of child evacuees.[26] Evensong was brought forward to 3 p.m. in order to cope with black-out regulations, and fire-fighting equipment provided. Procedures were devised for evacuation during a sung service which included leading the choir boys to safety and then continuing the service without music. The Air Raid Precaution authorities refused to allow the Chapter House and cathedral to be used as air-raid shelters, but money was set aside to equip the sacristy as a blast-proof and gas-proof shelter for the members of Chapter and their families.[27] This time the war in the air posed a threat to the fabric. Little could be done to protect the building as whole, but the glass was removed and windows boarded over. Christ Church was not alone, of course, in its concerns. Cathedrals across the country were busy moving treasures, libraries and archives

> [Form II] For the use of the Clergy only
> ## THANKSGIVING AND DEDICATION
> ### WHEN THE VICTORY IS WON IN EUROPE
>
> PRAYERS, LECTIONS, AND PSALMS
> APPOINTED BY AUTHORITY, TOGETHER WITH OTHER DIRECTIONS AND HELPS FOR INCUMBENTS AND THOSE CONDUCTING SERVICES
>
> 1. THE SPECIAL ORDER OF SERVICE which has been prepared and is printed separately (Form I) should be used on the Sunday or appointed day following the "armistice" as authority shall direct, and at united services. The rubrics apply to a service in a church or cathedral and will require small adaptations if the service is held in the open air or in a public hall. If there is an address it should be short, and should prepare for and lead into the confession, intercession, and dedication. The silences should be carefully observed and ample time allowed for the congregation to kneel or stand and become still before the next words are spoken. The doxology should follow the saying of the psalm without pause or playing over of the tune.
>
> 2. A SHORT ACT OF THANKSGIVING
> *For use on the day when the end of the war with Germany is declared, when people may be expected to come to the churches in large numbers throughout the day to give thanks, or to assemble in their places of work. It is desirable that incumbents and others should announce in advance the times when these short services will be held.*
>
> SENTENCES
> Not unto us, O Lord, not unto us: but unto thy Name give the praise.
> The Lord hath done great things for us: whereof we rejoice.
> Praise the Lord, O my soul: and forget not all his benefits.
>
> THANKSGIVING FOR VICTORY
> As in the Occasional Thanksgivings or in the Forms of Prayer to be used at Sea, or the first Collect authorised for use at the Holy Communion (cf. page 2).
>
> LESSON
> See Lessons authorised for Morning and Evening Prayer (page 3).
>
> PRAYERS
> O FATHER of infinite mercy and goodness, we praise thee for the men and women by whose sacrifice victory has been won. Grant them thy peace. And uphold with the arms of thy compassion and heavenly succour all those to whom this war has brought pain and grief; through Jesus Christ our Lord. *Amen.*

A form of service was prepared for the Sunday after the end of the Second World War, along with an order for a brief thanksgiving service to be held on the day that the war was formally declared to be over.

to places of safety.[28] Some cathedrals were damaged in air raids, either as collateral damage in industrial centres or as deliberate targets in the 'Baedeker' raids in 1942. Canterbury, Norwich and Exeter suffered particularly.[29] Oxford, apparently destined to be Hitler's capital after the war, was spared, although there were still fire-watchers positioned on the roofs, just in case. At the end of hostilities there were services of thanksgiving and commemoration, and a second set of tablets was set up opposite those from the First World War.[30]

Dean Lowe had steered Christ Church through the difficulties of the war – perhaps more a 'college' than 'cathedral' dean – and set the college on a path of academic change and physical modernisation. He resigned in 1959, and his place in the deanery was taken by Cuthbert Simpson, who had been a canon and regius professor of Hebrew since 1954. Simpson was a popular choice of dean, both on the academic and clerical side. He loved the dignity and beauty of services, was an active supporter of the choir and its school and was always working to promote the cathedral to its diocese.[31] According to Dr Mascall, one of the college chaplains, the vergers were scandalised when Simpson instructed them to pin a notice to the cathedral door advising latecomers to services that they were still welcome and to come in and take a seat. The vergers (then) considered that their role was to marshall the congregation in 'disciplined ranks' and to guard the doors against anyone who failed to turn up for the start of worship.

Since the middle of the twentieth century the combination of clergyman, academic and administrator in a single person has become far less common, and the character and interests of the deans often reveal them to be either a 'college' dean or a 'cathedral' dean. Dean White was thought to be a 'cathedral' dean, leaving the administration of the collegiate side of Christ Church life to its officers. Henry Chadwick is said to have struggled with decision-making but was a scholar second to none; under him, it is said, links between the college and the cathedral were weakened. Deans Williams and Simpson, on the other hand, involved themselves zealously on both sides, whereas Deans Lowe and Heaton were, perhaps, more 'college' men.[32] History has yet to decide where the three deans since Heaton will stand: perhaps one for 'college' and two following in the footsteps of Williams and Simpson.

In 1978 Christ Church, as a college of the University, and under the leadership of Dean Henry Chadwick, opened its doors to its first female academic, but it took two further years for women to arrive as undergraduates and as Students (Fellows). It was a signal step for the institution, but more than a decade would pass before the Church of England allowed the ordination of women.[33] In 1994, as soon as Synod agreed to the change in its canons, twelve women were ordained as priests in Oxford, including Anne Ballard, who was appointed as Precentor.[34] The sub-dean's address to the Friends of Christ Church Cathedral that year recalled this service, for which the Chapter wore red copes given by the Friends. He believed that this 'enlargement of the ministry [...] will be a means of great enrichment to our church'.[35] The first woman canon was Marilyn Parry, who joined the cathedral as Director of Ordinands in 2001, and the first woman canon professor was Revd Marilyn McCord Adams, the regius professor of divinity, appointed in 2004. These pioneers at Christ Church have been followed by more professorial and non-teaching canons and by a woman chaplain. It can only be a matter of time before there is a woman dean and a woman bishop.

* * * * *

It was not just the administration and finances of cathedrals that concerned the Church Assembly, or the General Synod, as the Assembly was renamed in 1970. The care of cathedral buildings and treasures, or perhaps the lack of it, had come to the fore when, in order to make cathedral interiors more suitable for modern worship, alterations, such as the removal in the 1960s from Hereford and Salisbury cathedrals of Victorian screens designed by Gilbert Scott and manufactured by Skidmore, were made without consultation.[36]

The Cathedrals Advisory Committee had been on hand to give advice from 1949, and was upgraded to a Commission of the General Synod in 1981. In 1984 it was decided that supervision should become mandatory. The near-sale of the Mappa Mundi from Hereford Cathedral in 1988 – for perfectly legitimate and understandable reasons – underlined how important it was for our buildings and cathedral artefacts to be protected.[37] The Care of Cathedrals Measure of 1990, which stipulated that cathedrals need to make formal proposals to carry out changes to the fabric, and to have an approved surveyor and archaeologist at least as consultants, does not, once again, apply specifically to Christ Church, because of its dual nature. However, Christ Church Cathedral has had a consultant architect for many years – at least from the 1930s, when Harold Rogers advised and designed the Regimental Chapel – and an advisory archaeologist from the 1980s.

Martin Stancliffe, Cathedral Architect in the 1980s, put forward a report with recommendations for internal modifications, particularly to the Lady Chapel. The work undertaken included a new stone altar, a candelabrum, free-standing candlesticks, a new carpet woven specially for the chapel to complement the Vyner window and a comprehensive rebuilding and move of the shrine, which involved much archaeological investigation and discovery, and was not completed until 2002.[38] In 2007 the Governing Body revisited the management of Christ Church's built environment, setting up a Buildings Sub-Committee and, employing a consultant architect to the whole Foundation (in 2008) and a professional surveyor (from 2009) to manage the maintenance programme across the site.[39]

Although Christ Church is not bound by the Measure, it has the same problems as other cathedrals in adapting its space for different needs and new styles of worship. Hereford and Salisbury cathedrals removed their screens in order to end the separation of congregation from the clergy in the sanctuary. Many have installed a new altar at the crossing so that the greater part of a service can be conducted close to the congregation. Christ Church still has its Scott–Skidmore screens; they do not divide nave from chancel, but do separate college from diocese. Its size and odd dual function make Christ Church a difficult place to alter and to make work. Simple things have been achieved to present a more open feel, not least the glass doors at the west end, installed in 2005, and innumerable special events and exhibitions bring the cathedral and its work alive. Other plans look to the future and the further opening-out of the nave and chancel.[40]

Much of the work in the cathedral, on its fabric and its furnishings in the post-war years, has been assisted by the generosity of the Friends of Christ Church Cathedral. The Friends were formed in 1937 at the suggestion of Dean Williams, as part of a wave of such groups appearing in cathedrals up and down the land. The first of these was created by George Bell at Canterbury in 1926, soon followed by others at York, Exeter and Norwich, with the aim of fostering good relations between the dioceses and the cathedrals, and to help with the huge tasks of 'decoration and enrichment' beyond everyday maintenance.[41] At Oxford the dean would chair the

> ### Cathedral volunteers
>
> Over 600 volunteers contribute their time and expertise to the cathedral, including Stewards and Welcomers (now Guides, from 2018), sidesmen and -women, flower arrangers, embroiderers, tea makers, collection counters, servers, readers, singers, bell-ringers, education volunteers and advisers, day chaplains and building advisers.

organisation, and the bishop would be President.[42] Christ Church is small when compared with most other ancient cathedrals, and the possibilities for large new installations like a communion table at the crossing like the one at Exeter or an infinity font such as the one at Salisbury are limited, but that has not stymied the Friends who have contributed to a huge variety of projects, including new lighting schemes to enhance the enjoyment of the cathedral's unusual architecture, the provision of altar frontals, copes and other textiles, and purchasing or facilitating the acquisition of service books and plate. The list is endless, and Friends' groups and visitors have helped with the legal requirements of Chapters to maintain their buildings appropriately, and to beautify them.

Visitors can, of course, be a problem as well as a blessing, and Christ Church, like all cathedrals, has seen tourists from the earliest days. Visitors came not just to pray at the shrine of the saint during the medieval period but also, like Chaucer's pilgrims, to socialise and to see new sights. In the seventeenth and eighteenth centuries intrepid travellers such as Celia Fiennes and Daniel Defoe toured the country keeping diaries and writing of their experiences. With the arrival of the railway, travel was made easier for everyone, and tourism began to increase noticeably, encouraged by the publication of Bradshaw's handbooks. At the dawn of the twentieth century picture postcards became popular, and Christ Church soon featured on many. Guidebooks began to appear for all cathedrals, but Christ Church was quite late to follow suit. Percy Dearmer wrote probably the first guide to the fabric of the cathedral and the diocese in 1899; then there was a contribution to the

College History series by Henry Thompson in 1900, although this was more concerned with the college than the cathedral.[43] It was not until 1924 that S. A. Warner produced his history and architectural survey of the cathedral, and in 1935 E. W. Watson wrote another slim volume. Since then, innumerable mini-guides, often produced by that famous name of English tourism, Pitkin, have appeared.

As early as 1881, the Governing Body had made a decision that visitors would have to pay a small fee.[44] Christ Church was not alone: cathedrals across the country were beginning to charge for entry, except on Sundays, and others were employing special guides.[45] In 1976 the tourist entrance on Meadow Gate was established, with a rate of 30p per person, and the first custodial staff appeared. The cathedral Treasury was installed in the Chapter House for the display of cathedral and parochial plate in 1972, and a shop was incorporated in 1980.[46] In 2017 over 400,000 people paid to come in to Christ Church, with most visiting the cathedral as tourists rather than as worshippers.[47]

The 'Heritage and Renewal' report drawn up for the Archbishops' Council in 1994 looked at cathedral finances. The incomes of the most prosperous cathedrals, it found, were derived in almost equal parts from investment and tourism, with over 60 per cent coming from just these two sources. Christ Church was not included in the report, but it still has to deal with the impact of mass tourism.[48] Tourists may have taken the place of medieval pilgrims, but their physical needs are the same: staff, volunteers, shops, toilets, security and education all have to be taken into consideration without losing the essence of the cathedral as a place of worship or the importance of the cathedral to members of college, cathedral and diocese who come together to celebrate both the great events of the liturgical calendar and more private ceremonies such as a funerals, weddings and baptisms. One of the most recent additions to the cathedral has been the 'new' font installed in the south transept in April 2018 and blessed by Bishop Steven Croft at the Easter Vigil Service.[49] The inscription around its foot reads: 'The water that I shall give shall be in them a well of water springing up into eternal life.' It brings full circle the history of the priory and cathedral in Oxford – from the healing springs used by St Frideswide for the benefit of pilgrims to the baptism of the children of the diocese into the future.

* * * * *

The Cathedral Church of Christ in Oxford of the Foundation of King Henry VIII is a unique place. There is no other institution that combines a university college with a diocesan cathedral. The scheme drawn up by Henry VIII in the sixteenth century has been both a blessing and a curse, but it has given Christ Church an unparalleled independence. Nevertheless, for much of its history the cathedral was little more than a college chapel and lecture facility, with few from outside the walls – just the occasional intrepid traveller or diplomatic guest – finding their way to services.

The author of the 1847 article in *The Ecclesiologist* criticised Christ Church for not taking care of its cathedral – either its fabric or its congregation. No sooner had the words been written than its guardians most certainly did 'awake to a sense of its beauty and its degradation' and act accordingly, but it took a little longer for Christ Church to take on board its lack of connection with the diocese. Henry Liddell began the work of opening out the cathedral, physically first and then socially, to a wider community. Two world wars brought the community of the diocese closer together, and during the later twentieth century and into the twenty-first – not least with the help of the Friends of the cathedral – through new services, events and exhibitions, more social awareness, a greater interest in ecumenism and ever-increasing tourism, the cathedral has reached out to its diocese and beyond.

However, it is not easy to do this when the cathedral is enclosed within the walls of the college. Several times in Christ Church's history it has been proposed that college and cathedral go their separate ways. *The Ecclesiologist* made its feelings very clear: 'But better than all would be the separation of the two incongruous elements. Let the present cathedral remain simply the chapel of the college, and let the diocese be either furnished with a new church and a new Chapter in Oxford, or return to its ancient seat at Dorchester.'[50] Hugh Cecil, one of the creators of the Church Assembly, suggested in

1925 that 'it might be wise to look forward to setting up a great collegiate church in the diocese of Oxford to perform the diocesan functions for which Christ Church is unsuited [...] But this would probably be judged too revolutionary, or might most undeservedly vex the feelings of the Chapter of Christ Church, which no one would wish.'[51]

At every point in its history when the notion of separation has reared its head, Christ Church has stepped back from the brink; to separate college and cathedral would be to destroy the uniqueness that both parts of the establishment have fought to protect for centuries and have, on frequent occasions, found useful for its very survival. It is not always convenient; it can cause confusion and sometimes friction. But it is what makes Christ Church the extraordinary place it is.

Epilogue

Christ Church and the future ministry of English cathedrals: the House becomes a home

It is fair to say that most cathedrals in the Church of England possess their own unique and complex 'ecclesial DNA'. Some began as monasteries, others as parish churches. Some were purpose-built, but others may no longer reside in the bounds of the original span of the diocese. Some are ancient, some modern. Most are a mixture of the two.

Christ Church is, of course, quite unique. As a foundation it has evolved from being a convent to a priory church and then a college chapel – and then finally to become a cathedral. It is an assemblage of memorials and memories, of art and architecture, of space and spirit. The eminent sociologist David Martin comments that

> We in England live in the chill religious vapours of northern Europe, where moribund religious establishments loom over populations that mostly do not enter churches for active worship even if they entertain inchoate beliefs. Yet these establishments guard and maintain thousands of Houses of God, which are markers of space and time.[1]

For many English people in the twenty-first century, religious establishments are perceived to have weathered rather badly. Secularisation and consumerism, coupled to a declining number of those who follow faith, and a perceived loss of integrity in the religious institutions, have led many to question the future of public religion. However, Martin suggests that the buildings – these very stones – still speak to us:

> Not only are they [i.e., churches] markers and anchors, but also the only repositories of all-embracing meanings pointing beyond the immediate to the ultimate. They are the only institutions that deal in tears and concern themselves with the breaking points of human existence. They provide frames of reference and narratives and signs to live by and offer persistent points of reference. They are repositories of signs about miraculous birth and redemptive sacrifice, shared tables and gift-giving; and they offer moral codes and exemplars for the creation of communal solidarity and the nourishment of virtue. They are places from which to launch initiatives which help sustain the kind of networks found, for example, in the inner city; they welcome schools and regiments and rotary clubs; they are islands of quietness; they are places in which unique gestures occur of blessing, distribution and obeisance; they offer spaces in which solemnly to gather, to sing, to lay flowers, and light candles. They are – in Philip Larkin's phrase – serious places on serious earth.[2]

Cathedrals are primary examples of this: ultimate places of spiritual space. Yet there is no denying that in the twenty-first century there is general anxiety about apparently declining numbers of attendees at regular Sunday worship in the Church of England.

However, at least one group of churches has bucked the trend: the cathedrals. Consistently, the numbers worshipping in English Anglican cathedrals have been resilient, immune to the decline seen elsewhere. Indeed, many cathedrals report an increase in the number of worshippers. But what do these numbers actually show? As with much statistical analysis, it is the story behind the numbers that tells us how to interpret the bare arithmetic. To understand the growth of worshippers in cathedrals, one needs to have some grasp of the nuanced ecology of English church-going.

Sociological exchange theory can help us here with some interpretation. Classic cathedral worship is typically a 'low threshold' pursuit – that is to say, anyone can come, without any need or pressure to join a rota, group, class or any other supplementary activity. However, 'low threshold' is probably combined with 'high reward': the music will invariably be superb, the preaching of a consistently high calibre and the liturgy predictable and elegant.

So cathedrals in the future, wherever they are, will need to avoid the temptation – and the fate – of becoming little more than the leading diocesan flagship in the bishop's fleet, there to hoist up the latest ideas and initiatives to signal to the other ships. Cathedrals are places of alterity, not homogeneity. They are here to provide an alternative from standardised ecclesial fare.

To be sure, every bishop has their 'throne' in the cathedral. Christ Church is no exception. But this throne is a symbol, not just furniture. It is a 'seat of learning', or a 'chair in theology'. The primary function of the bishop is to pastor and to teach. And the cathedral church witnesses to the bishop's calling as a theologian and pastor, underpinning that vocation by providing a space that invites us to convene and to trespass, to dwell and delight in poetry and silence, to witness acts of hope and lament, to participate in worship that can provide both blessing and censure.

Ultimately, our cathedrals stand as a proto-sign of a profoundly incorporative ecclesiology. As Albert van den Heuvel argued, they are a symbol of diversity in unity, theatres of basic drama, Pentecostal laboratories, temples of dialogue, centres of creativity, clinics for public exorcism, places of international exchange, broadcasting stations for the voice of the poor; towers of reconciliation, motels for pilgrims and houses of vicarious feasts. A cathedral is the hut of the Shepherd, and so the House of Christ.[3]

I am continually confounded by the thousands who attend Christ Church Cathedral at Christmas. I suspect we should not be surprised at the continuing rise in the number of attendees and worshippers during the festive season. But there is a sense in which the spirit of Christmas – the cathedral that is offering the 'low-threshold high-reward' experience – expresses the *true* essence of English Anglicanism. That is to say, the services will embody a quality and commitment in pastoral and liturgical endeavour for *all* those attending, quite independent of any reciprocation on their part.[4] In that sense, the ecclesiology expresses the theology: the Christ Child is for all, and not just the committed.

At Christmastide, the Church of England, led by its cathedrals, rediscovers and renews itself as a form of ecclesiology that expresses the particularity and theology of the incarnation, dwelling in the midst of the communities they serve. In gift, festivity and exuberance, new life and hope are celebrated in the darkest of seasons. Charity to all is affirmed, and the church once again resumes its vocation as the social skin of the nation. The word made flesh dwells among us once again, full of grace and truth, and a symbol of enduring light amid the darkness.

In such contexts I am reminded of the vocation given to St Francis of Assisi in the early years of the thirteenth century: 'come and attend to my house'. In Francis's case, his local church was in ruins, and his call was to restoration and renewal. But this was a spiritual restoration and renewal too, and for this work, early in the ministry of Francis, he continues to be celebrated.

Our cathedral at Christ Church is not in ruins, or in any way challenged in the manner that Francis sought to address. But 'attend' is the key. For the attentiveness that Francis brought was not only a wisdom for fabric and structure but also a realisation that to attend to the House of Christ was to offer hospitality and openness beyond the normal tribal boundaries of the church of his day. The care for the marginalised and the poor, and the engagement with the world's first sense of ecology – a care for creation – remind us that wisdom is not just about thinking. It is doing. It is being. It is living.

Francis was therefore open to other ideas and cultures. He was one of the first Christians to foster Christian–Muslim encounter about eight hundred years ago – the beginnings of inter-religious dialogue. The call of Francis to 'attend to my house' was not one of mere inward reordering; it was an outward call. God intends his House – whatever shape it may be in – to become a home of wisdom for all.

So for Jesus and Francis the 'House of God' was both a vision and a project: to be capacious – a house of many rooms in which all could find a place. But more than that – Aedes Christi, the 'house of Christ', or 'The House', as it is more usually known – is to be not just a house but a *home*. It is to be a place of hospitality, a place of development, a habitat for wisdom.

Homes, of course, are only as good as the warmth and wisdom they share with the wider world. There is little point in a nice home if you keep it all to yourself. That's not what Christ Church is here for. Our resources are here for the world: for education and social transformation, as well as for our own individual illumination.

Jesus, John's gospel tells us, made his *home* among us. His whole way of being, sharing, loving and wisdom is an exemplary way to live. So the wisdom we seek is not merely about information, so much as our formation – as people, a community and wider society. That's why Christ Church Cathedral is about *our* character and formation: beginning in this cathedral, spreading out into this diocese, radiating out into our city and counties.

Because Jesus is the body language of God, the life Jesus leads expresses the wisdom of God. It is not just what he says; it is also what he doesn't say. It is not just what he does but also what he doesn't do. His silence speaks as much as his words do. His wisdom is embodied. And that is our calling: to let the Spirit of God dwell in us – to become a people where God is truly at home. The houses and homes that Jesus lived and stayed in tended to be pretty busy places. Because many came to these spaces for teachings, conversations and encounters that were utterly transformative. Individuals and societies were changed. There is a sense in which Christ Church Cathedral is just as committed to following this call – through gathering, convening and drawing all in, becoming an agent of God's gracious, proactive hospitality.

One could perhaps be forgiven for thinking that this is all very well, but, laden with such a history, how does a House of Prayer like Christ Church Cathedral, with such an illustrious pedigree, ever move forward? Yet our great art and architecture are not just for preserving; they are also for fostering care and critical thinking. Appreciating our history is not supposed to keep us locked into the past. It is supposed to cause us to pause and think – but then to open our eyes to face the present, and the future.

So, we have a real opportunity – not only to be faithful to the past, and stewards of the mysteries of God in the present, but to think beyond. We are also called to pledge an allegiance to what God intends this place still to become: to the future God wills for it. Because, like all houses, Christ Church Cathedral can never be completely finished. So as the twenty-first century stretches ahead, there is more work for us to do to 'attend' to this unique House of Christ – God willing.

The Very Revd Professor Martyn Percy

Appendix 1: Priors of St Frideswide's

Guimond	1122
Robert of Cricklade	1139
Philip	1175
Simon	*c.*1195
Elias (Scotus)	1228
William of Gloucester	1236
Robert of Weston	1249
Robert of Olney	1260
John of Lewknor	1278
Robert of Ewelme	1284
Alexander of Sutton	1294
Robert of Thorveston	1316
John of Littlemore	1338
Nicholas of Hungerford	1349
John of Wallingford	1362
John of Dodford	1374
Thomas Bradwell	1391
Richard of Oxford	1405
Edmund Andever	1434
Robert Downham	1439
John Westbury	1458
George Norton	1479
Richard Walker	1484
Thomas Ware	1496
William Chedill	1501
John Burton	1513–24

Appendix 2: Bishops of Oxford and Deans of Christ Church

Sixteenth century

Bishops

Robert King, 1542–57: died in office

Thomas Goldwell, 1558: died before institution

(See remained vacant for nine years)

Hugh Curwen, 1567–8: died in office

(See remained vacant for 21 years)

John Underhill, 1589–92: died in office

(See remained vacant until 1604)

Deans

Richard Cox, 1546–53: then bishop of Ely

Richard Marshall, 1553–9: then Catholic priest

George Carew, 1559–61: then dean of the Chapel Royal and Exeter

Thomas Sampson, 1561–5: deprived for non-conformity

Thomas Cooper, 1565–7: then bishop of Lincoln

John Piers, 1570–76: then bishop of Rochester and archbishop of York

Toby Matthew, 1576–84: then bishop of Durham and archbishop of York

William James, 1584–96: then dean of Durham

Thomas Ravis, 1596–1605: then bishop of Gloucester

Appendix 2: Bishops of Oxford and Deans of Christ Church

Seventeenth century

Bishops

John Bridges, 1604–18: died in office

John Howson, 1619–28: translated to Durham

Richard Corbett, 1628–32: translated to Norwich

John Bancroft, 1632–41: died in office

Robert Skinner, 1641–63: translated to Worcester

William Paul, 1663–5: died in office

Walter Blandford, 1665–71: translated to Worcester

Nathaniel Crew, 1671–4: translated to Durham

Henry Compton, 1674–5: translated to London

John Fell, 1676–86: died in office

Samuel Parker, 1686–8: died in office

Timothy Hall, 1688–90: died in office

John Hough, 1690–99: translated to Lichfield and Coventry

William Talbot, 1699–1715: translated to Salisbury

Deans

Thomas Ravis, 1596–1605: then bishop of Gloucester

John King, 1605–11: then bishop of London

William Goodwin, 1611–20: died in office

Richard Corbett, 1620–28: then bishop of Oxford

Brian Duppa, 1628–38: then bishop of Chichester

Samuel Fell, 1638–48: ejected by the Visitors and died 1649

Edward Reynolds, 1648–51 and 1660: then bishop of Norwich

John Owen, 1651–60

George Morley, 1660: then bishop of Worcester

John Fell, 1660–86: died in office

John Massey, 1686–8: fled the country

Henry Aldrich, 1689–1710: died in office

Eighteenth century

Bishops

William Talbot, 1699–15: translated to Salisbury

John Potter, 1715–37: translated to Canterbury

Thomas Secker, 1737–58: translated to Canterbury

John Hume, 1758–66: translated to Salisbury

Robert Lowth, 1766–7: translated to London

John Butler, 1777–88: translated to Hereford

Edward Smallwell, 1788–99: died in office

John Randolph, 1799–1807: translated to Bangor

Deans

Henry Aldrich, 1689–1710: died in office

Francis Atterbury, 1711–13: then bishop of Rochester

George Smalridge, 1713–19: died in office

Hugh Boulter, 1719–24: then archbishop of Armagh

William Bradshaw, 1724–32: died in office

John Conybeare, 1733–55: died in office

David Gregory, 1756–67: died in office

William Markham, 1767–7: then archbishop of York

Lewis Bagot, 1777–83: then bishop of Norwich

Cyril Jackson, 1783–1809: resigned and retired

Nineteenth century

Bishops

John Randolph, 1799–1807: translated to Bangor and London

Charles Moss, 1807–11: died in office

William Jackson, 1812–15 – died in office

Edward Legge, 1816–27: died in office

Deans

Cyril Jackson, 1783–1809: died in office

Charles Henry Hall, 1809–24: died in office

Samuel Smith, 1824–31: died in office

Thomas Gaisford, 1831–55: died in office

Appendix 2: Bishops of Oxford and Deans of Christ Church

Charles Lloyd, 1827–9: died in office
Richard Bagot, 1829–45: translated to Bath and Wells
Samuel Wilberforce, 1845–70: translated to Winchester
John Mackarness, 1870–89: died in office
William Stubbs, 1889–1901: died in office

Henry Liddell, 1855–92: retired
Francis Paget, 1892–1901: then bishop of Oxford

Modern times

Bishops
William Stubbs, 1889–1901: died in office
Francis Paget, 1901–11: died in office
Charles Gore, 1911–19: retired
Hubert Burge, 1919–25: died in office
Thomas Banks Strong, 1925–37: retired
Kenneth Kirk, 1937–55: died in office
Harry Carpenter, 1955–70: retired
Kenneth Woollcombe, 1971–8: retired
Patrick Rodger, 1978–86: retired
Richard Harries, 1987–2006: retired

Deans
Francis Paget, 1892–1901: then bishop of Oxford
Thomas Banks Strong, 1901–20: then bishop of Ripon and Oxford
Henry White, 1920–34: died in office
Alwyn T. P. Williams, 1934–9: then bishop of Durham
John Lowe, 1939–59: retired
Cuthbert Simpson, 1959–69: died in office
Henry Chadwick, 1969–79: then regius professor of divinity, Cambridge
Eric Heaton, 1979–91: retired
John Drury, 1991–2003: retired, chaplain of All Souls College

John Pritchard, 2006–14: retired
[Colin Fletcher, 2014–16: acting bishop]
Steven Croft, 2016–

Christopher Lewis, 2003–14: retired
Martyn Percy, 2014–

Appendix 3: Organists at Christ Church

John Taverner (1525–30). Choir master from Tattershall.
John Benbow (1530–*c*.1548).
Bartholomew Lant (1548–89).
There must have been an organist following Lant, but no specific record survives in the disbursement books for an organist, and the role may have been performed by the master of choristers until 1605. From 1605 the list of organists (who usually held the position of choir master as well) is as follows:
Leonard Major (1605–8).
William Stonard (1608–sometime in the 1630s).
Edward Lowe (some time before 1641–82). Organist throughout the Civil War and Interregnum. He was also an organist at the Chapel Royal.
William Husbands (1684–92).
Richard Goodson I (1692–1718). Professor of music, and University organist.
Richard Goodson II (1718–41). Son of the above. Also Professor as well as organist.
Richard Church (1741–76). A 'good musician but not a very brilliant player'. Organist at New College too.
Thomas Norris (1776–90). A renowned tenor soloist who performed at the Handel commemorations in Westminster Abbey. He was organist at St John's College.
William Crotch (1790–1807). A child prodigy who played at Buckingham House and St James's Palace aged only three, and was appointed to Christ Church when he was fifteen.
William Cross (1807–25). Organist at St Martin's Church at Carfax, then at St John's and Christ Church.

William Marshall (1825–46). Organist at St John's College and All Souls College as well as Christ Church.

Charles William Corfe (1846–82). From a family of cathedral organists, he was famed for using a particular selection of organ stops.

Charles Harford Lloyd (1882–92). The first Christ Church organist to have an Oxford BA. After retirement he became precentor at Eton College, but later returned to employment as organist of the Chapel Royal.

Basil Harwood (1892–1909). Before coming to Oxford, Harwood was organist at Ely. The first conductor of the Oxford Bach Choir.

Henry Ley (1909–1926). An organ scholar at Keble College, he was appointed to Christ Church before he had received any degrees on the recommendation of Dean Strong, who was a staunch supporter of the choir.

Noel Ponsonby (1926–8). Later organist at Ely Cathedral.

William Harris (1929–32). Later organist at St George's Chapel, Windsor.

Thomas Armstrong (1933–55). The first organist to be appointed a Student of Christ Church.

Sydney Watson (1955–70). Music teacher at Stowe School and the Royal College of Music. Organist at New College.

Simon Preston (1970–81). Left Christ Church on his appointment as organist at Westminster Abbey.

Francis Grier (1981–5). Left Christ Church to travel to India to study Hinduism. He later entered the Benedictine abbey of Quarr.

Stephen Darlington (1985–2018). Organ scholar at Christ Church, then assistant organist at Canterbury and master of music at St Albans.

Stephen Grahl (2018–). Director of Music at Peterborough Cathedral.

Shaw (1991), 208–18

Conventions and monetary values

Conventions

In England, Wales and Ireland, the Julian calendar was replaced by the Gregorian calendar in 1752. Before this date, the civil or legal year began on 25 March, rather than 1 January. In this volume, however, all years, even before 1752, are assumed to have begun on 1 January.

All archival references, unless otherwise prefixed, are to Christ Church sources.

References to the *Oxford Dictionary of National Biography* are to the name in context unless otherwise indicated.

A note on monetary values

Calculations of equivalent values have been derived from Lawrence H. Officer and Samuel H. Williamson, 'Five Ways to Compute the Relative Value of a UK Pound Amount, 1270 to Present', on www.measuringworth.com. It is not always easy to pick the correct comparator, which is why, in some cases, two values have been given.

Notes

Introduction and acknowledgements
1. Warner (1924); Curthoys (2017).
2. Blair (1990). Thanks are also due to Stephen Mileson, editor of *Oxoniensia*.

1. St Frideswide and the beginnings of the priory
1. There are many books and papers that discuss the life of St Frideswide, including Parker (1885), Wigram (1895), Warner (1924), Jacob (1953), Blair (1987), Blair (1990), Blair (1994) and *ODNB*. Any doubt about Frideswide's existence derives from Bede's failure to mention her in his *Historia Ecclesiastica*. Blair (1987) compares and contrasts the content of the Lives and Malmesbury.
2. Life A is recorded in: BL MS Cotton Nero E 1 (fols 156–157v), a book of *vitae* written at Worcester; BL MS Lansdowne 436 (fols 101–103), a chronicle and collection of *vitae* from Romsey Abbey; Balliol College MS 228 (fol. 300); and a breviary at Hereford Cathedral, MS P.9.vi. See Blair (1987), 73.
3. Life B is recorded in full in three manuscripts: Bod MS Laud Misc. 114 (fols 132–140) written at Pershore Abbey; Gonville & Caius MS 129 (fols 167–177v), of unknown but monastic origins; and the Gotha collection at the Forschungsbibliotek, Mm. I.81 (fold 225v–230). See Blair (1987), 73–4.
4. Chadwick et al. (2012), 3, 224; Radford (2018), 36–7.
5. This incident is said to be the source of the legend that kings of England were afraid to enter Oxford. Medieval writers say that this fear persisted until Henry III came in 1263 to hold a council. It is, of course, nonsense; even Anthony Wood, who liked a good legend, admitted that Alfred, Aethelred and Stephen had all come to Oxford before Henry III. See Clark, Andrew (ed.), *Survey of the Antiquities of the City of Oxford, Composed in 1661–6, by Anthony Wood*, vol. ii: *Churches and Religious Houses* (Oxford, 1890) [hereafter Wood, *Survey*], 130.
6. The famous 'treacle well' at the church of St Margaret's of Antioch in Binsey. Margaret had been tortured after refusing the approaches of Olybrius, the Roman governor in the Diocese of the East, as he required her to renounce Christianity. The parallels are obvious, and Margaret is said to have been one of the saints to whom Frideswide prayed regularly. 'Treacle' comes from a Middle English word for a medicinal compound.

Notes

7. 19 October is still the feast day of St Frideswide. Some sources have suggested that she was buried at Binsey – see Warner (1924), 6 – but both Life A and Life B say that she was buried in Oxford.
8. Thacker and Sharpe (2002), 483–5.
9. Blair (1994), 56–63; Parker (1885), 87–8; Thacker and Sharpe (2002), 460–61.
10. Stenton [1953]; Nash Ford (2001). The church in Frilsham, not far from Reading, is dedicated to Frideswide and has a holy well near by, and Benson, in south Oxfordshire, has also been associated with her.
11. Blair suggests that the contiguity of the earliest of Eynsham Abbey's estates to those of St Frideswide's shows that there was a real connection between the two, possibly right from their foundations. Blair (1987), 90; Blair (1994), 54; CCA DP iv.b.1, fol. 39; *Valor Ecclesiasticus*, ii (1814).
12. Henig, in Carr et al. (2014), 80.
13. Chadwick et al. (2012), 3, 224; Radford (2018), 36–7.
14. Blair (1987), 88.
15. Foot (2006), 97.
16. Blair (1994), 63.
17. Foot (2006), 96.
18. Gittos (2013), 149, 159, 160. Principal churches were becoming more complex, with a longer nave, more chapels, aisles and a more cruciform appearance, while other, subsidiary, chapels remained simple.
19. One is visible on the inside wall of the north choir aisle too. It was uncovered in 1888 by the verger, William Francis, during alterations to the window above. See Dearmer (1899), 83.
20. Blair (1987), 87–8; Royal Commission on Historical Monuments England (1939) [hereafter RCHME *Oxford*], 35. Apses tend to be post-Norman but to have fallen out of fashion by the beginning of the twelfth century. There are, however, surviving mid-late Saxon apses at Deerhurst and Brixworth, for example. At the end of the nineteenth century eminent men went to great lengths to prove that elements, at least, of Aethelred's church survived in the fabric of the existing cathedral. More modern archaeologists and architectural historians disagree, and it has been suggested that the arches may be twelfth-century barrow holes built to allow access by the Norman workmen and then rendered over when the work was complete.
21. Blair (1987), 89; Blair (1994), 63; Yarrow (2006), 170; Foot (2006), 111.
22. Foot (2006), 106.
23. If there are two separate cemeteries, they could equally be monastic and lay burial places. The double house lasted for such a short period that there cannot have been all that many interments.
24. Foot (2006), 107–10, 117–19.
25. What was to become the Banbury Road was diverted to join up with the Woodstock Road and create one major route north–south. If it was Offa who improved the ford, then it was he who established the precedence of Oxford over the episcopal seat at Dorchester-on-Thames: see Briggs et al. (1986), 110.
26. Blair (1994), 87–92; Blair (1990), 236. An intramural road ran round the east and south sides of the priory precinct too into the twelfth century, until Henry I permitted

the new canons to close the road and gate their precinct to isolate them from the town.
27. Blair (1994), 99–101.
28. A hide is, technically, a fiscal unit but is usually described as the amount of land needed to feed a peasant family for a year, and considered to be about 120 acres.
29. Blair (1987), 89–90.
30. Foot (2006), 125.
31. Wood, *Survey* (1890), 135. But Wood also suggests that a community of women was not suitable alongside a university, an errant nonsense as scholars were not to appear for another four hundred years.
32. Roach (2016), 131 ff.
33. St Brice was a fifth century bishop of Tours, whose feast day was 13 November.
34. It is not certain whether the decree was aimed at all Danes or just Danish men. The very existence of Gunhilde is in doubt, and her relationship with Swein is mentioned only by William of Malmesbury much later. There is some evidence for Danes living in Oxford, possibly concentrated in the south-west corner of the town and its suburbs, particularly in the St Clement's area: Blair (1994), 167.
35. Roach (2016), 187–200; Williams (2003), 52–4. In 2008 the bodies of thirty-eight young men, most of whom were shown to have Scandinavian origins, were discovered in excavations at St John's College. They bore the marks of both battle and slaughter. The number of Danes killed on St Brice's Day, in Oxford or nationwide, is not known.
36. Roach (2016), 203–10. Much of the Eynsham Abbey estate was given to Christ Church when it was founded in 1546, as part of its endowment. The archive holds the cartulary of the abbey, dated to *c*.1186, which includes a copy of the 1005 charter: CCA D&C vi.a.2 (see Hanna and Rundle (2017), 405–8).
37. Roach (2016), 259, 276–7, 284, 290.
38. CCA D&C vi.c.1, 7 & 8; Wigram (1895), 2–6. See also Hanna and Rundle (2017), 412.
39. A tile was found during the construction of Meadow Buildings in 1863 (now in the Ashmolean Museum) that was long thought to be eleventh-century. This has now been reviewed, and the tile is more likely to be from the early sixteenth century (personal communication from Blair). Biddle and Biddle, in Blair (1990), 259–63, and Blair (1990), 266–8.
40. Blair (1987), 116; Halsey, in Blair (1990), 117; Harrison (1891).
41. Bolton (2009), 78–94; Bolton (2017), 108–13.
42. Another possible date is 1040, when Harthacnut may have made some gift to Abingdon. See Bolton (2017), 184, 200.
43. Blair (1990), 226–7; Page (1907) [hereafter *VCH Oxon*, ii], 97. Over the next two centuries Oxford was filled with religious houses and the early monastic colleges that formed the beginnings of the University.

2. Patronage and pilgrimage: the twelfth century
1. Warner (1924), 187.

Notes

2. Warner (1924), 187–8; Parker (1885), 224; Williams and Martin (2002), 422, 430.
3. Warner (1924), 189–90. The date of the refoundation is traditionally set at 1122, but Corpus Christi College's version of the cartulary includes a charter made out to the prior and canons as early as 1116.
4. VCH Oxon, ii (1907), 97.
5. Warner (1924), 189–90; Hibbert (1988), 138; Crossley and Elrington (1979) [hereafter VCH Oxon, iv] (1979), 310–11; Wigram (1894), 12; CCA D&C vi.c.1, 16. The fair predates the refoundation in 1122; its profits formed part of the king's revenue in the early twelfth century. The date of the fair was changed to October in 1228.
6. Hibbert (1988), 139; VCH Oxon, iv, 311.
7. ODNB.
8. Warner (1924), 191. St Mildred's was demolished to make way for Lincoln College in the early to mid-fifteenth century.
9. VCH Oxon, iv (1979), 48–9.
10. Warner (1924), 192; VCH Oxon, ii (1907), 90. Adrian IV was the only Englishman to have been pope.
11. Warner (1924), 195; Briggs et al. (1986), 109; Blair (1994), 39–41, 44–5, 111–12.
12. Yarrow (2006), 169.
13. Blair (1987), 116; Warner (1924), 196.
14. Blair (1987), 93. The account is found in a continuation to a version of Life A in BL MS Lansdowne 436, fols 101–103.
15. Fragments of the bones of the saint were taken, either in 1180 or at the second translation in 1289, to Winchester, Reading and Waltham abbeys: Blair (1990), 247.
16. Warner (1924), 196; Yarrow (2006), 169; Jacob [1953], 9; VCH Oxon, ii (1907), 98.
17. Yarrow (2006), 174–6; Blair (1994), 182.
18. An account of the ceremony was penned by Prior Philip, and can be found in the Bodleian Library's MS Digby 177. Blair (1987), 117.
19. Yarrow (2006), 177–8.
20. Warner (1924), 196.
21. Mayr-Harting (1985), 197; Thacker and Sharpe (2002), 490.
22. Blair (1990), 248–50. The shrine was probably elevated over the saint's grave on columns or a table, so it would still have been possible for pilgrims to prostrate themselves as they prayed.
23. Blair (1987), 117; Yarrow (2006), 169; Catto (1984), 10–11; Wood, *Survey*, 165.
24. Blair (1994), 183; Yarrow (2006), 178; Mayr-Harting (1985), 195. The saint was popular not just with the locals of Oxfordshire but also with scholars at the newly emerging University.
25. Wood, *Survey*, 167.
26. Mayr-Harting (1985), 198–202.
27. Yarrow (2006), 178–89.
28. Catto (1984), 11–13; Brockliss (2016), 12.
29. Catto (1984), 15–19.
30. The city walls were altered and realigned several times between the eleventh century and the thirteenth. Hibbert (1988), 91.

31. Much of the work on the twelfth-century priory church was done by Richard Halsey and is written up in Blair (1990), 115–67.
32. Blair (1990), 248. It is possible that three small columns survive from the 1004 church used as shafts in a western triforium in the south transept: Warner (1924), 22.
33. Sturdy, in Blair (1990), 83, 91–2.
34. Halsey, in Blair (1990), 119–20; Curthoys (2017), 197–8; *ODNB*. John Chessell Buckler (1793–1894) was an artist and architect who wrote the text of *Views of the Cathedral Churches of England and Wales* (1822) to accompany engravings by his father, also John Buckler.
35. Halsey, in Blair (1990), 153, 160–67. Very little, if anything, survives of the great medieval abbey and priory churches close to Oxford such as Reading, Abingdon and Oseney, so comparison is difficult.
36. Blair (1990), 266–8. The grave slab was found in the east choir wall and is now on long-term loan to the City Museum. Bishop Roger's diocese included the quarries at Purbeck.
37. Halsey, in Blair (1990), 120; Blair (1990), 236–7.
38. Halsey, in Blair (1990), 123, 155; Blair (1990), 237.
39. Blair (1990), 239–42; Scull, in Blair (1990), 65.
40. Tyack (1998), 20; Halsey, in Blair (1990), 135–6. The spire may be from the early thirteenth century, and was one of the first stone spires in the country. The pinnacles on the corners are a feature of churches in Normandy.
41. Alexander Neckam was a theology teacher in Oxford during the 1190s, before moving to Cirencester Abbey around 1200. Celestine III was pope from 1191 to 1198.
42. Warner (1924), 196; Halsey, in Blair (1990), 134–5. There is some fire staining on the exterior of the north-east tower turret (which indicates that the tower was at least at this height by 1190) and, of course, there is some reddening to the outside of the Chapter House doorway.
43. Blair (1990), 242–4.
44. Blair (1990), 240.
45. Blair (1990), 242. The doorway to the Chapter House shows that the work was extended downwards after the fire. The material excavated from the garth may well have been used to build up the levels to the south allowing for the extension of the precinct in that direction.
46. Blair (1990), 244.
47. Halsey, in Blair (1990), 155–8.
48. Halsey, in Blair (1990), 149. This would suggest that the room over the slype is unlikely to have been used as a sacristy; security would have been rather compromised. The south transept probably contains the only pre-rebuild elements – the shafts in the triforium above the Littleton monument. These were originally thought to be Saxon, but probably date from around 1120 and were reinserted rather than representing in-situ masonry.
49. Halsey, in Blair (1990), 151–2.
50. Halsey, in Blair (1990), 154.

51. The ground beneath the sanctuary bay is unstable, possibly having been excavated in Neolithic times and then re-excavated and refilled at various times throughout its history, and would hardly have been the ideal foundation for the east end had it been possible to build elsewhere. Sturdy, in Blair (1990), 90.
52. Blair (1990), 241; Halsey, in Blair (1990), 133–7, 160.
53. Halsey, in Blair (1990), 159.
54. Halsey, in Blair (1990), 138–9; Chadwick et al. (2012), 16; RCHME *Oxford* (1939), 37. Possible footings for the west end of the priory church were found under the terrace during excavations in 2006–7.

3. Crown and convent: the thirteenth century

1. Catto (1984), 30–32; Brockliss (2016), 15.
2. Catto (1984), 89, 267, 274, 279; Brockliss (2016), 26; Warner (1924), 197. Although it appears that very little had been done with the annual payment between 1214 and 1240, the capital received from the burgesses was not large, and loans from the chest would have been limited. Many scholars would, if necessary, have borrowed from Oxford's Jewish community, which was settled in properties immediately surrounding St Frideswide's. The chest remained in the priory until 1320, when it and the other eleven or so chests were moved into the Congregation House at St Mary's on its completion. The first Chancellor of the University was Geoffrey de Lucy, appointed around 1213/14; this may be the reason why there is a Lucy Chapel in the cathedral – Brockliss (2016), 16.
3. Catto (1984), 382; Warner (1924), 218; *ODNB*.
4. Dearmer (1899), 116; Catto (1984), 177, 226–7. Urban and Bekes halls were bought by Bishop Fox in the early sixteenth century as part of the site of Corpus Christi College.
5. Pandulf was papal legate and bishop-elect of Norwich. It was he who had negotiated the peace between King John and the barons, and the lifting of the interdict.
6. Warner (1924), 198.
7. The succession of the early priors is uncertain. After Philip there may have been a John, who remained only for five years, followed by William of St Aldate's until 1210. See Warner (1924), 178; Wigram (1895), xiii; Wood, *Survey*, 162. The succession of the canons used within this text is taken from David Knowles's volume of 1957 and from its successor volumes by Smith and London (2001 and 2008).
8. Warner (1924), 199.
9. Salter (1960), 230–31. Copin of Worcester founded Oxford's synagogue *c*.1228. Rather than a purpose-built synagogue, it was more likely to have been a room or rooms at the back of commercial properties – inns or shops – on the street front. Much of the area around the north-west of the present Christ Church site was occupied by the Jewish community.
10. It is also said that Elias was dismissed for fornication, rather than mere financial misdemeanours. Grosseteste deposed eleven heads of houses in his first year as bishop, ten of whom were heads of Augustinian abbeys or priories. See Southern (1992), 260.

11. A mark was a unit of account, rather than an actual coin, equivalent to two-thirds of a pound sterling, so 13s. 4d.
12. Salter (1922), ix, xvi, xviii, 4.
13. Warner (1924), 199–200.
14. Wigram (1895), 213, 364; Salter (1969), 186.
15. Warner (1924), 200; Wigram (1895), 291
16. Wigram (1895), 364.
17. Warner (1924), 200; Wigram (1895), 58. This privilege was carried forward to modern times; when Warner was writing in 1924, members of Chapter were still permitted to wear an 'almuce', or fur tippet, in spite of the garment being forbidden by the Church of England in 1571.
18. Wigram (1895), 113–15.
19. Warner (1924), 201–2; Wigram (1895), 64; Jacob [1953], 10.
20. Maddicott (1994), 336. The money never reached de Montfort; his son was attacked at Kenilworth by Prince Edward's forces.
21. Warner (1924), 202.
22. Warner (1924), 203–4. The plaque is said to have remained in place for 150 years, possibly somewhere near Merton College.
23. Warner (1924), 205.
24. Wigram (1895), 412; Nilson (1998), 21. The property was on the north side of St John's Street, the present Merton Street. The shrine casket would have been removed either at the suppression of the priory by Wolsey or later, by Henry VIII. Preparations for a translation could take years, especially if new building work was required. The shrine of Edward the Confessor took thirty years to construct, and work on Thomas Becket's shrine at Canterbury took at least five years, even after all the materials had been assembled.
25. The naturalistic decoration is rare for the period, with examples dating only from a very brief period at the end of the thirteenth century.
26. Nilson (1998), 23.
27. William de la Corner was bishop of Salisbury from the spring of 1289 to the autumn of 1291. Prior Robert was lucky to catch him as, during his thirty-month tenure of the bishopric, Corner was away from England for two extended periods. He was probably on his way from his consecration in Canterbury in May and his enthronement in Salisbury on 18 September.
28. Nilson (1998), 31–3.
29. Bond (2004), 332. Taynton stone was being supplied to the priory by the early thirteenth century.
30. Blair (1990), 28. A footing in this position uncovered in excavations may be the base for the 1180 shrine.
31. Blair (1990), 245.

4. 'Misrule and adversities': the fourteenth century

1. Alexander of Sutton had been appointed prior in 1294 and remained so until 1316.

Notes

2. Warner (1924), 207. Twelve marks, using the RPI, would now be worth in the region of £6,000.
3. Warner (1924), 207. Perhaps Geoffrey or one of his ancestors had held a position at court in charge of napery.
4. Warner (1924), 208; *VCH Oxon*, ii (1907), 98; Public Record Office (PRO), *Calendar of Patent Rolls, Edward II, vol. iii (1903)*, 296. Thorveston resigned in 1337.
5. Wigram (1895), 70.
6. Warner (1924), 209.
7. Using the RPI, this would now be in the region of £900,000.
8. *VCH Oxon*, ii (1907), 98. Apparently, the men of Oxford did not even eat the pigs, but kept them in such poor conditions that thirty of them died.
9. Salter (1922), xviii–xix, 18.
10. Warner (1924), 209.
11. *VCH Oxon*, ii (1907), 98; *VCH Oxon*, iv (1979), 311.
12. Wood, *Survey*, 170–71; Bill (1960), 8–12. Elizabeth was also buried in the priory church. Her highly decorated tomb is between the Lady and Latin chapels.
13. Warner (1924), 62; Clark (1890), 62. Anthony Wood lists the guild among his notes on St Frideswide's parish church, rather than the priory, but the parish had already been amalgamated with St Edward's by 1348.
14. Smith and London (2001). The two chantry priests charged with the masses for the Montacute family were reduced to one in 1363 as a consequence of the plague.
15. *VCH Oxon*, iv (1979), 18–19. The Black Death left Oxford in June 1349. Somewhere between 45 and 60 per cent of the population of England may have perished during the 1348–9 outbreak.
16. Warner (1924), 210. Gynwell was the bishop of Lincoln who was later charged with resolving the town and gown problems after the St Scholastica's Day riot in 1355.
17. Warner (1924), 214.
18. The priory's charter was confirmed by Edward III in 1335.
19. Warner (1924), 210–11; *VCH Oxon*, ii (1907), 98. The misdoings of Hungerford are colourfully described in Ann Swinfen's novel *The Merchant's Tale* (2017).
20. Warner (1924), 208.
21. Islip founded Canterbury College in 1362 as a stadium for the monks of Christ Church in Canterbury. The present Canterbury Quad marks its site.
22. Warner (1924), 210–13; *VCH Oxon*, ii (1907), 98–9; Smith (2008), 501; Wigram (1896), 373–4; Storey (1991), 81–2. Control of the convent was given to King John of Castile and Leon for three years from 1377.
23. Warner (1924), 213; Wigram (1895), 477–80; Smith and London (2001), 445; Logan (2002), 224; Storey (1991), 81–2. This all seems to have revolved around negotiations between Edward III and Gregory XI concerning royal rights of patronage.
24. Wigram (1895), 73.
25. Logan (2002), 120n.
26. Wigram (1895), 80–81. Prior Dodford's petition to the king telling of the attack is in both French and Latin.

27. Hibbert (1988), 139, 242. The University held control over the market until well into the nineteenth century, and there is still an honorary position within the University of Clerk of the Market. The St Frideswide's Fair passed to the monarch before the foundation of Christ Church around 1540. Edward VI granted the fair to the city. It declined rapidly and consisted of only a couple of stalls by the mid-nineteenth century, when it finally vanished.
28. Warner (1924), 214, 215; VCH Oxon, ii (1907), 99.
29. Warner (1924), 214; Brockliss (2016), 113.
30. Warner (1924), 215–216; Broad and Hoyle (1997), 8, 13. St Frideswide's held the patronage and rectory of Oakley, Buckinghamshire.
31. Smith (2008), 501.
32. About £1,000 today, using the RPI.
33. Warner (1924), 216–17; VCH Oxon, ii (1907), 99. Fleming founded Lincoln College in Oxford in 1427.
34. Knowles (1957), 171. A papal chaplaincy carried, as well as the honour and spiritual advantages, exemption from the regular life and obedience usual in a monastery. Thus chaplaincies could lead to men taking positions outside. The gift of papal chaplaincies was rare before the Western Schism in the church, but several hundred were granted (or bought) from the 1380s to the resolution of the Schism in about 1417.
35. Logan (2002), 52.
36. Smith (2008), 501; Cross and Livingstone (2005), 847. After the Investiture disputes of the eleventh and twelfth centuries a truce had been established between the popes and secular rulers over the conferring of rights to bishops and abbots; the pope retained the rights to present the spiritualties and the symbols of office, while the secular rulers kept the right to present temporalities.
37. Warner (1924), 217.
38. Donald, in Blair (1990), 100–02; Warner (1924), 81–3; Wood, *Survey*, 170. Burghersh left the priory the rectory of the church in Churchill, Oxfordshire, to fund his chantry.
39. Blair (1990), 245; Morris, in Blair (1990), 182.
40. The statue of the saint and the niche in which is stands are now severely eroded.
41. Blair (1990), 252–2; CCA BR 2/5/12.
42. The location of a prior's burial inside the church is unusual, and suggests that Sutton was held in high regard by the canons and perhaps had a significant role in the 1289 translation of the relics. The tomb is elaborate and has similarities to the 1289 shrine.
43. Blair (1990), 252; Tyack (1998), 36; Wood, *Survey*, 175–6.
44. Willis (1730); Warner (1924), 60; Dearmer (1899), 89–91; Kennedy (2012); Nilson (1998), 53.
45. The Lucy Chapel had an altar probably from 1122 until the sixteenth century – probably 1538, when Henry VIII decreed that all veneration of the saint must cease. The window survived probably because the canons removed the single pane showing the saint's head. It was restored in the 1980s: see below.
46. Tyack (1998), 20.
47. Tyack (1998) 69, for example.

48. I am grateful to Dr Simon Bradley for sharing his thoughts (and those of Christopher Wilson and John Goodall) ahead of the publication of the revised Pevsner volume on Oxfordshire. See also Tyack and Goodall (2017).
49. ODNB.
50. Jacob [1953], 2.
51. Warner (1924), 218.

5. Finance and finality: the fifteenth and early sixteenth centuries

1. Wigram (1895), 484–9.
2. Warner (1924), 219; Wigram (1895), 91–3; *VCH Oxon*, ii (1907), 99–100. So few animals on the 'home' farm may be one indication of the small size of the priory.
3. Jacob [1953], 2–3. The Common of a Virgin was a standard (Common) service in the Mass celebrating virginity, rather than a special (or Proper) service commemorating a specific event or person.
4. Tyack (1998), 69.
5. Dendrochronological dating was carried out on the roof timbers of the north transept in March 2018 by Dr Dan Miles.
6. Curthoys (2017), 7; Munby (forthcoming).
7. Smith (2008), 501. Walker had been a canon of St Augustine's in Bristol. Almost all of the priors had been canons at St Frideswide's before their election.
8. Emden (1974). Burton had both a bachelor's and a doctoral degree in canon law.
9. Knowles (1959), 68; Salter (1922), xxxvi. It is not known whether the 1521 Chapter was actually held. Where Warner acquired the information about Pole coming to St Frideswide's is uncertain (Warner (1924), 219; ODNB). It is not mentioned in the cartulary or in the 1690 *Vita Reginaldi Poli Cardinalis* or in the records at Magdalen College. Another suggestion is that Pole was sent to the Carmelites before going up to Magdalen College, with Henry VIII paying his stipend at least for 1512: see Mayer (2000), 47.
10. Gunn and Lindley (1991), 107.
11. Knowles (1959), 157–60; Bernard (2005), 229–30.
12. Salter (1909), iv, xi.
13. Lesnes Abbey, near present-day Bexley, was a substantial landowner but had only five canons and struggled financially to manage its marshy site and the large number of corrodies charged to it; *VCH Kent*, ii (1926), 165–7.
14. Bernard (2005), 230.
15. Youings (1971), 27. Bishop Fisher of Rochester was also diverting the proceeds from two poor nunneries to St John's College, Cambridge, in 1524.
16. Wigram (1896), 374–9.
17. Curthoys (2017), 17–18; Smith (2008), 502.
18. Warner (1924), 221; *VCH Kent*, ii (London, 1926), 167–9; ODNB. Tonbridge School was not founded until 1553.
19. Warner (1924), 222; Bernard (2005), 230.

Interlude: From priory to cathedral

1. Warner (1924), 223; Gutch.
2. The west end of the twelfth-century church would have been a little way further west of the present double-arch entrance to the cathedral.
3. The wooden shuttering may be seen as another indication that Wolsey had no intention of retaining the priory church.
4. Curthoys (2017), 44–8. The size of the new chapel is debatable. Aubrey suggested that it was to stretch from the college to the Blue Boar Inn. This is surely impossible. Agas's map of Oxford from 1578 and recent excavations suggest a building perhaps twice the width of the other three sides of the quadrangle: see Chadwick et al. (2012), 234. Odd fragments of decorative masonry survive in the garden walls of the archdeaconry.
5. Wayment, in Gunn and Lindley (1991), 126; Warner (1924), 49. The glass was definitely given to Balliol in 1529.
6. Curthoys (2017), 49, 61.
7. The seal of Cardinal College shows the Trinity, the Madonna and Child, and St Frideswide with an ox at her feet, much as she is represented in the lectionary held in Christ Church Library: MS 101. The dedication of the college is almost the same as that of the priory, just swapping All Saints for St Frideswide.
8. Tattershall College was a grammar school for church choristers established in 1439 and formally dissolved in 1545.
9. *ODNB*. Thomas Cromwell commented in 1528 on the quality of the college's services and music.
10. PRO, *Letters and Papers, Foreign and Domestic, of the reign of Henry VIII*, vol. iv (ii), 2457. Batey (1989), 33. Batey suggested instead that the choice of 19 October for the opening celebrations may indicate that Wolsey intended to keep the priory church for pilgrims to visit the shrine, but to keep it separate from the college chapel.
11. Glanville, in Gunn and Lindley (1991), 140–48; CCA DP iv.b.2; Gutch, (1781), vol. ii, 304–6; Curthoys (2012), 8–14. The plate ordered for Cardinal College was not just for the chapel but included a great drinking horn embellished in silver-gilt with a stand of three eagle's feet; a salt engraved with portcullises and roses; silver and gilt plates and dishes; and cruets.
12. Haigh (1993), 61, 66; Curthoys (2012), 8.
13. Taverner returned home to Lincolnshire. At least two men who had been appointed to Cardinal College retained positions at both King Henry VIII College and Christ Church: William Tresham (canon) and Robert Benbow (informator and chaplain).
14. Curthoys (2012), 15–21.
15. Higden died before Christmas 1532.
16. *ODNB*; Curthoys (2012), 17.
17. *Valor Ecclesiasticus*, ii (1814), 250–53.
18. *Valor Ecclesiasticus*, ii (1814), 250–53.
19. Curthoys (2012), 19.

Notes

20. Orme (2017), 111; Bernard (2005), 489–90. The Becket window in the Lucy Chapel is a rare survival of Henry's determination that any memorial to the saint should be destroyed.
21. Curthoys (2017), 78.
22. Dearmer (1899), 86.
23. Bernard (2005), 491–2, 500–04. The king held on firmly, however, to the doctrine of transubstantiation in the Act of Six Articles in 1539. The Act also confirmed clerical celibacy, vows of chastity, private masses and confession. He was not a European Protestant.
24. Gwyn (2002), 464.
25. Orme (2017), 100; Ryrie (2017), 125.
26. Orme (2017), 103.
27. And Lincoln, out of which Oxford diocese was to be carved, was the richest of all.
28. Gwyn (2002), 466.
29. Gwyn (2002), 468–9.
30. Cole (1838), 14–16.
31. Three readers *were* included in the first election list for Christ Church, dated 12 March 1549: Peter Martyr Vermigli (Divinity), Richard Bruarne (Hebrew) and George Etheridge (Greek). CCA D&C i.b.1, f01.1.
32. Bernard (2005), 457–8; Orme (2017), 104. The six new dioceses were Bristol, Chester, Gloucester, Oxford, Peterborough and Westminster. It must have been the same financial constraints that persuaded the king to abandon Oseney and place the cathedral at the heart of his new college.
33. Cole (1838), xiii.
34. Hibbert (1988), 296–7. The abbey was surrendered to the Crown in November 1539. Nothing remains of the abbey church today. Its area is marked out in the cemetery to the west of the railway line just south of Oxford station.
35. *ODNB*. It was London who had kept Cromwell and Wolsey informed of progress on the building of Cardinal College in 1525/6: see Curthoys (2017).
36. Ironically, statutes for Oxford were not drawn up – another indication, perhaps, that plans for Christ Church college and cathedral were already advanced. Cox was appointed tutor to Prince Edward in 1540.
37. Orme (2017), 107. The Great Bible, in English, was authorised for use in churches in 1539.
38. Much of this section is derived from Haigh (1996).
39. Wigram (1896), 380–83.
40. Pantin (1985), 22; Curthoys (2017), 147–51.
41. The account records that a Nicolson was installing new glass. It seems unlikely that this was the same James Nicholson who had installed the windows for Wolsey – see Curthoys (2017), 51 – as he had probably died before 1544. Perhaps it was a son or other relative. Harrison (1952), 16.
42. An account book in the Christ Church archives (CCA iii.b.99) – 'The accownte of all charges and receyttes both of Frediswydes and Oseney after theyr dissolution by Alexander Belsyre for one hole yere and one halfe ended att mychaelmas yn

the xxxviiith yere of Kyng Henry yhe eyght' – records the income from estates and expenditure, including stipends, during this interim period.
43. Haigh (1996). I am grateful to Roger Bowers of Jesus College, Cambridge, for his thoughts on this interim period. He has described this section of the accounts (CCA iii.b.99) as the 'single most crucial document for understanding the genesis of Christ Church – and of Trinity [College, Cambridge] also'.

6. Trouble and turmoil: the later Tudors

1. Curthoys (2012), 42–7.
2. The canons were not prebendaries paid from the income from land or property specifically attached to a canonry. At Christ Church the dean and canons were paid a stipend (as were canons in all the new foundation cathedrals) and then received dividends on top, derived from entry fines (periodic payments for the renewal of leases, designed to offset the effects of inflation) and profits from assets such as timber, coal and manorial dues.
3. Curthoys (2012), 43; CCA DP xii.c.5, fols 35v–36; *ODNB*.
4. Haigh (1996), 8.
5. Orme (2017), 109.
6. Perhaps the first occasion when Christ Church's dual foundation caused it to differ from other cathedrals.
7. Orme (2017), 113.
8. CCA xii.b.1; MacCulloch (1999), 67; Devereux (1969). Not only did the Dean and Chapter buy copies of the *Paraphrases* for use in the cathedral, but at least one was purchased for a patronal church.
9. Curthoys (2012), 55.
10. Curthoys (2012), 57–66.
11. CCA D&C i.b.2, 100; Haigh (1996).
12. *ODNB*; Cross, in Duffy and Loades (2006), 59; CCA D&C i.b.2, 100.
13. CCA D&C i.b.1. The first list of Students and other men paid by the endowment includes places – usually counties – of origin. John ab Ulmis, from 'Helvetius', is one of the third group of Students (*philosophiae secondi vicenarii*).
14. *ODNB*; MacCulloch (1999), 89–92; Brockliss (2016), 186. The second exhortation to communion in the 1552 Prayer Book is a translation of Vermigli's *Adhortatio ad coenam Domini mysticam*.
15. Catherine and Vermigli had married in 1545. Vermigli's two-storeyed study, built in the garden of the Priory House and visible on David Loggan's engraving of Christ Church from 1673, was demolished in 1684 by Henry Aldrich. Wood, *Athenae Oxonienses*, i, col. 329.
16. Curthoys (2017), 9. Tresham extended the Priory House, filling a gap between the Chapter House and the medieval prior's lodgings partly with the present choir practice room and spreading into the dormitory over the Chapter House. He also funded the building of the wall between Christ Church and Blue Boar Lane: see CCA DP i.a.15, fol. 4v.

17. Curthoys (2017), 43–5; Brockliss (2016), 190. The other Catholic college was Trinity.
18. *ODNB*.
19. Haigh (1996).
20. Haugaard (1968), 46.
21. Orme (2017), 115.
22. Le Neve (1996), 105; Lehmberg (1988), 124–5; CCA DP i.a.16.
23. *ODNB*; Cross, in Duffy and Loades (2006), 62.
24. *ODNB*. Marshall, or Martiall, had been one of the short-lived diocesan scholars and then was elected to a Studentship at Christ Church in 1546.
25. *ODNB*; CCA DP i.a.1. After the death of Mary, Newton was made a canon of Canterbury cathedral; Pullain came home to be a reforming archdeacon in Colchester; Whittingham was appointed first a fighting chaplain with the Earl of Warwick at Le Havre, and then dean of Durham. Goodman remained unpopular even after the accession of Elizabeth; during his time away he had written a book justifying resistance to the Crown and questioning the legitimacy of female rulers. He returned home, but spent much of the rest of his life in Scotland, Ireland and the north of England.
26. Loades, in Duffy and Loades (2006), 34–5, 46; *ODNB*. King died in 1557 and Thomas Goldwell, bishop of St Asaph and an associate of Cardinal Pole, was nominated to take his place. Papers were drawn up, but the death of Mary prevented his institution. He would barely have been resident, however, as the plan was to send him to Rome as ambassador. Goldwell was exiled in 1559, became a pensioner of Philip II and died – the last surviving member of the Marian episcopal bench – in 1585.
27. *ODNB*; Charles-Edwards and Reid (2017), 66–7. Jewel was a close friend and supporter of Vermigli and was expelled from his college for that friendship, as well as for refusing to attend Mass and subscribing to heretical doctrines. He tried to remain a quiet scholar in England, but, in spite of a reluctant acceptance of Catholic articles of faith, found that exile was the only way. He met up with both Cox and Vermigli in Frankfurt and Strasbourg, returning to England with the other exiles after Mary's death, to be appointed bishop of Salisbury in 1560.
28. CCA D&C i.b.2, 89.
29. CCA D&C i.b.2, 90 and 255.
30. CCA D&C i.b.2, 256.
31. CCA DP i.a.1. The deans' admissions books form a continuous sequence from 1546 until the Second World War. However, those recording admissions before 1660 appear to have been compiled retrospectively around that date, sometimes apparently using documents that do not survive but also drawing on the Chapter Books, the battels books and the disbursement books.
32. Cross, in Duffy and Loades (2006), 66; CCA MS Estates 35, fol. 1. The grant was allegedly correcting a fault in the original endowment. Mary also discharged the Dean and Chapter of an annual rent to the Crown of over £73 per annum. The total grant today would be worth about £58,000 using the RPI or £1.5 million using per-capita GDP. It is not always easy to choose which comparator to use when giving

modern equivalents of costs or income. Throughout this book the choice has been made using the guidance on the website www.measuringworth.com.

33. *ODNB*; Cross, in Duffy and Loades (2006), 65–9; Brockliss (2016), 189.
34. Orme (2017), 115. About 280 people were executed by burning, including five bishops and five canons.
35. Lehmberg (1988), 127.
36. Cross, in Duffy and Loades (2006), 70.
37. Orme (2017), 116.
38. *ODNB*; Wood, *Survey* (1890), 169; Calfhill (1562).
39. Lehmberg (1998), 137; *ODNB*; and see footnote 26 above.
40. Warner (1924), 227; Haugaard (1968), 46, 157. Oversight was directly by Archbishop Whitgift from 1583. Whether Elizabeth really did leave the see vacant for the income is debatable; Oxford was only a very small diocese and not wealthy.
41. Haugaard (1968), 47. Kennall had also been archdeacon of Oxford before the creation of the new diocese.
42. Cross, in Duffy and Loades (2006), 73.
43. Cross, in Duffy and Loades (2006), 74; Orme (2017), 117.
44. Haigh (1993), 255.
45. *ODNB*.
46. CCA D&C i.b.2, 100; Hanna and Rundle (2017), 38.
47. *ODNB*; Curthoys (2012), 71; Cross, in Duffy and Loades (2006), 73; Lehmberg (1988), 157.
48. *ODNB*; Haugaard (1968), 137.
49. Orme (2017), 117.
50. The regius professorship of Hebrew was not annexed to a canonry at Christ Church until 1630.
51. *ODNB*.
52. *ODNB*; CCA DP i.a.16, fol. 3v; CCA DP i.a.1, fol. 23.
53. Warner (1924), 227–9; *ODNB*; Calfhill (1562); Blair (1990), 254–5.
54. *ODNB*; CCA DP i.a.16, 7. Belsyre also owed Christ Church about £50: CCA D&C i.b.2, 216–217.
55. CCA DP i.a.16, 13 and 15; *ODNB*. Bernard had been appointed, before and after Mary, to the living of Pyrton in south Oxfordshire. Twice he was responsible, like so many of his contemporaries, for whitewashing the interior of the church, replacing the service books and changing the altar for a wooden communion table.
56. Curthoys (2017), 24–5. The rule about seniority broke down fairly quickly, and the Chapter Books are riddled with discussion and debate about occupancy. Chaplains' Quad was roughly where the western end of Meadow Buildings now is.
57. Curthoys (2017), 24–7.
58. Curthoys (2012), 78–9.
59. Orme (2017), 128–9.
60. Lehmberg (1988), 193–225. The quarterly stipends of the three groups of choristers are recorded in the disbursement books, along with those of the precentor and of the organist and schoolmaster, who were often one and the same man.

61. Curthoys (2017), 57–9. There is nothing in the disbursement books concerning the organ itself until the early seventeenth century. However, the presence of an organist suggests that there was an instrument from the earliest days.
62. Nichols, *Progresses*, i (2014).
63. ODNB.
64. CCA D&C i.b.2, 223.
65. ODNB.
66. CCA D&C i.b.2, 229–231; Haigh (1993), 273.
67. CCA xii.b.24.
68. CCA xii.b.25.
69. CCA D&C i.b.2, 338.
70. Orme (2017), 127–8.
71. Lehmberg (1988), 271.
72. The burial records of the cathedral do not begin until the mid-seventeenth century, but there are only four sixteenth-century monuments, all for members of Christ Church.
73. CCA DP xii.c.5,fsee footno fol. 36r. The covenant also permitted the removal of ornaments, plate, jewels, glass, iron, bells and all outstanding moneys due in from the estates.
74. Curthoys (2017), 81–2; CCA xii.b.25; CCA D&C vi.c.4, fol. 24; CCA xii.b.24, fol. 54v; CCA MS Estates 143, fol. 1. Work was going on all over Christ Church at this period, presumably making use of the building materials that were available from Oseney. There was certainly work in the Buttery and the cellars, with new walls and gates in many places, paving and slating, repairs to Chaplains' Quad and the almshouse etc.
75. Curthoys (2012), 79.
76. Nichols, *Progresses*, iii (2014).
77. Ryrie (2017), 157, 187. Cathedrals might not have survived the Edwardian regime had the young king lived longer. Orme (2017), 118, 124. 'Cathedral' is here being used as a noun, rather than as an adjective to describe the seat of the bishop (as in 'cathedral church').
78. Orme (2017), 130–33.

7. Revolution and restoration: the seventeenth century
1. Curthoys (2012), 83; Warner (1924), 230.
2. Moore and Reid (2011), 45.
3. Orme (2017), 133. Jacob Arminius (1560–1609) was a Dutch Protestant, but anti-Calvinist, theologian.
4. Spurr (2006), 39; Moore and Reid (2011), 47.
5. Cross and Livingstone (2005), 1094.
6. Moore and Reid (2011), 47; Cross and Livingstone (2005), 738.
7. Spurr (2006), 40.
8. Campbell (2010), 28, 34–42.
9. Cross and Livingstone (2005), 136.
10. Moore and Reid (2011), 66.

11. Moore and Reid (2011), 79, 86; Spurr (2006), 41.
12. CCA xii.b.60, fol. 38.
13. ODNB.
14. ODNB.
15. Fincham (1994), xxv, 188–99; Fincham (1998), 277. While several Stuart bishops conducted diocesan Visitations, none appears to have been conducted at the cathedral.
16. CCA xii.b.65. The pew cost £3 10s., perhaps around £700 today.
17. Curthoys (2012), 88; ODNB. It is possible, even likely, that there was some resentment between Corbett and Duppa anyway. Corbett was made bishop so that the deanery could be freed up for Duppa.
18. Moore and Reid (2011), 44.
19. ODNB.
20. Orme (2017), 134–5.
21. CCA xii.b.69, fol. 7; Hiscock (1946), 216.
22. CCA xii.b.71, fol. 20.
23. CCA xii.b.59. A list of requirements produced for newly arriving undergraduates in 1546 included a copy of Leo Judas's psalter: see Curthoys (2012), 49–50.
24. Warner (1924), 231; ODNB. Cuddesdon was later annexed to the diocese in perpetuity by royal warrant. Corbett had lived at Cassington, where he held the vicarage, but where his predecessors had lived is unknown.
25. Fincham (1998), 39n. The bishopric of Oxford was never well funded. Cuddesdon and perhaps the rich living of Witney were its principle sources of revenue.
26. VCH Oxon, v (1957), 100. It was destroyed during the Civil War, in 1644, to avoid it being used as a Parliamentary base for an attack on Oxford.
27. Warner (1924), 230.
28. In 1628 Samuel Fell had seen and approved of the new screen at St Helen's Church in Abingdon – see CCA MS Estates 145, fol. 247. Other colleges were making alterations too. University College installed a sequence of van Linge windows in its new chapel in the 1640s. See Darwall-Smith (Oxford, 2008), 162. At Oriel a complete rebuilding of the chapel along Laudian lines was begun in the 1630s (although probably not completed until after the Restoration). At the same time Laud was purging the University church of St Mary the Virgin of all its secular University functions, again not completed until the construction of the Sheldonian Theatre in the 1660s. See Catto (2013), 359, and Crook (2008), 74–5.
29. CCA xi.b.35, fol. 81; Hiscock (1946), 213–14; ODNB. Stone worked with his cousin Gabriel Stacy, and the men received payment not just for the new floor, new columns, battlements and rails but also for a new door which was opened somewhere in the cathedral. The north aisle roofs were reslated at the same time.
30. Curthoys (2017), 175. There were also some stalls in the nave that were transferred to Cassington after the nineteenth-century refurbishment.
31. Only one of the windows survives intact, although sufficient fragments of others allow some sense of what the cathedral must have looked like when all were in place.
32. CCA xii.b.75, fols 17, 41.
33. Spurr (2006), 238–40.

Notes

34. Curthoys (2017), 39–40.
35. *The Ecclesiologist* (1847), 55, 56.
36. Orme (2017), 135
37. Warner (1924), 232; Wood, *Life & Times*, iv (1895), 56.
38. Orme (2017), 136.
39. *ODNB*. Laud was executed on 10 January 1645.
40. Orme (2017), 138.
41. Curthoys (2012), 57–67. The almshouse is now the lodgings of the Master of Pembroke College.
42. Orme (2017), 137–8. And the function of the cathedral as college chapel, which, arguably, has been its primary function for much of the last five hundred years, would have necessitated different practices.
43. Wood, *Life & Times*, i (1891), 58, 61, 68; Curthoys (2012), 102–4.
44. Robinson (1992), 39. James II was probably the last monarch to actually perform the *pedilavium* – the washing of the feet of the poor at the Maundy Thursday ceremonies. The service took place in Oxford in 1644 too, and then not again until 2013. CCA D&C ix.b.1 – burials recorded in the cathedral in 1643 and 1644 are markedly higher than in other surrounding years.
45. Hiscock (1946), 214; CCA xii.b.58. The Vice-Chancellor's stall was made in 1614 by William Bennett. Charles I used the stall when attending services during his residence at Christ Church from 1642 to 1646. As part of Scott's restoration of the cathedral the stall was moved to the Latin Chapel, where it was used by the regius professor of divinity to deliver his lectures. It was restored to its former position opposite the pulpit in 1962, during a programme of work and archaeological excavation in the Latin Chapel.
46. Orme (2017), 139–42, 146–7.
47. Curthoys (2012), 58–9; CCA D&C i.b.3, 33. Appointments to the almshouse were made by the monarch, except during the Commonwealth, when the patents were issued by the Committee for Public Revenue. The position was reversed immediately at the Restoration.
48. *ODNB*; Warner (1924), 235. Skinner had been translated to Oxford in 1641, succeeding John Bancroft, who died that year and was buried at Cuddesdon.
49. College prayers were moved from 10 a.m. and 3 p.m. to 5 a.m. and 5 p.m. – CCA D&C i.b.3, 23.
50. CCA xii.b.52.
51. CCA D&C i.b.3, 1v.
52. CCA D&C i.b.3, 40; Curthoys (2012), 110; Curthoys (2017), 175–6. John Evelyn, visiting Oxford in 1654, reported that the once famous windows were 'much abused': E. S. de Beer, *The Diary of John Evelyn*, iii (Oxford, 1955), 104–9; Orme (2017), 141. Evelyn also suggests that the college communion tables were turned 'table-wise', after the Puritan requirement, but otherwise were in 'pontifical order'. The Bishop King window, also by van Linge, but not part of the main series, survived the war and Commonwealth.
53. Wood, *Life & Times*, i (1891), 148.
54. *ODNB*.

55. Le Neve (1996); *ODNB*.
56. CCA D&C i.b.3, 1.
57. CCA D&C i.b.3. The first Chapter Book (D&C i.b.1) runs from 1548 to 1619, but includes very few accounts of meetings. The second book (D&C i.b.2) is called a Chapter Book, covering 1549–1646, but is more a collection of miscellaneous decrees bound together almost at random and certainly not chronologically. It is only the third (D&C i.b.3), covering 1648–1688, that begins a real sequence of minutes.
58. Curthoys (2012), 108.
59. Curthoys (2012), 109; Curthoys (1995).
60. CCA D&C i.b.3, 23. There appears to have been a dearth of chaplains, as Mr Segary, one of the Censors, was thanked, and paid, for conducting prayers: CCA D&C i.b.3, 5.
61. CCA D&C i.b.3, 24–25.
62. Canon Edward Pococke also refused the engagement, and was deprived of his positions. His canonry was taken first by Peter French, until his death in 1655, and then by John Poynter.
63. *ODNB*; CCA D&C i.b.3, 39.
64. CCA D&C i.b.3, 39.
65. CCA D&C i.b.3, 49. Henry Cornish took over as proxy the following year, followed by Ambrose Upton (a fellow of All Souls who had been made a canon in 1651) and Henry Wilkinson.
66. *ODNB*.
67. CCA D&C i.b.3, 91–93.
68. CCA D&C i.b.3, 93.
69. CCA xii.b.103, fols 36v and 39. Bonfires were a regular part of any celebration. In particular, one was lit every year on 5 November.
70. *ODNB*; Cross and Livingstone (2005), 463; Orme (2017), 150.
71. Orme (2017), 149.
72. Bennett (1975), 3–5, 8.
73. The almsmen were all swapped around again too: Curthoys (2012), 59.
74. Curthoys (2012), 114–16.
75. *ODNB*; Warner (1924), 236.
76. Wood, *Life & Times*, i (1891), 347, 356, 358.
77. CCA D&C i.b.3 (decree of 1 August 1660)
78. CCA xii.b.103, fol. 91; xii.b.105, fol. 17.
79. CCA xii.b.103, fol. 91. The two verges are still in use today.
80. Charles also visited, and stayed for some months, during the plague outbreak of 1665, and then again in 1681. There is no indication that he visited the cathedral during the 1681 visit. The Prince of Orange attended a service in December 1670 and was assisted with the liturgy by Henry Compton, future bishop of Oxford.
81. CCA D&C vi.c.3, fols 54–62; CCA DP ii.c.2, fol. 22.
82. Curthoys (2012), 126.
83. CCA MS Estates 143, fols 4–20.
84. Wood, *Life & Times*, i (1891), 432, 445; Curthoys (2017), 96–8, 102–15.
85. Curthoys (2012), 116; Wood, *Life & Times*, ii (1892), 3, 195. Apple-sellers had evidently been a problem for many years; Wolsey had laid down a rule that they,

along with seamstresses and stocking menders, were not to be admitted to the college under any circumstances.
86. CCA D&C i.b.3.
87. Le Neve (1996), 71.
88. ODNB. The rectory of Witney, which was very lucrative, often went with the bishopric of Oxford at this period.
89. ODNB. Three other deans held the bishopric after resigning the deanery: Corbett, Paget and Strong.
90. Fell was buried in a brick-lined vault on the left side of the Divinity (Latin) Chapel under the seat where he had heard Latin prayers twice a day – Wood, *Life & Times*, iii (1894), 191–2. There is an impressive memorial to him in the ante-chapel (originally in the north transept) with an inscription by Henry Aldrich.
91. The duke had visited the dining hall in 1683 but not the cathedral.
92. Bennett (1975), 8–9.
93. Hiscock (1960), 43.
94. Wood, *Life & Times*, iii (1894), 201–2; Le Neve (1996), 71; Darwall-Smith (Oxford, 2008), 210; Hiscock (1960), 43. It was only at Magdalen and Christ Church that bells were rung to celebrate the arrival of the royal baby in 1688.
95. ODNB; Warner (1924), 236–7.
96. Darwall-Smith (Oxford, 2008), 211; Brockliss (2016), 208.
97. Only one of the nine non-juring bishops (those who could not swear the oath of allegiance to William and Mary) had been educated at Christ Church. None of the canons was a non-juror.
98. Bennett (1975), 27.
99. Curthoys (2012), 138; Warner (1924), 237.
100. Brockliss (2016), 208.
101. ODNB.

8. Torpidity and tranquillity: the eighteenth century

1. Lehmberg (2005), 271; Orme (2017), 160.
2. Curthoys (2012), 141.
3. In the eighteenth century these were the regius professorships of divinity (from 1605), Hebrew (1630) and Greek (1546).
4. It was this arrangement that prompted the changes to the constitution in the mid-nineteenth century and the separation – to a certain degree – of the finances of the Chapter from that of the collegiate establishment.
5. Orme (2017), 163. Pluralism was socially acceptable: a clergyman who had a parish in the town and a parish in the country was a reflection of the movement of the gentry and aristocracy between their town and country residences.
6. The location of the Audit House is uncertain, although considerable evidence points to it being on the east side of the Chaplains' Quad, in a continuation of the Priory and Cloister Houses. It appears to have been used as a meeting and/or dining room by the canons until the demolition of Chaplains' Quad in the 1860s.
7. ODNB.

8. Curthoys (2012), 147–53.
9. ODNB; Warner (1924), 238. Smalridge had also followed Atterbury as dean of Carlisle before returning to Oxford. It was said that, where Atterbury had set fires, Smalridge had followed with a bucket of water.
10. Baker (1980), 235; Halévy (1971); ODNB.
11. CCA MS Estates 145, fol. 308; Curthoys (2012), 88; Warner (1924), 239.
12. Curthoys (2012), 165.
13. ODNB.
14. Potter's first child, John, was baptised on 22 November 1710 but did not survive. John junior was buried on 5 January 1711. His daughter, Elizabeth, was baptised on 8 November 1711.
15. ODNB.
16. Orme (2017), 165–6.
17. CCA D&C i.b.5; MS Estates 143, fols 21–26; Warner (1924), 127–8. Three old bells were evidently sent to Gloucester in part-exchange for the new ones.
18. Curthoys (2017), 183; CCA D&C i.b.5, 228. The window was designed by James Thornhill, executed by William Price and funded by Peter Birch, who had been an undergraduate and then a chaplain. Two memorials in the south transept – that of the Narborough brothers, who died with Sir Cloudesley Shovell in 1707, and that of John Torksey, precentor, who died in 1702 – were made by William Townsend, who was the master mason for both Peckwater Quad and the Library.
19. Two or three old silver tankards were to be melted down for the purpose.
20. CCA D&C ix.b.1.
21. Aldrich may have had some influence on the designs for the Old Ashmolean, Trinity College Chapel, the Fellows' Building at Corpus Christi College and Queen's College too.
22. ODNB; Hiscock (1960), 13–31; Wollenberg (2001), 45.
23. Curthoys (2017), 122–4, 128–31.
24. Orme (2017), 171–4. The first history of the cathedral was not published until 1899 (by Percy Dearmer). H. L. Thompson's brief account of Christ Church (1900) included the cathedral, and S. A. Warner produced a rather dry and equally brief description of the building and its history in 1924.
25. Defoe (1779), 191–2; Morris (1947), 34.
26. Willis (1730), 407–14.
27. CCA MS Estates 143, fol. 30; Curthoys (2017), 197–8, 135–7. Henry Keene, surveyor to the Dean and Chapter of Westminster Abbey, was the architect charged with converting the open loggia under the New Library into a picture gallery.
28. ODNB; Orme (2017), 175–6.
29. Andrews (1970), 171.

9. Reform and renewal: the nineteenth century
1. Orme (2017), 186; Curthoys (2012), 229.
2. Lehmberg (2005), 278.
3. Orme (2017), 187.

Notes

4. *ODNB*; Orme (2017), 187. Van Mildert had already established Durham University, in 1832, as a means to increase the influence of the Dean and Chapter in Durham and to protect ecclesiastical revenues. He had by then been passed over for the archbishopric of Canterbury, possibly because of his reluctance to adapt to changing political times.
5. *Reports from His Majesty's Commissioners Appointed to Consider the State of the Established Church with Reference to Ecclesiastical Duties and Revenues* (London, 1840), 96. Durham's exceeded £32,000 and Westminster's was more than £17,000.
6. CCA DP ii.b.1, fols 31–34; CCA D&C i.c.2. Memorial of the Dean and Chapter of Christ Church, Oxford, 1840.
7. Curthoys (2012), 230.
8. *The Ecclesiastical Commissioners Act*, 3 & 4 Victoria, Ch.113, dated 11 August 1840.
9. Lehmberg (2005), 279. All cathedrals were restricted to four canons except Canterbury, Christ Church, Durham and Ely (which were allowed six), and Winchester and Exeter (five). Minor canons (or vicars choral) were limited to six in each cathedral, with a minimum of two. The stipends of deans were fixed at £1,000 except at Durham (£3,000) and St Paul's, Westminster and Manchester (£2,000).
10. Lehmberg (2005), 280; Orme (2017), 201.
11. The battlements on the east side of the cathedral were repaired in 1805; rainwater spouts on the Chapter House were repaired and the organ loft fitted up for the choristers in 1806; and the Clerk of Works was directed in 1815 to make substantial repairs to the cathedral roof and spire. Stoves were installed in 1821 for warmth. Dean Jackson's memorial, paid for by subscription, was installed in the north transept in the 1830s; it shows the dean sitting with his back to the east end. A window was also proposed but finally rejected as no one could agree about the designs submitted by Francis Chantrey. The statue was moved from the cathedral to the library in the 1870s and then to the ante-Hall in 1957. See CCA D&C i.b.8, fols 43v, 50v and 146; CCA D&C i.b.9, fol. 16.
12. Whyte (2017), 21. The Oxford Movement (a group also known as the Tractarians), prominent from the 1830s to the 1850s, was led by John Henry Newman, of Oriel College, and Edward Bouverie Pusey, the regius professor of Hebrew at Christ Church.
13. *The Ecclesiologist* (1847), 50.
14. *The Ecclesiologist* (1847), 52–5.
15. *The Ecclesiologist* (1847), 47, 56.
16. Bill (2013), 130.
17. CCA MS Estates 143, fol. 103. The identity of Mr Coddington is uncertain. He is possibly Henry Coddington (1798–1845), the linguist and scientist from Trinity College, Cambridge, for whom see *ODNB*.
18. Installed by the Gérente Brothers in 1854 to commemorate the 300th anniversary of the foundation of Christ Church, this window was short-lived, being removed by Scott when he reconstructed the east end in a more Romanesque style. The fragments of glass were placed into the transept clerestory windows until 1961, when they were once more removed, broken up and reinstated in geometric patterns by S. E. Dykes Bower in the windows of the lantern. The clerestory windows now hold some of the fragments of van Linge glass from the 1630s.

19. Curthoys (2017), 166–72.
20. Thompson (1899), 154; Orme (2017), 200.
21. *The Ecclesiologist* (1847), 58.
22. Curthoys (2012), 46.
23. *Jackson's Oxford Journal*, 2 August 1856.
24. Thompson (1899), 156.
25. CCA DP vii.c.1, fols 2–3. Billing was Borough Surveyor in Reading, but when he was made an FRIBA in 1854, he moved his practice to 12 Abingdon Street, Westminster.
26. Orme (2017), 202.
27. CCA DP vii.c.1, fols 4–10.
28. Orme (2017), 198.
29. *Jackson's Oxford Journal*, 23 August 1856.
30. CCA DP vii.c.1, fol. 19.
31. *Jackson's Oxford Journal*, 23 August 1856.
32. Thompson (1899), 157.
33. CCA MS Estates 143, fols 188–192.
34. *Jackson's Oxford Journal*, 2 August 1856.
35. CCA GB ii.b.10.
36. CCA DP vii.c.1, fols 21–22.
37. Unfortunately, the 1867 Decennial Survey does not survive.
38. CCA GB i.b.2, fol. 19.
39. Curthoys (2017), 179; Thompson (1899), 156.
40. CCA DP vii.c.1, fol. 23.
41. CCA DP vii.c.1, fols 26–28.
42. George Gilbert Scott, 'Report of George Gilbert Scott, Esq. RA on the Cathedral of Christ Church, Oxford', printed for private circulation, 3 June 1869.
43. In 1871 Scott abandoned the idea of rebuilding the high roofs externally. He still wanted to construct stone vaults to match the choir, but appears to have settled for retaining the existing timber roofs: see DP vii.c.1, fols 133–134.
44. Using the RPI, this represents just over £3 million. If a GDP comparator is used, the figure is closer to £21 million.
45. Barnwell et al. (2014). Scott did major work at Ely, St David's, Ripon, Salisbury and St Albans cathedrals, and at Westminster Abbey.
46. CCA DP vii.c.1, fols 66–69.
47. CCA D&C i.b.2, 59. The appeal was extended out to include the diocese only in January 1872, this time including the elements that had been missed from the old members' letter. That the appeal had not been sent to the diocese immediately is another, if small, indication of the disconnection between Christ Church and the wider community.
48. CCA DP vii.c.1, fols 85–86.
49. CCA DP vii.a.5, fol. 106. Revd Rogers had a short memory; the Dean and Chapter had contributed to the work on the chancel at Batheaston, but had not given as much as Rogers had hoped.
50. CCA DP vii.c.1, fols 272–276. Barclay Thompson was a Student of Christ Church, and Lee's Lecturer in Anatomy.

Notes

51. Law (1998), 49–51.
52. The glass in the east end windows is by Clayton and Bell, funded by Henry Liddon and John Mowbray (who also funded the statue of Dean Liddell on the Fell Tower).
53. Thompson (1899), 157.
54. Warner (1924), 74–5; Thompson (1899), 158.
55. *The Ecclesiologist* (1847) 55.
56. Halsey, in Blair (1990), 147.
57. CCA DP vii.c.1, fols 254–257.
58. Curthoys (2017), 187; Thompson (1899), 158.
59. The firm of Skidmore also constructed the glass and metal roof of the Oxford University Museum of Natural History and the choir screen of Hereford Cathedral. Francis Skidmore was a proponent of the Gothic Revival style. The wooden carvings of the new stalls were made by John Chapman, a local man, employed by Symm for this contract.
60. Impractically, the iron grilles separating the choir from the aisles were originally solid. It was not until 1928 that gates were made to allow the passage of communicants: see CCA D&C xvii.b.1.
61. Barnwell et al. (2014), 133; CCA DP vii.c.1, fol. 226. Other marble floors were laid by the firm of Farmer and Brindley. Pevsner incorrectly attributed the design to the church of the Knights of St John in Malta.
62. CCA DP vii.c.1, fols 181–182.
63. Tom Quad was known as the Great Quadrangle in all official documents at least until the end of the nineteenth century and then in most into the 1970s.
64. There is no reference to the quotation in the Governing Body minutes or the Chapter minutes for 1872. The matter was probably handled by the dean and Thomas Vere Bayne for the Restoration Committee.
65. CCA DP vii.c.1, fols 213, 218, 233.
66. Curthoys (2017), 185.
67. CC DP vii.c.1, fol. 199.
68. CCA DP vii.c.1, fols 215–217; Dearmer (1899), 80. The altar table was moved to the north choir aisle and then to the Lucy Chapel. Bright stuck by his offer to pay for the altar.
69. The bishop's throne was dedicated, as is the present one, to Bishop Samuel Wilberforce, who died in 1873.
70. In 1847 *The Ecclesiologist* (p. 55) had commented that the previous episcopal throne was 'meanness itself, and can hardly be distinguished without a most diligent search: on the prayer-books nearest to it, and nowhere else, are inscribed the words "Christ-church chapel", as if to warn the Bishop off the forbidden ground'.
71. CCA DP vii.c.1, fols 244a; CCA MS Estates 143, fols 271–273; CCA Maps ChCh 85. The heating system installed by Billing was altered from hot air to hot water, with the heating apparatus moved from the south side of the church to a vault specifically built for it under the entrance at the west end.
72. This did make some of the rooms over the east cloister walk barely usable.
73. Thompson (1899), 163–4; Curthoys (2017), 200–02; Wakeling, vol. vii (2003), 306. Chapter meetings moved to the small room off the Chapter House (now the

choir practice room) via a new stone staircase. The room had been added to the Priory House in the sixteenth century by Canon Tresham: see Curthoys (2017), 196.
74. CCA D&C ii.b.11, 54 and 57. The font had a very elaborate canopy which was not included in the original design or cost of £112 9s. 3d. The font was moved from the Lucy Chapel to the north transept in the mid-twentieth century, and the canopy was lost. A replacement was ordered in 1950, but both it and the font were removed in 1991, and the cathedral returned to using a silver bowl.
75. CCA D&C ii.b.11, 109.
76. Dearmer (1899), 104. The sepulchre may also have been the tomb of a highly honoured person, perhaps the founder or patron of the chapel.
77. Dearmer (1899), 84–5.
78. Mason, in Brock and Curthoys (2000), 225.
79. For a more in-depth discussion of the 1850 commission and nineteenth-century reform in the University in general, see Brockliss (2016), 347ff. For reform at Christ Church, see Bill and Mason (1970) and Curthoys (2012).
80. Depending on the comparator used, an income of £12,500 is the equivalent of between £2 million and £9 million today. The Students' stipends would average between £35,000 and £57,000.
81. *Third Report of Her Majesty's Commissioners for Inquiring into the State of Cathedral and Collegiate Churches in England and Wales* [1855], 22.
82. Curthoys (2012), 256–7.
83. The Chapter Fund was set at £17,000, of which £13,500 was considered to be the stipends of the dean and canons. The remaining money had to meet the costs of the six chaplains, the organist, the lay clerks, the choristers, the vergers and other cathedral staff, pensioners, almsmen, charitable giving and the expenses of services, plus the maintenance of the cathedral and Chapter House. Needless to say, it was difficult to make ends meet. The Governing Body later assisted with the costs of the School, and the cost of building maintenance was met from a Fabric Fund set up after the 1882 Statute revisions were ratified.
84. *Christ Church Oxford Act*: 30 & 31 Victoria, lxxvi, 30 & 31 Victoria, lxxvi, 12 August 1867. The Chapter Fund was to cover the stipends of all the cathedral and cathedral school staff, the expenses of services, the payment of alms and pensions and payment of the cathedral portion of the stipends of the Dean and Canons: clauses V and VIII. The cathedral fabric fund would be determined after the newly established decennial survey of the whole fabric: clause VII.
85. CCA MS Estates 143, fol. 218; Thompson (1900), 217; Curthoys (2012), 231; Rothblatt, in Brock and Curthoys (1997), 304. Attendance at 'chapel' prayers during the week at 8 a.m. and 9.15 p.m. was technically compulsory, at least in the 1850s, although there was considerable laxity. Sunday services were not compulsory, and after 1871 – with the passing of the Test Act, which permitted non-Anglicans to be matriculated – absence even from college chapel was no longer a disciplinary issue, and attendance was poor.
86. *The Ecclesiologist* (1847), 47.
87. Wollenberg (2001), 29, 35, 80–85; *Gentleman's Magazine*, 14 (1744), 619.
88. Barrett (1993), 146–7, 158, 161; *The Ecclesiologist* (1847), 56.

89. Barrett (1993), 188.
90. CCA MS Estates 143, fol. 137.
91. CCA MS Estates 143, fols 138ff.
92. Barrett (1993), 169, 54.
93. CCA MS Estates 143, fol. 151.
94. CCA MS Estates 143, fols 164.
95. Wollenberg (2001), 195.
96. Wollenberg (2001), 196.
97. Barrett (1993), 254.
98. Wakeling (1997), 262, and (2001), 265. *Jackson's Oxford Journal*, 15 November 1873.
99. Barrett (1993), 237. Worcester Cathedral was refurbished by George Gilbert Scott and W. A. Perkins. As at Christ Church, seventeenth-century screens and panelling were removed.
100. CCA D&C xii.c.1ff.

10. Openness and outreach: modern times

1. *ODNB*. Strong was an energetic supporter of the choir, not least in providing support for William Walton, who was later to become organist and a composer of renown.
2. Orme (2017), 204–6.
3. *Christ Church 1899–1900*; CCA GB ii.b.11, 257.
4. CCA BR 3/1/1. It was decided that no ranks would be included on the memorial; all men who died in the service of their country were equal.
5. The Oxfordshire and Buckinghamshire Light Infantry is now a territorial Battalion (the 5th) of the Royal Green Jackets. Eleven regimental colours have been laid up in the cathedral, of which those in the best condition hang in the Military Chapel. It is usual practice to allow the colours to decay.
6. Paget was the son of Francis Paget, dean of Christ Church and bishop of Oxford.
7. Harold Sidney Rogers (1877–1953) set up in private practice in Oxford in 1912. He lived in a Christ Church property on Iffley Road, with offices first at 119 St Aldate's, and then at number 88. He acted as advisory architect to the cathedral. Much of his work was ecclesiastical, including the design of St Luke's Church in Cowley (now the Centre for Oxfordshire Studies). He served as mayor of Oxford in 1937 and 1938.
8. Limonofides and Belcher (2007). A short memorial service is held four times a year.
9. The Act allowed the Church Assembly to bring 'Measures' to Parliament for approval so that the process of changes could be managed directly by the Church while maintaining the link between Church and State.
10. Orme (2017), 226–7.
11. Christ Church had already, in 1867, placed the management of its landed estate into the control of the Governing Body (on which members of the Chapter sit). The statutes were reformed in 1926, but the relationship between the Governing Body and the Dean and Chapter remained the same as had been established in 1867 and remains so today. Other peculiars (churches outside the direct control of the diocese

or archdiocese), such as Westminster and St George's, Windsor, had requested to be excluded from the measure; CCA D&C x.c.1.

12. CCA D&C xvii.b.1. Much of the work done in the 1920s is recorded in this interleaved and annotated copy of Warner's 1924 history of the cathedral. In 1921 the cloister garth had been tidied up and laid to grass.
13. Curthoys (2012), 303–4.
14. Ela Longespée was the daughter of William Longespée, 3rd Earl of Salisbury, natural son to Henry II. Among Ela's benefactions were grants to the canons of Oseney and the nuns of Godstow. In 1295 she gave land to the University of Oxford, part of which was to be paid to the fellows of Merton College that they might perform masses for her soul.
15. Clement Oswald Skilbeck (1865–1954), painter and designer, was a friend of William Morris and Edward Burne-Jones. In 1911 he published a catalogue of the armour held by the Honourable Artillery Company.
16. *ODNB*. Tristram recorded almost all known wall-paintings across the country in the course of his career, and conserved many. His work at Christ Church is reported in *The Walpole Society's 16th Volume* (1928).
17. Comper also designed the memorial to Henry Scott Holland, using an inscription by Dean Strong.
18. The altar was the gift of the Mothers' Union and included not just the altar table but a gilded and decorated reredos, oak platform with riddel posts, an oak communion kneeler, frontal and frontlet, and a tapestry dorsal to be fitted into the reredos.
19. Stenton [1953].
20. Astonishingly, there were only three dean's vergers throughout the whole of the twentieth century. After Francis's death, the position was taken by John Holloway until 1978. Edward Evans stepped into his shoes until 2009, to be followed by Matthew Power from 2009 to 2018.
21. CCA GB i.b.6, 370; CCA Cen v.c.26.
22. Goudge had been principal of the theological college in Ely before coming to Christ Church as regius professor of divinity in 1923. Hodgson had been tutor in theology at Magdalen, professor of Christian apologetics at the General Theological Seminary in New York and canon of Winchester before his appointment as canon professor at Christ Church in 1938.
23. CCA GB i.b.6, 384–389.
24. Another paper – by N. P. Williams, the Lady Margaret professor of divinity – included a section on the 'geography' of the clean-cut proposal, with quite radical suggestions for closing off the cathedral from the new King's College, with independent access somehow agreed with Merton or Corpus Christi colleges. The cathedral would only be used for college services until such time as a separate chapel was built.
25. Curthoys (2012), 312–14, 326–7. The Governing Body in 1939 consisted of the dean, six canons and twenty-eight Students. The subject was raised again in 1969 and in 1978/9, but there seems to have been no more stomach for the proposals then than there had been in 1939. Even Hugh Trevor-Roper, not known for his enthusiasm for clerics, felt that the cost of separation – whether financial, administrative or social – should be avoided. He foresaw a time when radicals might

attempt to oust a dean by isolation until such point as his position became untenable, but suggested that this would involve greater radicalism than even the radicals would wish.
26. Curthoys (2012), 314–15.
27. CCA D&C ii.b.12, 444.
28. The cathedral has never really had a library of its own, as it has always been attached to the academic college. The Chapter Books and cartularies may well have been kept in the Chapter House until modern times; certainly some volumes in the archive carry a Chapter House number. Other papers were kept in the deanery.
29. Orme (2017), 235.
30. Curthoys (2017), 208–10. The tablets were carved on this occasion by Darsie Rawlins.
31. A Canadian, Simpson had many North American friends who helped to fund the reordering of the sanctuary in 1962/3. The high altar candlesticks, for example, were given by the Roebling family, who had built the Brooklyn Bridge.
32. Curthoys (2012), 327.
33. Orme (2017), 241.
34. Women could be ordained as deacons from 1985; the first was appointed in 1987.
35. *Friends of Christ Church Cathedral, Oxford 1993–94.*
36. Orme (2017), 245–8. Salisbury's screen was sent for scrap, but Hereford's was saved and is now in the Victoria & Albert Museum.
37. Orme (2017), 239.
38. Curthoys (2017), 186; *Christ Church 2002*. The carpet was woven by Simon Cooper in memory of his brother Joseph.
39. Curthoys (2017), 221.
40. Curthoys (2017), 186–7. Also in 2005 the pews were removed from the crossing, to be replaced by chairs.
41. Orme (2017), 232.
42. CCA D&C xi.a.3; Curthoys (2012), 95.
43. Dearmer (1899); Thompson (1900); Warner (1924); Watson (1935).
44. GB i.b.2, 290 and 296.
45. Orme (2017) 211–14.
46. Curthoys (2017), 202. The shop was not popular in all circles, and is on the verge (December 2018) of moving out to a purpose-built facility.
47. In 2012 the figure was 250,000: see Curthoys (2012), 328. Many tourists also come to services, particularly Evensong. Members of the diocese can apply for a pass to give them free access to the cathedral at any time.
48. Orme (2017), 250–52.
49. The font is late seventeenth-century and is on long-term loan from Ely Cathedral. Its location in the south transept is harmonious with the 'Cavalier' monuments around the walls.
50. *The Ecclesiologist* (1847), 58–9.
51. CCA D&C x.c.2.

Epilogue: Christ Church and the future ministry of English cathedrals

1. David Martin, 'Believing without Belonging', cited in Grace Davie, *Religion in Britain since 1945* (Oxford, 1991), 189.
2. Martin in Davie, *Religion in Britain since 1945*, 190.
3. Extract from Albert van den Heuvel's sermon to dedicate Coventry Cathedral, 1962.
4. For a discussion of the concept 'low-threshold high-reward', see Martyn Percy, 'The Household of Faith', in Paul Avis and Benjamin Guyer (eds.), *The Lambeth Conference: Theology, History, Polity and Purpose* (London, 2017), 316–40.

Bibliography

Manuscript sources

Christ Church Archives (CCA)

There are few sections of the archive that do not include some information about the cathedral. Archival documents used are referenced throughout the text, prefixed with CCA. However, the principal series used are as follows:

Annual Reports	Series cited as *Christ Church [date]*
BR	Buildings Records series
Cen	Records of the Censors of Christ Church
D&C	Dean and Chapter papers, particularly:
D&C i.b.1–12	Dean and Chapter act books
D&C ii.b.1–15	Dean and Chapter minute books
DP	Deanery papers
GB	Governing Body records
Maps and Plans ChCh	Architectural drawings, etc.
MS Estates	Estates correspondence
xii.b.1–119	Disbursement books
xii.c.120–308	Disbursement books

Christ Church Library (CCL)

MS 101	Cardinal Wolsey's lectionary

Printed sources

Abbreviations

L&P	*Letters and Papers, Foreign and Domestic*
ODNB	*Oxford Dictionary of National Biography*, ed. H.C.G. Matthew and B. Harrison (Oxford, 2004). Also available and updated on-line at http://www.oxforddnb.com/
RCHME	Royal Commission on Historical Monuments of England
VCH	Victoria County History. Volumes are indicated in the notes as, for example, *VCH Oxon*, iv

Ady, C. M., *Some Early Bishops of Oxford* [Oxford, 1953]
Andrews, C. Bruyn (ed.), *The Torrington Diaries, Containing the Tours through England and Wales of the Hon. John Byng (Late Fifth Viscount Torrington) between the Years 1781 and 1794*, vol. iii (London, 1970)
Arkell, W. A., *Oxford Stone* (London, 1947)
Baker, Frank (ed.), *The Works of John Wesley*, vol. xxv: *Letters, I, 1721–1739* (Oxford, 1980)
Barlow, Frank, *The English Church, 1000–1066* (New York, 1979)
Barnwell, P. S., Tyack, Geoffrey, and Whyte, William (eds.), *George Gilbert Scott, 1811–1878: An Architect and His Influence* (Donington, 2014)
Barrett, Philip, *Barchester: English Cathedral Life in the Nineteenth Century* (London, 1993)
Batey, Mavis, *The Historic Gardens of Oxford and Cambridge* (London, 1989)
Bennett, G. V., *The Tory Crisis in Church and State, 1688–1730: The Career of Francis Atterbury, Bishop of Rochester* (Oxford, 1975)
Bernard, G. W., *The King's Reformation: Henry VIII and the Remaking of the English Church* (New Haven, CT, 2005)
Bill, E. G. W., 'Lady Montacute and St Frideswide's Priory', in Friends of Christ Church Cathedral, Oxford, *Cathedral Record* (1960), 8–12
Bill, E. G. W., ed. Howell, Peter, 'Sir Gilbert Scott's restoration of Christ Church Cathedral', *Oxoniensia*, 78 (Oxford, 2013), 127–55
Bill, E. G. W., and Mason, J. F. A., *Christ Church and Reform, 1850–1867* (Oxford, 1970)
Blair, John, 'St Frideswide reconsidered', *Oxoniensia*, lii (1987), 71–127
Blair, John, *Saint Frideswide: Patron of Oxford. The Earliest Texts* (Oxford, 1988)
Blair, John (ed.), *Saint Frideswide's Monastery at Oxford: Archaeological and Architectural Studies* (Gloucester, 1990)
Blair, John, *Anglo-Saxon Oxfordshire* (Stroud, 1994)
Blair, John, *The Church in Anglo-Saxon Society* (Oxford, 2005)
Bliss, Philip (ed.), *Athenae Oxonienses by Anthony Wood*, i (Oxford, 1813) [Wood, *Athenae*]
Bolton, Timothy, *The Empire of Cnut the Great: Conquest and Consolidation of Power in Northern Europe in the Early Eleventh Century* (Leiden, 2008)
Bolton, Timothy, *Cnut the Great* (New Haven, CT, 2017)
Bond, James, *Monastic Landscapes* (Stroud, 2004)
Briggs, Grace, Cook, Jean, and Rowley, Trevor (eds.), *The Archaeology of the Oxford Region* (Oxford, 1986)
Britton, John, *The History and Antiquities of the Cathedral Church of Oxford* (London, 1821)
Broad, John, and Hoyle, Richard (eds.), *Bernwood: The Life and Afterlife of a Forest* (Preston, 1997)
Brock, M. G., and Curthoys, M. C., *The History of the University of Oxford*, vol. vi: *Nineteenth-Century Oxford, Part 1* (Oxford, 1997)
Brock, M. G., and Curthoys, M. C., *The History of the University of Oxford*, vol. vii: *Nineteenth-Century Oxford, Part 2* (Oxford, 2000)
Brockliss, L. W. B., *The University of Oxford: A History* (2016)
Calfhill, James, *Historia de Exhumatione Catharinae nuper uxoris Doctissimi Theologi D. Petri Martyris, ac eiusdem ad honestam sepulturam restitutione* (London, 1562)
Campbell, Gordon, *Bible: The Story of the King James Version, 1611–2011* (Oxford, 2010)

Bibliography

Carr, Linda, Dewhurst, Russell, and Henig, Martin (eds.), *Binsey: Oxford's Holy Place. Its Saint, Village, and People* (Oxford, 2014)
Catto, J. I., *The History of the University of Oxford*, vol. i: *The Early Oxford Schools* (1984)
Catto, Jeremy (ed.), *Oriel College: A History* (Oxford, 2013)
Chadwick, A. M., Gilbert, D. R., and Moore, J. (eds.), *'... quadrangles where wisdom honours herself'. Archaeological Investigations at Tom Quad, Peckwater Quad and Blue Boar Quad, Christ Church, Oxford* (Oxford, 2012)
Charles-Edwards, Thomas, and Reid, Julian, *Corpus Christi College, Oxford: A History* (Oxford, 2017)
Clark, Andrew (ed.), *Survey of the Antiquities of the City of Oxford, Composed in 1661–6, by Anthony Wood*, vol. ii: *Churches and Religious Houses* (Oxford, 1890) [Wood, *Survey*]
Clark, Andrew (ed.), *The Life and Times of Anthony Wood, Antiquary, of Oxford, 1632–1695, Described by Himself*, vols i–iv (Oxford, 1891–5) [Wood, *Life & Times*]
Cole, H. (ed.), *King Henry VIII's Scheme of Bishopricks* (London, 1838)
Crook, J. Mordaunt, *Brasenose: The Biography of an Oxford College* (Oxford, 2008)
Cross, F. L., and Livingstone, E. A. (eds.), *The Oxford Dictionary of the Christian Church* (Oxford, 2005)
Crossley, Alan, and Elrington, C. (eds.), *The Victoria County History of the County of Oxford*, vol. iv (1979) [*VCH Oxon*, iv]
Curthoys, Judith, '"To perfect the college...": the Christ Church almsmen, 1546–1888', *Oxoniensia*, lx (1995), 379–95
Curthoys, Judith, *The Cardinal's College: Christ Church, Chapter and Verse* (London, 2012)
Curthoys, Judith, *The Stones of Christ Church: The Story of the Buildings of Christ Church, Oxford* (London, 2017)
Darwall-Smith, Robin, *A History of University College, Oxford* (Oxford, 2008)
Dearmer, Percy, *The Cathedral Church of Oxford: A Description of its Fabric and a Brief History of the Episcopal See* (London, 1899)
de Beer, E. S., *The Diary of John Evelyn*, vol. iii (Oxford, 1955)
Defoe, Daniel, *A Tour through the Island of Great Britain*, vol. ii (Dublin, 1779)
Devereux, E. J., 'The publication of the English *Paraphrases* of Erasmus', *Bulletin of the John Rylands Library*, 52 (2) (Manchester, 1969), 348–67
Dictionnaire d'histoire et de géographie ecclésiastiques, vol. ii (Paris, 1914)
Doble, C. E., *Remarks and Collections of Thomas Hearne*, vols i & ii (Oxford, 1885 & 1886) [*Hearne*]
Duffy, Eamon, *Fires of Faith: Catholic England under Mary Tudor* (New Haven, CT, 2009)
Duffy, Eamon, and Loades, David, *The Church of Mary Tudor* (Aldershot, 2006)
The Ecclesiologist, lvi [n.s., iv] (February 1847), 47–59
Emden, A. B., *A Biographical Register of the University of Oxford to AD 1500* (Oxford, 1957)
Emden, A. B., *A Biographical Register of the University of Oxford, AD 1501–1540* (Oxford, 1974)
Farmer, David Hugh, *The Oxford Dictionary of Saints* (Oxford, 2011)
Fincham, Kenneth (ed.), *Visitation Articles and Injunctions of the Early Stuart Church*, vols i & ii (Woodbridge, 1994, 1998)
Foot, Sarah, *Monastic Life in Anglo-Saxon England, c.600–900* (Cambridge, 2006)
Gittos, Helen, *Liturgy, Architecture, and Sacred Places in Anglo-Saxon England* (Oxford, 2013)

Godfrey, Jim, 'Reference files 1–4' [unpublished notes produced for the cathedral's guides and stewards]

Goldring, Elizabeth, Eales, Faith, Clarke, Elizabeth, Archer, Jayne Elisabeth, Heaton, Gabriel, and Knight, Sarah (eds.), *John Nichols's The Progresses and Public Processions of Queen Elizabeth I: A New Edition of the Early Modern Sources*, vol. i: *1533–1571* (Oxford, 2014) [Nichols, Progresses, i (2014)]

Goldring, Elizabeth, Eales, Faith, Clarke, Elizabeth, Archer, Jayne Elisabeth, Heaton, Gabriel, and Knight, Sarah (eds.), *John Nichols's The Progresses and Public Processions of Queen Elizabeth I: A New Edition of the Early Modern Sources*, vol. iii: *1579–1595* (Oxford, 2014) [Nichols, Progresses, iii (2014)]

Gunn, S. J., and Lindley, P. G., *Cardinal Wolsey: Church, State and Art* (Cambridge, 1991)

Gutch, John, *Collectanea Curiosa: or Miscellaneous Tracts, Relating to the History and Antiquities of England and Ireland, the Universities of Oxford and Cambridge, and a Variety of Other Subjects*, 2 vols (Oxford, 1781)

Gwyn, Peter, *The King's Cardinal: The Rise and Fall of Thomas Wolsey* (London, 2002)

Gwynn, Dominic, 'The seventeenth century organs at Christ Church Cathedral, Oxford', unpublished paper in CCA D&C xvii.a.1

Haigh, Christopher, *English Reformations: Religion, Politics, and Society under the Tudors* (Oxford, 1993)

Haigh, Christopher, '1546 Before and after: the making of Christ Church', unpublished lecture, 1996

Halévy, Elie, *The Birth of Methodism in England* (Chicago, 1971)

Hanna, Ralph, and Rundle, David, *A Descriptive Catalogue of the Western Manuscripts, to c.1600, in Christ Church, Oxford* (Oxford, 2017)

Harrison, James Park, *The Pre-Norman Date of the Design and Some of the Stone-Work of Oxford Cathedral* (1891)

Harrison, James Park, *An Account of the Discovery of the Remains of Three Apses at Oxford Cathedral* (1891)

Harrison, J. Park, *On a Pre-Norman Window and Some Additional Early Work in Oxford Cathedral* (1892)

Harrison, Kenneth, *The Windows of King's College Chapel, Cambridge: Notes on Their History and Design* (Cambridge, 1952)

Haugaard, William P., *Elizabeth and the English Reformation: The Struggle for a Stable Settlement of Religion* (Cambridge, 1968)

Hearne, Thomas – see Doble

Hibbert, Christopher (ed.), *The Encyclopaedia of Oxford* (London, 1988)

Hiscock, W. G., *A Christ Church Miscellany: New Chapters on the Architects, Craftsmen, Statuary, Plate, Bells, Furniture, Clocks, Plays, the Library and Other Buildings* (Oxford, 1946)

Hiscock, W. G., *Henry Aldrich of Christ Church, 1648–1710* (Oxford, 1960)

Ingram, James, *Memorials of Oxford*, vol. i (London, 1837)

Jacob, E. F., *St Frideswide: The Patron Saint of Oxford* (Oxford, 1953)

James, M. R., and Tristram, E. W., 'Medieval wall-paintings at Christ Church, Oxford', in *The Sixteenth Volume of the Walpole Society* (1928)

Jenkins, Simon, *England's Cathedrals* (London, 2016)

Bibliography

Kennedy, Jane, 'Vault repairs to the tomb of Sir Robert Danvers, Christ Church Cathedral, Oxford', *ASCHB Transactions*, 35 (2012), 18–21

Knowles, David, *The Religious Orders in England*, 3 vols (Cambridge, 1948–59)

Knowles, David, and Hadcock, R. Neville, *Medieval Religious Houses: England and Wales* (London, 1971)

Knowles, David, Brooke, C. N. L., and London, Vera C. M. (eds.), *The Heads of Religious Houses, England and Wales*, vol. i, *940–1216*, 2nd edn (Cambridge, 2001)

Lane, Richard, and Lee, Michael, *The History of Christ Church Cathedral School, Oxford* (Oxford, 2017)

Law, Brian R., *Building Oxford's Heritage: Symm & Company from 1815* (Oxford, 1998)

Le Neve, John (compiled Joyce N. Horn), *Fasti ecclesiae anglicanae, 1541–1857*, vol. vii: *Bristol, Gloucester, Oxford and Peterborough Dioceses* (London, 1996)

Lehmberg, Stanford E., *The Reformation of Cathedrals: Cathedrals in English Society, 1485–1603* (Princeton, 1988)

Lehmberg, Stanford E., *Cathedrals under Siege: Cathedrals in English Society, 1600–1700* (Exeter, 1996)

Lehmberg, Stanford E., *English Cathedrals: A History* (London, 2005)

Limonofides, Dino, and Belcher, Ken, 'The Regimental Chapel in Christ Church Cathedral, Oxford', in Jenkins, Stanley C. (ed.), *Bugle and Sabre* (Lydney, 2007), 43–5

Lobel, Mary D., *A History of the County of Oxford, vol. v: Bullingdon Hundred* (London, 1957) [*VCH Oxon*, v]

Logan, F. Donald, *Runaway Religious in Medieval England, c. 1240–1540* (Cambridge, 2002)

Mabey, Richard, *Flora Britannica* (London, 1996)

Mabey, Richard, *Weeds: How Vagabond Plants Gatecrashed Civilisation and Changed the Way We Think about Nature* (London, 2012)

MacCulloch, Diarmaid, *Tudor Church Militant: Edward VI and the Protestant Reformation* (London, 1999)

Maddicott, J. R., *Simon de Montfort* (Cambridge, 1994)

Matthew, H. C. G., and Harrison, Brian, *Oxford Dictionary of National Biography* (Oxford, 2004) [*ODNB*]

Mayer, Thomas F., *Reginald Pole: Prince and Prophet* (Cambridge, 2000)

Mayr-Harting, Henry, 'Functions of a twelfth-century shrine: the miracles of St Frideswide', in *Studies in Medieval History Presented to R. H. C. Davis* (London, 1985), 193–206

Moore, Helen, and Reid, Julian, *Manifold Greatness: The Making of the King James Bible* (Oxford, 2011)

Morris, Christopher (ed.), *The Journeys of Celia Fiennes* (London, 1947)

Munby, Julian, *The Bishop, the Shopkeeper, and the Cloister; Robert Shirborne and St Frideswide's* [forthcoming]

Nash Ford, David, 'St Frideswide: folklore or fact?' in *Royal Berkshire History* (2001). Online at http://www.berkshirehistory.com/legends/frideswide02.html. Accessed 15 June 2018

Nichols, *Progresses* – see Goldring et al.

Nilson, Ben, *Cathedral Shrines of Medieval England* (Woodbridge, 1998)

ODNB – see Matthew, H. C. G., and Harrison, Brian

Orme, Nicholas, *The History of England's Cathedrals* (Exeter, 2017)

Oxford Archaeological Unit, 'Christ Church Cathedral: St Frideswide's Shrine, measured survey', unpublished report, 2000
Page, William (ed.), *The Victoria County History of the County of Oxford*, vol. ii (1907) [*VCH Oxon*, ii]
Page, William (ed.), *A History of the County of Kent*, vol. ii (London, 1926) [*VCH Kent*, ii]
Pantin, W. A., *Canterbury College Oxford*, vol. iv (Oxford, 1985)
Parker, James, *The Early History of Oxford, 727–1100* (Oxford, 1885)
Pestell, Tim, *Landscapes of Monastic Foundation: The Establishment of Religious Houses in East Anglia, c.650–1200* (Woodbridge, 2004)
Pevsner, Nikolaus, *Buildings of England: Nottinghamshire* (London, 1997)
PRO [Public Record Office], *Calendar of Patent Rolls, Edw. II*, vol. iii (1903)
Radford, David, *The Archaeology of Oxford in 20 Digs* (Stroud, 2018)
RCHME *Oxford* – see Royal Commission on Historical Monuments England
Roach, Levi, *Aethelred the Unready* (New Haven, CT, 2016)
Robinson, Brian, *Silver Pennies and Linen Towels: The Story of the Royal Maundy* (London, 1992)
Rodwell, Kirsty (ed.), *Historic Towns in Oxfordshire: A Survey of the New County* (Oxford, 1975)
Rowse, A. L., *Oxford in the History of the Nation* (London, 1975)
Royal Commission on Historical Monuments England, *An Inventory of the Historical Monuments in the City of Oxford* (1939) [RCHME *Oxford*]
Ryrie, Alec, *The Age of Reformation: The Tudor and Stewart Realms 1485–1603* (Abingdon, 2017)
Salter, H. E. (ed.), *A Subsidy Collected in the Diocese of Lincoln in 1526* (Oxford, 1909)
Salter H. E. (ed.), *Chapters of the Augustinian Canons* (Oxford, 1922)
Salter, H. E., *Survey of Oxford*, vol. i (1960)
Salter, H. E., *Survey of Oxford*, vol. ii (1969)
Scott, George Gilbert, 'Report of George Gilbert Scott, Esq. RA on the cathedral of Christ Church, Oxford' (printed for private circulation, 3 June 1869)
Shaw, Watkins, *The Succession of Organists of the Chapel Royal and the Cathedrals of England and Wales from c.1538* (Oxford, 1991)
Sherwood, Jennifer, and Pevsner, Nikolaus, *The Buildings of England: Oxfordshire* (London, 1974)
Smith, David M. (ed.), *The Heads of Religious Houses, England and Wales*, vol. iii: *1377–1540* (Cambridge, 2008)
Smith, David M., and London, Vera C. M. (eds.), *The Heads of Religious Houses, England and Wales*, vol. ii: *1216–1377* (Cambridge, 2001)
Smyth, W. H., 'II. Description of an astrological clock, belonging to the Society of Antiquaries of London: in a letter to the president', *Archaeologia*, 33 (London, 1849), 8–30
Southern, R. W., *Robert Grosseteste: The Growth of an English Mind in Medieval Europe*, 2nd edn (Oxford 1992)
Spurr, John, *The Post-Reformation: Religion, Politics and Society in Britain, 1603–1714* (Harlow, 2006)
Stenton, Frank, *St Frideswide and Her Times* [Oxford, 1953]

Bibliography

Stevenson, W. E., and Salter, H. E., *The Early History of St John's College, Oxford* (Oxford, 1939)

Storey, R. L., 'Papal provisions to English monasteries', *Nottingham Medieval Studies*, xxxv (1991)

Swinfen, Ann, *The Merchant's Tale* (Shakenoak, 2017)

Tapsell, Grant (ed.), *The Later Stuart Church, 1660–1714* (Manchester, 2012)

Thacker, Alan, and Sharpe, Richard (eds.), *Local Saints and Local Churches in the Early Medieval West* (Oxford, 2002)

Thompson, Henry L., *Henry George Liddell, DD, Dean of Christ Church, Oxford: A Memoir* (New York, 1899)

Thompson, Henry L., *Christ Church* (London, 1900)

Tyack, Geoffrey, *Oxford: An Architectural Guide* (Oxford, 1998)

Tyack, Geoffrey, and Goodall, John, 'How Oxford University's buildings evolved, and how its "chiefest wonder" came into being', *Country Life* (10 April 2017)

Valor Ecclesiasticus, ii (London, 1814)

VCH Kent, ii – see Page, William

VCH Oxon, ii – see Page, William

VCH Oxon, iv – see Crossley, Alan, and Elrington, C.

VCH Oxon, v – see Lobel, Mary D.

Wakeling, Edward (ed.), *Lewis Carroll's Diaries: The Private Journals of Charles Lutwidge Dodgson*, vols i–x (Luton, 1993–2007)

Warner, S. A., *Oxford Cathedral* (London, 1924)

Watson, E. W., *The Cathedral Church of Christ in Oxford* (London, 1935)

Whyte, William, *Unlocking the Church: The Lost Secrets of Victorian Sacred Space* (Oxford, 2017)

Wickham, C., *Common Plants as Natural Remedies* (London, 1981)

Wigram, Spencer Robert, *The Cartulary of the Monastery of St Frideswide at Oxford*, vol. i: *General and City Charters* (Oxford, 1895)

Wigram, Spencer Robert, *The Cartulary of the Monastery of St Frideswide at Oxford*, vol. ii: *The Chantry and Country Parish Carters* (Oxford, 1896)

Williams, Ann, and Martin G. H. (eds.), *Domesday Book: A Complete Translation* (London, 2002)

Williams, Ann, *Aethelred the Unready: The Ill-Counselled King* (New York, 2003)

Willis, Browne, *A Survey of the Cathedrals of Lincoln, Ely, Oxford, and Peterborough ...* (London, 1730)

Winkles, Benjamin, *Architectural and Picturesque Illustrations of the Cathedral Churches of England and Wales*, vol. ii (1851)

Wollenberg, Susan, *Music at Oxford in the Eighteenth and Nineteenth Centuries* (Oxford, 2001)

Wood, *Athenae Oxonienses* – see Bliss, Philip

Wood, *Life and Times* – see Clark, Andrew

Wood, *Survey* – see Clark, Andrew

Yarrow, Simon, *Saints and Their Communities: Miracle Stories in Twelfth-Century England* (Oxford, 2006)

Youings, Joyce, *The Dissolution of the Monasteries* (London, 1971)

Index

All places are in Oxford unless otherwise stated. *Italic* page numbers refer to black and white illustrations; colour plates are indicated by 'Pl.'; and note numbers are preceded by '*n*'.

A
abdication crisis (1936) 142
Abingdon (Berkshire/Oxfordshire) 71
   Abbey 12, 14–15, 20, 30
   St Helen's Church 226*n*28
Act of Uniformity (1558) 89
Acts of Supremacy (1558) 89
Adams, Marilyn McCord 188
Adelaide, Queen consort 177
Adrian IV, Pope 20, 213*n*10
Aelfgifu, abbess of Winchester 4
Aethelflaed, Lady of the Mercians 10
Aethelred II (the Unready), King 10, 12–14, 210*n*5
   St Frideswide's foundation charter 3, 6, *11*, 13, 14
air-raid shelters 185
Alasco, Prince of Siradia 97
Albert Memorial (London) 160
Alcock, John, bishop of Ely 59
Aldrich, Dean Henry 127–8, 130, 135, 146, 203, 222*n*15, 229*n*90
   memorial 131, *131*

Alexander IV, Pope 35
Alexander V, Pope 49, 50
Alexander of Sutton, prior of St Frideswide's 33, 40, 42, 43, 50, 201, 216*n*1, 218*n*42
   tomb *40*, 50, 52, 218*n*42
Alexius (papal legate) 22
Alfred the Great, King 10, 210*n*5
Algar, Prince of Leicester 4–5, 6
Algiva, abbess of Winchester 4
All Saints Church 17, 135
All Souls College 83, 125
Allestree, Richard 123
alms-giving 81, 98, 111
almshouse 111, 115, 225*n*74, 227*n*41, 227*n*47
altars 50, 71, 80, 161–2, 180, 181, 218*n*45, 236*n*18
Amadas, Robert 65–6, *66*
Anarchy, The (1135–53) 24, 26–7
Andever, Edmund, prior of St Frideswide's 56, 201
Andrew, Richard 36

Anglo-Spanish War (1585–1604) 91, 99, 101
Anne, Queen 129, 130
Anne of Denmark, Queen consort 100
apses 8, 211*n*20
Archbishops' Council, 'Heritage and Renewal' report (1994) 191
Arminianism 101, 104, 105
Arminius, Jacob 225*n*3
Armstrong, Thomas 208
Ashmolean Museum 230*n*21
Aston, Hugh 65
Atterbury, Dean Francis, bishop of Rochester 130–32, 134, 204, 230*n*9
Audit House 130, 229*n*6
Augustinians 16, 18, 26, 49, 215*n*10
  General Chapter 34–5, 44, 58
Aylesbury (Buckinghamshire) 112

B
Bach, Johann Sebastian 173
Bagot, Dean Lewis, bishop of St Asaph 129, 204
Bagot, Richard, bishop of Oxford (*later* bishop of Bath and Wells) 142, 160, 205
Bailey, Samuel Grant 183, 184–5
Ballard, Anne 188
Balliol College 86, 89
  chapel 64
Bampton (Oxfordshire) 5, 6
Banbury (Oxfordshire) 112
Banbury Road 211*n*25
Bancroft, John, bishop of Oxford 69, 105, 119, 203, 227*n*48
Bancroft, Richard, archbishop of Canterbury 102, 105
Bankes, Sir John 115
Bankes, Mary, Lady 115
Bankes, Robert 83, 84, 92
Bannyge, John 50
baptisms 113, 135, 164, 185, 191–2
Barking Abbey (Essex) 9
Barons' Wars 35–6, 215*n*5
Barraud, F. P., drawing of nave and chancel *163*
Bass, Irene 177
Batheaston (Somerset) 157, 232*n*49
battlements 226*n*29, 231*n*11
Bayham Abbey (Sussex) 60
Beaufort, Henry, bishop of Winchester 54
Becket, Thomas, archbishop of Canterbury 20, 21, 52
  shrine 20, 52, 68
  writings on 21
Becket window (Lucy Chapel) 52, 221*n*20, Pl.
Bedford, Samuel 118
Bekes Hall 33, 215*n*4
Bell, George, bishop of Chichester 189
bells:
  Christ Church Cathedral 71, 95, 125, 135, 159, 172
  St Frideswide's Priory 33
Belsyre, Alexander 73, 83, 84, 91, 221*n*42, 224*n*54
Benbow, John 207
Benbow, Robert 220*n*13
Bennett, J., map of Christ Church Meadow Pl.

Index

Bennett, William (joiner) 114, 227n45
Bensington, Battle of (777) 30
Benson (Oxfordshire) 211n10
Bentham, Thomas 90
Bercheroft (Oxfordshire) 33
Bernard, Thomas 83, 84, 92, 224n55
Bernwood Forest (Oxfordshire/
  Buckinghamshire) 48–9
Berry, Richard 125
Beverley Minster (Yorkshire) 31
Bible:
  Bishops' Bible 102, 103
  Christ Church Cathedral's copies 80,
    95–6, 103, 105
  Geneva Bible 102, 103
  Great Bible 95–6, 221n37
  King James/Authorised Version
    102–3
  Zwingli/Zurich Bible 80
Billing, John 232n25
  Christ Church Cathedral restoration
    122, 147–9, 150, *150*, 171,
    233n71
Binsey (Oxfordshire) 5, 6–7, 16, 17,
  49, 211n7, Pl.
  St Margaret's Church 51, 210n6
  'treacle well' 21, 210n6
Birch, Peter 146, 230n18
Birinus, bishop of Dorchester 30
bishopric of Oxford *see* diocese of
  Oxford
bishops of Oxford:
  list of 202–6
  residence 69, 105, 106, 160
Black Death 44–5, 217n14–15
Blackmore Priory (Essex) 60

Blandford, Walter, bishop of Oxford
  (*later* bishop of Worcester) 125, 203
Blomfield, Charles, bishop of London
  141
Bloxham, Thomas 50–51
Blue Boar Inn 220n4
Blue Boar Lane 222n16
Blue Boar Quadrangle 106
Bodley, Thomas 164
Bokyngham, John, bishop of Lincoln
  47
Bolles 48
Bolton, John 114
Bomy (Pas-de-Calais) 6
bonfires 121, 123, 228n69
Book of Common Prayer 67, 80,
  81–2, 87, 90, 114, 116, 121, 123,
  222n14
Boteler, Dr 50–51
Boulter, Dean Hugh, archbishop of
  Armagh 129, 131, 132, 204
Brackley (Northamptonshire),
  Magdalen College School 92
Bradshaw, Dean William 129, 132,
  204
Bradwell, Thomas, prior of St
  Frideswide's 43, 49, 56, 201
Bradwell Abbey (Buckinghamshire) 60
'Bread and Butter Row' (1865) 168
Brice, St 13, 212n33
Bridges, John, bishop of Oxford 103,
  203
Bright, William 151–2, 162, 233n68
Bristol 185
  diocese of 70, 129, 134, 141,
    221n12

St Augustine's Abbey 219*n*7
Brixworth (Northamptonshire) 211*n*20
Broad Walk 125
Broadgates Hall 85
Brouncker, William, 1st Viscount 115
Brown, Matthew 115–16
Bruarne, Richard 83, 85, 90, 221*n*31
Bucer, Martin 67, 81
Buckingham, George Villiers, 1st Duke of 105
Buckler, John 214*n*34
Buckler, John Cheswell 26, 214*n*34
Bull, John (treasurer) 146, 149, 171
Burge, Hubert, bishop of Oxford 205
Burghal Hidage (Anglo-Saxon document) 10
Burghersh, Henry, bishop of Lincoln 50, 218*n*38
burial grounds *see* cemeteries and burial grounds
Burne-Jones, Sir Edward, Christ Church Cathedral window designs 149–50, 159, 177, 180, Pl.
burning, execution by 85, 86, 224*n*34
Burton, John, prior of St Frideswide's 33, 56, 58, 61, 201, 219*n*8
Burton, Robert, memorial 179
Buss, Robert, engraving of Cathedral chancel Pl.
Butler, John, bishop of Oxford (*later* bishop of Hereford) 132, 204
Buttery 225*n*74
Button, Ralph 118, 120
Byland Abbey (Yorkshire) 31
Byng, John, 5th Viscount Torrington 138–9, 140
Byrd, William 94

C

Cadíz, sack of (1596) 91
Calceto Priory (Sussex) 60
Calfhill, James 91
  reburial of Catherine Vermigli *87*, 91
Cambridge Camden Society 144, 151
  A Few Words to Church Builders 144
  see also Ecclesiologist, The (journal)
Cambridge University 32, 69, 74, 165–6
  see also individual colleges
Candelar, John 73
canons' lodgings 92, 124–5, 181, 224*n*56
Canterbury (Kent) 9
  Christ Church 217*n*21
  diocese of 73
Canterbury Cathedral (Kent) 111, 115, 186, 189, 231*n*9
  Becket shrine 20, 52, 68
Canterbury College 71, 127, 217*n*21
Canterbury Quadrangle 92, 217*n*21
Canwell Priory (Staffordshire) 60
Cardinal College:
  construction 31, 61–2, 63–6, 122, 161, 162, 220*n*11, 221*n*35
  dedication 65, 220*n*7
  dissolution 30, 67, 71
  funding 59–62
  statutes 65

Index

Care of Cathedrals Measure (1990) 188
Carew, Dean George 89, 202
Caroline of Ansbach, Queen consort 134
Carpenter, Harry, bishop of Oxford 205
Carter, John 138
Cassington (Oxfordshire) 226*n*24, 226*n*30
Cathedral, Christ Church, history and development:
  foundation 67–75, 79
  16th century 80–99
  17th century 100–128
  18th century 129–39
  19th century 140–74
  20th century 174–91
  21st century 189, 191–3, 195–200
Cathedrals Act (1840) 141–2, 144, 165, 167
Cathedrals Advisory Committee 188
Cathedrals Measure (1931) 179
Catherine of Alexandria, St 4, 51
  St Catherine window 51, Pl.
Catherine of Aragon 23
Catte Street 10
Cavalier monuments (Lucy Chapel) 115
Cecil, Hugh, 1st Baron Quickswood 192–3
Cecilia, St 4, 169
Celestine III, Pope 29, 214*n*41
cemeteries and burial grounds 4, 9, 148, 211*n*23
Chadwick, Dean Henry 187, 205

Challoner divinity lectures 132
Chamberlain, Thomas 151
chancel:
  construction 27–8, 29, 30
  restoration and additions *108*, 109, 110, 148, *163*, 189, Pl.
Chancellorship of diocese of Oxford 32, 142
Chantrey, Francis 231*n*11
Chantries Act (1548) 74, 80
Chapel of Remembrance (*formerly* Military Chapel) *143*, 159, 177, 188, 235*n*5
Chaplains' Quadrangle 92, 94, 125, 224*n*56, 225*n*74, 229*n*6
Chapman, John (joiner) 233*n*59
Chapter Books 85, 94, *95*, 111, 118, 223*n*31, 228*n*57, 237*n*28
Chapter House 28, 29, 31, 33, 52, 164, 179, 191, 231*n*11, 233*n*73, 237*n*28
  doorway 26, *27*, 31, 52, 153, 214*n*45, Pl.
  paintings 178, 179, Pl.
  windows 26, 27
Chapter meetings 96, 118, 130, 233*n*73
Charles I, King 109–110
  execution 114–15, 122, 123
  as Prince of Wales 105
  wartime residence at Christ Church 112–14, 116, 227*n*45
Charles II, King 121, 126
  visits Christ Church 124, 228*n*80
charters, Christ Church Cathedral, (1546) 74–5

charters, St Frideswide's Priory:
  (1004) 3, 6, 10, *11*, 13, 14, 212*n*36
  (1122) 16, 20, 25, 213*n*3
  (1335) 47, 217*n*18
Chaundler, Thomas 33
Chedill, William, prior of St
  Frideswide's 33, 56, 57, 58, 201
Chedsey, William 82, 92
Chester (Cheshire), diocese of 70, 73,
  221*n*32
chests, university, keepers of 32–3,
  215*n*2
Chichele, Henry, archbishop of
  Canterbury 56
Chichester Cathedral (Sussex)
  111
Childrey (Berkshire) 121
choir (singers) 65, 69, 84, 88, 93–4,
  132, 169–70, 171, 173, 187
  practice room 222*n*16, 234*n*73
  school 170, 187
choir (architecture) 80, 97, 109, 137,
  149, 160
  vault 52–4, 56–7, 112, Pl.
choir aisles 29
  north choir aisle 8, 137, 149, 159,
    165, 211*n*19, 233*n*68
  south choir aisle 148, 159, 177,
    179
choristers *see* choir
Christ Church Cathedral *see* Cathedral,
  Christ Church
Christ Church Cathedral School (prep
  school) 170
Christ Church Oxford Act (1857) 151,
  168–9, 234*n*84

Church Assembly (*later* General
  Synod) 178–9, 187–8, 192, 235*n*9
Church, Richard 207
Church of England Assembly (Powers)
  Act (1919) 178, 235*n*9
Churchill (Oxfordshire) 218*n*38
Cirencester Abbey (Gloucestershire)
  21, 214*n*41
city walls 25, 27, 31, 213*n*30
Civil Law School 33
Civil War, English 111–17, 119, 124–
  5, 226*n*26
  Cavalier monuments 115
Clarendon, Edward Hyde, 1st Earl of 125
Clarendon Press 177
Clayton and Bell (stained glass
  manufacturers) 160, 233*n*52
Clement VII, Pope 60, 61
clerestory 51, 56, 150, 180,
  231*n*18
Clerke, Charles 151, 159
clock, Christ Church Cathedral
  172
cloister:
  Christ Church 97, 156, 164,
    236*n*12
  St Frideswide's Priory 4, 7, 27, 28,
    29, 31, 57
cloister walks 29
  east 31, 233*n*72
  north 26, 137, *138*, 161
  south 27
  west 64–5
Cnut, King 14–15
Cobbett, William 140
Coddington, Henry 146, 231*n*17

Index

Colchester (Essex) 119
Cole, H., *King Henry VIII's Scheme of Bishopricks* 70
Commonwealth of England 114–21, 122, 123
communion tables 80, 104–5, 106, 110, 111, 116, 123–4, 190, 224n55, 227n52
Comper, Sir Ninian 180, 236n17
Compton, Henry, bishop of Oxford (*later* bishop of London) 126, 203, 228n80
constitution, Christ Church's 83–4, 150, 165–9
Conybeare, Dean John 129, 132, 204
Cooper, Dean Thomas, bishop of Lincoln 202
Corbett, Dean Richard, bishop of Oxford (*later* bishop of Norwich) 104, 105, 132, 203, 226n17, 226n24, 229n89
Corfe, Charles William 171, 173, 208
Corfe Castle (Dorset) 115
Corner, William de la, bishop of Salisbury 39, 216n27
Cornish, Henry 118, 228n65
Corpus Christi College 24, 83, 85, 102, 213n2, 215n4, 236n24
  Fellows' Building 230n21
  presidency 82, 92, 101
Courcy, John 35
Courthopp, James 83, 91–2
Cowley (Oxfordshire) 6, 10
  St Luke's Church 235n7
Cox, Dean Richard 30, 70, 73, 81, 82, 83, 84, 95, 202, 223n27

Cranmer, Thomas, archbishop of Canterbury 70, 80, 81, 83, 84, 85–6, 90
Creton, Henry de 42
Crew, Nathaniel, bishop of Oxford (*later* bishop of Durham) 126, 203
Cricklade (Wiltshire) 21
Croft, Steven, bishop of Oxford 191, 206
Croft, William, anthems 132
Croke, Richard 68
Cromwell, Oliver 119, 120, 121
Cromwell, Richard 121
Cromwell, Thomas 67, 70, 220n9, 221n35
Cross, William 207
Crotch, William 207
Cuddesdon Palace (Oxfordshire) 69, 105, 106, *106*, 125, 134, 160, 185, 227n48
Curle, Walter, bishop of Winchester 113
Curwen, Hugh, bishop of Oxford 88, 202
Cutteslowe (Oxfordshire) 6, 10

D

Dale, Thomas, engraving of Oseney Abbey *19*
Dallam, Thomas 105, 117, 122
Dammartin, Catherine *see* Vermigli, Catherine
Danes 10, 12–14, 30
  St Brice's Day massacre 13, 14, 212n34–5
Danvers, Sir Robert 51

Darlington, Stephen 208
Daventry Abbey (Northamptonshire) 59, 60, 68
Day, Thomas 73, 83, 91
de Montfort, Simon, 6th Earl of Leicester 35–6, 216n20
dean, use of title 63
Deane, Thomas 152
deans of Christ Church, list of 202–6
Dearmer, Percy, *The Cathedral Church of Oxford* 190, 230n24
Declaration of Indulgence (1687) 126, 127
Deerhurst (Gloucestershire) 211n20
Defoe, Daniel 135, 137, 140, 190
Denison, Edward, memorial window Pl.
Didan (7th-century sub-king; father of St Frideswide) 4, 6, 9, 10, 51
Dillwyn, Colin 183
diocese of Oxford:
    establishment 30, 69–70
    extent 142, 185
Directory for Public Worship 114, 116, *116*, 121
dissolution of monasteries 59–62, *61*, 68–9
Divinity School 53, 58, 94
Dodgson, Charles 159
Dodnash Priory (Suffolk) 60
d'Oilly, Robert 18
Dolben, John, archbishop of York 123
Domesday Book 16
Dorchester-on-Thames (Oxfordshire), diocese of 30, 185, 192, 211n25

Doune, William 46
Downham, Robert, prior of St Frideswide's 56, 201
Drury, Dean John 205
Dugdale, William, *Monasticum Anglicanum* 135
Dunstable Priory (Bedfordshire) 35
Duppa, Dean Brian, bishop of Chichester 104, 105–6, 109, 203, 226n17
    refurbishment of Cathedral 52, 105–8, *107*, *108*, 109, 110, *110*, 147, 159, Pl.
Durham (Co. Durham):
    Cathedral 134, 141, 231n9
    diocese of 73, 126, 141
    University 231n4
Dyar, John 73, 83

E

Ecclesiologist, The (Cambridge Camden Society journal) 144
    report on Christ Church Cathedral (1847) 144–6, 146–7, 148, 159, 169, 192, 233n70
Edes, Richard 102
Edgehill, Battle of (1642) 112
Edmund, 2nd Earl of Cornwall 39
Edmund of Abingdon, St 54
Edward the Confessor, King 15
    shrine 216n24
Edward I, King 36, 39, 42
    as Prince of Wales 36–7
Edward II, King 42
Edward III, King 43, 44, 46, 47–8, 217n23

254

Index

Edward VI, King 67, 69, 80, 83, 84, 218n27, 225n77
    July Injunctions 80
Edward, Prince of Wales (the Black Prince) 16
Eleanor of Castile, Queen consort, tomb 160
electric lighting 179–80, 190
Elias (Scotus), prior of St Frideswide's 33, 34–5, 201, 215n10
Elizabeth I, Queen 88, 89–90, 100, 103, 122, 224n40
    visits Christ Church 90, 92–4, 97
Elsfield (Oxfordshire) 16
Ely (Cambridgeshire):
    Cathedral 51, 231n9, 232n45, 237n49
    diocese of 73
Erasmus, *Paraphrases* 80, 222n8
Essex, Arthur Capell, 1st Earl of 112
Estwick, Sampson 169
Ethelreda, St 51
Etheridge, George 83, 221n31
Eton College (Berkshire) 58, 90, 122
    choir 173
Evans, Sir Arthur 8
Evans, Edward 236n20
Evelyn, John 227n52
Exeter Cathedral (Devon) 186, 189, 190, 231n9
Eynsham (Oxfordshire) 6
    Abbey 14, 211n11, 212n36

F

Fair, St Frideswide's 17, 18, 43, 48, 213n5, 218n27

Fairfax-Murray, Charles, Lady Chapel windows Pl.
Farmer and Brindley (architectural sculptors) 163, 233n61
Faussett, Robert 151, 152, 162
Felixstowe Priory (Suffolk) 60
Fell, Dean John, bishop of Oxford 121, 123, 124–5, 126, 128, 129, 203, 229n90
Fell, Dean Samuel 112, 118, 119, 123, 124, 203, 226n28
Fell Tower 233n52
Fell's Building 125
festivals, choral 173
Fiennes, Celia 135, 137, 140, 190
fires:
    (1002) 13
    (1190) 28, 29, 31, Pl.
    (1958) 106
First World War 174–5, *176*, 185
    commemoration 175–7, 235n2
Fisher, John, bishop of Rochester 219n15
Fisher, John and William (builders) 147
FitzOger, Richard 17
Fitzwalter, William 35
Fleming, Richard, bishop of Lincoln 49–50, 218n33
Fletcher, Colin, acting bishop of Oxford 206
fonts 135, 164, 191–2, 234n74, 237n49
Foster, Michael 183, 184–5
Fox, Richard, bishop of Winchester 215n4

Francis of Assisi, St 198
Francis, William 112, 181–2, *182*, 211*n*19, 236*n*20
French, Peter 228*n*62
Frideswide, St 3–6, 210*n*1–3, 211*n*10–11
  canonisation 56
  cult of 6, 20, 23, 213*n*24
  death and burial 5, 8, 9, 10–11, 20, 22, 26, 211*n*7
  feast days and celebrations 54, 56, 181, 217*n*7
  likenesses *3*, *15*, *37*, 38, 50, 51, 149–50, 220*n*7, Pl.
  relics and shrine 20–24, 28, 29, *37*, 38–40, 50–51, 68, 88, 91, 165, 189, 213*n*15, 213*n*22, Pl.
Friends of Christ Church Cathedral 189–90
Frilsham (Berkshire) 211*n*10

G

Gage, Sir Henry 115
Gaisford, Dean Thomas 143, *144*, 165–7, 170–71, 172, 178, 204
  memorial 179
Garbrand (bookseller) 96
Gardiner, Stephen, bishop of Winchester 67, 69, 70, 81
garth 29, 65, 214*n*45, 236*n*12
  burials 143, 148
General Synod *see* Church Assembly
Gerald of Wales 24
Gérente Brothers (glass-painters) 148, 231*n*18

Gibbs, W. H., engraving of Charles Wesley *133*
Gill, MacDonald 177
Gilpin, Bernard 83
Gilpin, James 91
Gladstone, William Ewart 166, 167
Glasgow, George Boyle, 6th Earl of 157
Glastonbury (Somerset) 9
Gloucester (Gloucestershire):
  Cathedral 173
  diocese of 70, 73, 221*n*32
Gloucester Hall 30, 69
Godstow Nunnery (Oxfordshire) 236*n*14
Godwin, Thomas, bishop of Bath and Wells 92–3
Godyngton, Richard 50
Goldwell, Thomas, bishop of Oxford 88, 202, 223*n*26
Goodman, Christopher 83, 85, 223*n*25
Goodson, Richard I 207
Goodson, Richard II 207
Goodwin, Arthur 112
Goodwin, Dean William 114, 203
  memorial 179
Gordon, Osborne 168
Gore, Charles, bishop of Oxford 205
Gothic revival architecture 137–8, 144, 151
Goudge, Henry 183, 236*n*22
Grahl, Stephen 208
Grandison, William Villiers, 2nd Viscount 115
Granville, Granville Leveson Gower, 2nd Earl 157–8

Index

Great Perambulation (1300) 49
Great Quadrangle (Tom Quad) 92, 98, 181, 233n64
   design and construction 31, 64, 92, 161, 162
   development and additions 106, 108, 124–5
Great Tom (bell) 71, 125, 172
Gregory XI, Pope 217n23
Gregory, Dean David 132, 204
Grey, Charles, 2nd Earl 140
Grey, Lady Jane 86
Grier, Francis 208
Griffiths, Davy 63
Grosseteste, Robert, bishop of Lincoln 32, 34, 215n10
guides to Christ Church Cathedral 190–91, 230n24
Guimond, prior of St Frideswide's 16, 17, 25, 201
Gunhilde (alleged sister of Swein of Denmark) 13, 212n34
Gynwell, John, bishop of Lincoln 45, 217n16

H

Haigh, Christopher 83
Hall (Christ Church) 109
   stairs 65, 159
Hall, Dean Charles Henry 204
Hall, Timothy, bishop of Oxford 127, 203
Halsey, Richard 214n31
Hampton Court Conference (1604) 100, 101–2
Hampton Court Palace (London) 172
Handel, George Frideric 170, 207
   Acis and Galatea 170
Harding, John 102
Harley, Robert, 1st Earl of Oxford 130
Harmar, John 102
Harries, Richard, bishop of Oxford 205
Harris, William 208
Harrod, Sir Roy 183
Harthacnut, King 212n42
Harwood, Basil 208
Haynes, William 73, 82, 83
Headington (Oxfordshire) 6, 16
Headship, Committee on (1939) 183–5
heating systems 149, 179, 231n11, 233n71
Heaton, Dean Eric 187, 205
Henley, Robert, 2nd Baron, 'Plan of Church Reform' 140–41
Henrietta Maria, Queen consort 109
Henry I, King 9, 16, 17, 18, 211n26
   St Frideswide's confirmation charter 16, 20, 25
Henry II, King 24, 33, 236n14
Henry III, King 33–4, 35–7, 54, 210n5
Henry VIII, King 58, 67–8, 79, 83, 92, 97, 99
   dissolution of monasteries and new bishoprics scheme 59–62, 68–74, 79
Hereford Cathedral (Herefordshire) 90, 137, 144, 188, 189, 233n59
   choir 173
Higden, John 64, 67, 220n15
Hilda of Whitby, St 51

Hodgson, Leonard 183–4, 236n22
Holgate, Robert, archbishop of York 84
Holland, Henry Scott, memorial 236n17
Holloway, John 236n20
Honorary Canons 166
Honorius I, Pope 30
Honorius II, Pope 17
Honorius III, Pope 34
Hooker, Richard, *Laws of Ecclesiastical Polity* 101
Horkesley Priory (Essex) 60
Hough, John, bishop of Oxford (*later* bishop of Lichfield and Coventry) 128, 203
Houghton (Oxfordshire) 18
Howard, Charles (*later* 1st Earl of Nottingham) 91
Howley, William, archbishop of Canterbury 141
Howson, John, bishop of Oxford (*later* bishop of Durham) 103–4, 134, 203
Hugall, John West 151, 152
Hume, John, bishop of Oxford (*later* bishop of Salisbury) 204
Humphrey, Laurence 89–90
Husbands, William 207
Hutchinson, G. T. 177
Hutten, Leonard 102
Huygens, Christiaan 172

I

Iffley (Oxfordshire) 26
Iffley Road 235n7
Inglis, Sir Robert 170
Interregnum *see* Commonwealth of England
intoning of prayers 170, 172–3
Ipswich (Suffolk):
　College 66
　Priory 60
Islip, Simon, archbishop of Canterbury 46, 217n21

J

Jackson, Dean Cyril 204
　memorial 231n11
Jackson, William, bishop of Oxford 204
Jackson's Oxford Journal 171–3
James I, King 100, 101–3, 104, 105
James II, King 121, 126–8, 227n44
James Powell & Sons (glassmakers) 149–50, 180
James, Dean William 97, 202
Jarrow Abbey (Co. Durham) 9
Jedburgh Abbey (Scotland) 27
Jelf, Richard William 151
Jewel, John 85, 89, 92, 223n27
Jewish community in England 34, 36–7, 215n2, 215n9
　expulsion of (1290) 34, 36
John, King 32
　Barons' War 215n5
John I, King of Castile and Leon 217n22
John Chrysostom, St 102
John of Baldington 47
John of Dodford, prior of St Frideswide's 43, 46, 47–9, 201, 217n26

Index

John of Elsfield 38
John of Lewknor, prior of St Frideswide's 33, 38, 201
John of Littlemore, prior of St Frideswide's 43, 44, 45, 201
John of Nowers 47
John of Reading 34
John of Sutton (porter) 42
John of Wallingford, prior of St Frideswide's 43, 47–8, 201
Jones, Robert (porter) 73
Judas, Leo, psalter 80, 105, 226n23

K
Keene, Henry 137, *138*, 230n27
Kenilworth (Warwickshire) 216n20
Kennall, John 88, 92, 224n41
Kent, Thomas 91
Key, Henry 208
Killcanon 106, 125, 181
King, Dean John, bishop of London 100, 203
King, Philip 103
King, Robert, bishop of Oxford 30, 69, 70, 84, 85, 100, 202, 223n26
  tomb 88, Pl.
  window 180, 227n52
King Henry VIII's College 30, 67–8, 71, 72
King's College (Cambridge) 64, 122
Kirk, Kenneth, bishop of Oxford 181, 185, 205
Knox, John 85

L
Lacock Abbey (Wiltshire) 137
Lady Chapel 8, 40–41, 45, 50, 52, 97, 189, Pl.
  altar 181, 189
  wall paintings 179
  windows 159, 189, Pl.
Lady Margaret professorship 91, 118, 167, 236n24
Lamprey, Thomas 133–4
Langley, Henry 118
Lant, Bartholomew 207
Laon Cathedral (Aisne) 159
Laski, Prince of Siradia 97
Latimer, Hugh, bishop of Worcester 86
Latin Chapel 28, 41, 132, 134, 145, 164–5, 179–80, 229n90
  stalls 64, 148, 227n45
  windows 51, 149–50, 181, Pl.
Laud, William, archbishop of Canterbury 103, 104–5, 109–110, 226n28
Launton (Oxfordshire) 116
Legge, Edward, bishop of Oxford 204
Legton, Thomas de 43
Leicester (Leicestershire):
  diocese of 30
  St Mary Newarke Church 65
Leicester, Robert Dudley, 1st Earl of 95
Leigh, Thomas 158
Lesnes Abbey (Kent) 59, 60, 219n13
Leveson Gower, Granville, 2nd Earl Granville 157–8
Lewis, Dean Christopher 206
Lichfield Cathedral (Staffordshire) 115
Liddell, Edith 177

Liddell, Dean Henry 144, 146–7, 150, 170, 171, 174, 177, 182, 205
   Christ Church reforms 167–8
   restoration of Cathedral 147–65, 171, 192
   sketch of Thomas Gaisford *144*
   statue 233*n*52
Liddon, Henry 233*n*52
Lincoln College 88, 89, 213*n*8, 218*n*33
Lincoln, diocese of 24, 221*n*27
Littlemore (Oxfordshire), St Nicholas' Priory 60
Littleton, Edward, 1st Baron 115
   monument 115, 214*n*48
liturgy and litany 56, 67, 70–71, 80, 87, 96, 100–101, 130, 170–71
   see also Book of Common Prayer; Directory for Public Worship
Lloyd, Charles, bishop of Oxford 160, 205
Lloyd, Charles Harford 208
Loggan, David, engraving of Christ Church 98, *98*, 172, 222*n*15
London, John 30, 70
Longland, John, bishop of Lincoln 65, 70
Lowe, Edward 207
Lowe, Dean John 182–3, 185, 187, 205
Lowth, Robert, bishop of Oxford (*later* bishop of London) 204
Lucy, Geoffrey de 215*n*2
Lucy Chapel 31, 35, 215*n*2
   altar cross 143
   altars 218*n*45
   Cavalier monuments 115
   font 164, 234*n*74
   wall paintings 179
   windows 52, 180–81, 218*n*45, 221*n*20, Pl.
Lutheranism 67

M

Mackarness, John, bishop of Oxford 205
Magdalen College 58, 59, 89, 102, 126, 127, 229*n*94
   choir 173
   presidency 102, 126, 127, 128
Major, Leonard 207
Malcolm IV, King of Scotland 21, 33
Maldon, Battle of (991) 12
Malta, Knights of St John Church 233*n*61
Manchester Cathedral 231*n*9
Mappa Mundi, proposed sale of 188
Marbeck, Roger 90–91
Margaret of Antioch, St 51, 210*n*6
Markham, Dean William, archbishop of York 129, 204
Marsh Baldon (Oxfordshire) 103
Marshall, Dean Richard 84, 86, 89, 202, 223*n*24
Marshall, William 208
Marston (Oxfordshire) 16
Martin, David 195, 196
Mary I, Queen 83, 84–8, 89, 90, 99, 223*n*26
Mary, Queen of Scots 101
Mascall, Eric 187
Mason, Sir John 85

Massey, Dean John 126–8, 131, 203
Masters, William 90
Matilda, Empress 24, 27, 33
Matthew, Dean Tobias, archbishop of York 94–5, 101
Maundy ceremonies 113, 227n44
Meadow, Christ Church 44, 55, Pl.
Meadow Buildings 10, 53, 146, 150, 177, 212n39, 224n56
Meadow Gate 191
Medley island 19
Merton College 23, 102, 236n14
Merton Field 53
Merton Street (*formerly* St John's Street) 38, 121, 216n24
Methodism 133
Michael, St 177
St Michael window 57, 159, Pl.
Middlesex, diocese of 70
Military Chapel *see* Chapel of Remembrance
Millenary Petition (1603) 101
Mills, John 118
Monck, George (*later* 1st Duke of Albemarle) 121
Monmouth, James Scott, 1st Duke of 126, 229n91
Montacute, Lady Elizabeth 44
tomb 50, *52*, 179, 217n12, Pl.
Montacute chantries 44, 80
Morley, Dean George, bishop of Worcester 121, 123, 203
Morris, William 149
Moss, Charles, bishop of Oxford 204
Mothers' Union 236n18
Mowbray, John 233n52

muniment rooms 26, 137, *138*, 161, 164
Museum of Natural History 233n59
Myres, J. N. L. 183, 184–5

N

Naperye, Geoffrey de la 42, 217n3
Narborough brothers, memorials 230n18
Naseby, Battle of (1645) 116
nave 80, *110*, *163*
construction 29
extension and restoration 148, 156, 161, 189
Neckam, Alexander 29, 214n41
Neile, Richard, archbishop of York 104, 109
Nevinson, Stephen 90
New, Edmund, engraving of Christ Church 172
New College 70, 71
choir 173
New Library 135, 230n18, 230n27
Newman, John Henry 231n12
Newton, Francis 85
Newton, Theodore 85, 223n25
Nicholas of Hungerford, prior of St Frideswide's 43, 45–7, 201, 217n19
Nicholson, James 64, 221n41
Norham (Oxfordshire) 33
Norman Conquest 14, 16, 30
Norris, Thomas 207
North, Edward 79
north transept 29–30, 39, 52, 56–7, 148, 180, 234n74, Pl.
St Frideswide statue *3*, 50

St Michael window 57, 159, Pl.
   Zouch tomb 56, *57*
Northampton (Northamptonshire) 24
Norton, George, prior of St Frideswide's 55, 56, 58, 201
Norwich Cathedral (Norfolk) 122, 186, 189
Nowell, Lawrence 83
Nowers, George/John 51
   tomb 51, 179

O

Oakley (Buckinghamshire) 33–4, 218*n*30
oath to the House, undergraduates' 74, 75
Offa, King of Mercia 10, 211*n*25
Oliver, John 67–8
Orchard, William 53, 57, 58
organists 65, 122, 169–70, 171, 173, 207–8, 225*n*61
organs 122
   Cardinal's College 122
   Christ Church Cathedral 105, *110*, 111, 117, 119, 122, 123, 135, 148, 225*n*61
Oriel College 83, 90
   chapel 226*n*28
Oriel Street 10
Oseney Abbey/Cathedral (Oxfordshire) 18–19, *19*, 20, 24, 30, 61, 83, 180, 236*n*14
   disputes with St Frideswide's 19–20, 33, 34
   dissolution 70, 72, 221*n*34
   removal of materials to Christ Church 71, 96–7, 225*n*74
   seat of bishops of Oxford 70–71, 73
Oseney Cemetery 148
Overton, William, bishop of Lichfield and Coventry 94
Owen, Dean John 119–21, *120*, 203
Owen, William 120
Oxenford, Richard 50
Oxford, history and development:
   origins 10
   early medieval period 10, 13–14, 212*n*34
   12th century 17, 23, 24, 29
   13th century 35–6, 215*n*2, 215*n*9
   14th century 44–5, 217*n*15
   17th century 112, 116
   18th century 169–70
   19th century 148
   20th century 185, 186
Oxford Architectural Society 151
Oxford Castle, St George's Chapel 18
Oxford Movement 143, 231*n*12
Oxford University *see* University of Oxford
Oxford University Act (1854) 166–7
Oxford University Commission (1850) 165–6, 234*n*79
Oxfordshire and Buckinghamshire Light Infantry (regiment) 176, 177, 235*n*5
Oxfordshire Yeomanry (regiment) 177

P

Paget, Sir Bernard 177, 235*n*6

Index

Paget, Dean Francis, bishop of Oxford 174, 205, 229n89, 235n6
Pandulf Verraccio, bishop of Norwich 34, 215n5
papal chaplaincies 50, 218n34
papal interdict (1208) 32, 34, 215n5
Paris, university of 24, 32
Parker, Matthew, archbishop of Canterbury 74, 96
Parker, Samuel, bishop of Oxford 127, 128, 203
Parks Road 10
Parry, Marilyn 188
Paul, William, bishop of Oxford 125, 203
Peckwater, Ralph 35
Peckwater Inn 35, 71
Peckwater Quadrangle 92, 135, 230n18
Peel, Sir Robert 140–41
Pembroke College 85, 127
  Master's lodgings 227n41
Pennyman, William 115
Percy, Dean Martyn 195–200, 206
Perkins, W. A. 235n99
Perrin, John 102
Peterborough (Cambridgeshire), diocese of 70, 73, 221n32
Pevsner, Sir Nikolaus, *Buildings of England; Oxfordshire* 28, 219n48, 233n61
Philip II, King of Spain 223n26
Philip, prior of St Frideswide's 17, 21–4, 28–9, 34, 201, 213n18, 215n7
Phillips, Morgan 82
Pickhaver, William (carpenter) 97
Piddington (Oxfordshire) 21, 33
Piers, Dean John, archbishop of York 100, 202
Pilgrimage (1934) 181
plagues 44–5, 113, 217n14–15, 228n80
plate, church 65–6, 66, 68, 71, 107, 125, 191, 220n11, 237n31, Pl.
Pococke, Edward 118, 121, 228n62
Pole, Reginald, archbishop of Canterbury 58, 87, 88, 219n9, 223n26
Ponsonby, Noel 208
Porters' Lodge 92
Potter, John, bishop of Oxford (*later* archbishop of Canterbury) 134, 204, 230n14
Poughley Priory (Berkshire) 60
Powell & Sons (glassmakers) 149–50, 180
Powell, Walter 169
Power, Matthew 236n20
Poynter, John 228n62
Pré Priory (Hertfordshire) 60
precincts, St Frideswide's Priory 7, 24–5, 211n26, 214n45
Presbyterianism 101, 103, 118, 119, 121
Preston, Simon 208
Price, William 146, 230n18
priors of St Frideswide's, lists of 17, 33, 43, 56, 201
Priory House 83, 92, 222n15–16, 234n73
Pritchard, John, bishop of Oxford 206
Prout, Thomas 168

Provisions of Oxford (1258) 35
Pullain, John 85, 223*n*25
pulpit 114, *114*
pulpitum 148
Purbeck (Dorset), stone quarries 22, 26, 214*n*36
Pusey, Edward Bouverie 142, 143, *143*, 151, 169, 231*n*12
  memorial 143, 179
Pusey, Philip E. 143
Pynham Priory (Sussex) 60

Q
Queen's College 230*n*21
Queen's Own Oxfordshire Hussars (regiment) 177

R
Rainolds, John 101, 102
Ralph of Brackley 35
Randolph, John, bishop of Oxford (*later* bishop of London) 204
Randolph, Thomas 85
Ravenstone Priory (Buckinghamshire) 60
Ravis, Dean Thomas, bishop of Gloucester 101, 102, 202
Rawlins, Darsie 237*n*30
Rawlyns, Richard 23
Reading (Berkshire) 32
  Abbey 26, 30, 213*n*15
  diocese of 185
  University 174
Reform Act (1832) 140, 141
Regimental Chapel *see* Chapel of Remembrance
reredos 161, 162, 164, 236*n*18
Restoration (1660) 121–3
Rewley Abbey 70
Reynolds, Dean Edward, bishop of Norwich 118–19, 121, 123, 203
Rich, Richard, 1st Baron 67
Richard of Dover, archbishop of Canterbury 22, 23
Richard of Oxford, prior of St Frideswide's 56, 201
Ridley, Nicholas, bishop of London 86, 91
Rieger (organ builders) 122
Ripon Cathedral (Yorkshire) 232*n*45
Robert, Earl of Gloucester 33
Robert of Cricklade, prior of St Frideswide's 4, 17, 20–21, 27–8, 201
Robert of Ewelme, prior of St Frideswide's 33, 38, 201
Robert of Olney, prior of St Frideswide's 33, 35, 36, 38, 201
Robert of Thorveston, prior of St Frideswide's 42–3, 201, 217*n*4
Robert of Weston, prior of St Frideswide's 33, 35, 201
Rochester (Kent):
  Cathedral 111
  diocese of 73
  Priory 12
Rodger, Patrick, bishop of Oxford 205
Roger of Salisbury 16, 17, 22, 23, 26, 214*n*36
Rogers, Christopher 118
Rogers, Harold 177, 188, 235*n*7
Royal Flying Corps 175

Index

Rudhall of Gloucester (bell-founders) 135
Rumburgh Priory (Suffolk) 60
Ruskin, John 146, 149
Ryle, Gilbert 183–4

S

sacristy 159, 185
Safrida (mother of St Frideswide) 4, 51
St Albans Abbey (Hertfordshire) 66, 232n45
St Aldate's 10, 34
  Bishop's Palace 69
St Aldate's Church 9
St Bernard's College *see* St John's College
St Brice's Day massacre (1002) 13, 14, 212n34–5
St Catherine window 51, Pl.
St Clement's 48, 212n34
St David's Cathedral (Pembrokeshire) 232n45
St Ebbe's 112, 148
St Ebbe's Church 7, 9, 25, 26
St Ebbe's Street 10
St Edward's parish church 39, 217n13
St Frideswide window 149–50, 180, Pl.
St Frideswide's parish church 39, 217n13
St Frideswide's Priory:
  administrative and domestic buildings 4, 7, 9, 53, 57
  bell 33
  charters 3, 6, 10, *11*, 13, 14, 16, 20, 25, 47, 212n36, 213n3, 217n18
  dedication 9, 220n7
  infirmary 18, 35, 53
  lists of priors 17, 33, 43, 56, 201
  precinct 7, 24–5
  properties and income 6, 10–11, 16–20, 21, 32–5, 42, 43, 44, 48–9, 55
  relations with university 32–3, 48
  seal 15, *15*
  site 7, *8*, 9–10, 64
St Frideswide's Priory, church:
  early medieval period 7–9, 14, 20, 26
  12th century 16, 26–31, 39
  13th century 38–41
  14th century 50–54
  15th and early 16th centuries 56–7, 64–5
  see also Chapter House
St Frideswide's Priory, history and development:
  foundation and beginnings 3–15, *8*
  12th century 16–31
  13th century 32–41
  14th century 42–54
  15th and early 16th centuries 49–50, 55–9, 64
  dissolution 59–63, *61*
St James's Church, Piccadilly (London) 134
St John's College (*earlier* St Bernard's College) 58, 70, 83, 103, 212n35
  organ and organists 122, 207, 208
  presidency 83, 91, 104
St John's College (Cambridge) 59, 219n15

St John's Street *see* Merton Street
St Mary Hall 82
St Mary Magdalen's Church 20, 33, 35
St Mary the Virgin, University church of 52, 94, 124, 135, 226n28
   Congregation House 215n
St Michael at the Northgate Church 17, 148
St Michael window 57, 159, Pl.
St Mildred's Church 17, 213n8
St Omer (Pas-de-Calais), Abbey of St Bertin 6
St Patrick's Schools 33
St Paul's Cathedral (London) 141, 231n9
St Peter in the Bailey Church 17, 148
St Peter in the East Church 26
St Radegund's Priory (Cambridgeshire) 59
St Scholastica's Day riots (1355) 48, 217n16
St Thomas's (parish) 148, 151, Pl.
Salisbury, William Longespée, 3rd Earl of 236n15
Salisbury Cathedral (Wiltshire) 188, 189, 190, 232n45, 237n36
Sampson, Richard, bishop of Chichester 69
Sampson, Dean Thomas 89–90, 91, 202
Sancroft, William, archbishop of Canterbury 126, 130
Sandford, Charles 151
Sandwell Priory (Staffordshire) 60
Sarum rite 56, 67
Savoy Conference (1661) 123

school, Christ Church's 73, 88, 111
Scott, Sir George Gilbert 112, 232n45, 235n99
   Christ Church Cathedral restoration 26, 107, 108, 122, 150–65, *154–5*, *158*, 188, 189, 232n43
Scott, Robert 146
seals:
   Cardinal College 220n7
   Christ Church 169
   St Frideswide's Priory 15, *15*
Secker, Thomas, bishop of Oxford (*later* archbishop of Canterbury) 134, 204
Second World War 185–7
   commemoration 186, *186*
Segworth, Richard 47–8
Selborne Priory (Hampshire) 59
sepulchre 165, 234n76
service sheets 173, 176, *176*, 186
Seven Bishops, petition of (1687) 126
Shaw, Archdeacon Edward 181
Sheldon, Gilbert, archbishop of Canterbury 125, 126
Sheldonian Theatre 226n28
Sherborne, Robert 57
shop, Cathedral 191, 237n46
Shovell, Sir Cloudesley 230n18
shrine, St Frideswide's 20–24, 28, 29, 37, 38–41, *41*, 50–51, 68, 88, 165, 189, 213n22, Pl.
shrine chapel 29, 38–41, *41*, 50
Siddall, Henry 83, 91
Sidney, Sir Philip 91
Siena Cathedral (Tuscany) 160
Simon, prior of St Frideswide's 17, 33, 34, 201

Index

Simon and Copin (moneylenders) 34
Simpson, Dean Cuthbert 122, 187, 205, 237n31
Skidmore, Francis 160, 161, 188, 189, 233n59
Skilbeck, Clement 179, 236n15
Skinner, Robert, bishop of Oxford (*later* bishop of Worcester) 116, 123, 125, 203, 227n48
Skippon, Philip 115
slype (passage) 26, 28, 31, 172, 214n48
Smallwell, Edward, bishop of Oxford 204
Smalridge, Dean George 129, 131–2, 134, 204, 230n9
Smith, Bernard ('Father Smith'; organ-maker) 122
Smith, John (Cavalier soldier) 115
Smith, Miles (canon at Exeter) 103
Smith, Richard (regius professor of divinity) 81, 86
Smith, Dean Samuel 204
Snape Priory (Suffolk) 60
Somerset, Edward Seymour, 1st Duke of 81
Sonning (Berkshire) 64
South African wars (1880–81; 1899–1902) 176
South, Robert 121
south transept 31, 145, 148, 156, 159, 164, 214n48
 clock 172
 memorials 230n18
 windows 28, 159

Spanish War (1585–1604) 91, 99, 101
Stacy, Gabriel 226n29
Stadhampton (Oxfordshire) 119
Stancliffe, Martin 189
Stanesfield, Laurence de 34
Stansgate Priory (Essex) 60
statutes, Christ Church 79, 133, 151, 166–7, 183, 184, 235n11
Stenton, Frank 181
Stephen, King 24, 26–7, 33, 210n5
Stockwell Mead 44
Stonard, William 207
Stone, Nicholas 106, 226n29
Strawberry Hill House (London) 137
Strong, Dean Thomas Banks, bishop of Oxford 142, 174–5, *175*, 185, 205, 229n89, 235n1
Stubbs, William, bishop of Oxford 174, 205
Sugworth (Oxfordshire) 71
surplices 80–81, 123
Swein, King of Denmark 13–14, 212n34
Swinfen, Ann, *The Merchant's Tale* 217n19
Symm & Co. (builders) 154, 158–9, 160, 161, 233n59

T

Tackley, Robert 42
Talbot, Edward, bishop of Winchester 164
Talbot, William, bishop of Oxford (*later* bishop of Durham) 134, 203
Tallis, Thomas 94

Tattershall College (Lincolnshire) 65, 220n8
Taverner, John 65, 122, 207, 220n13
   Gaude plurimum 93
Taynton (Oxfordshire), quarry 153, 216n29
Tenison, Thomas, archbishop of Canterbury 134
Thame Abbey (Oxfordshire) 70
Thoby Priory (Essex) 60
Thomas of Woodstock, 1st Duke of Gloucester 49
Thompson, Arthur B. 151
Thompson, Henry Lewis 151, 152
   Christ Church 164, 190–91, 230n24
   Henry George Liddell 147, 150, 152
Thompson, John Barclay 157, 232n50
Thornbury (Oxfordshire) 4, 6
Thornhill, James 146, 158, 230n18
Thornton, Thomas 91
throne, bishop's 114, 160, 161, 162–3, *163*, 197, 233n69–70
Tickford Priory (Buckinghamshire) 60
Tiptree Priory (Essex) 60
Tom Quad *see* Great Quadrangle
Tom Tower 125, 172
Tonbridge (Kent):
   Priory 60, 62
   School 62, 219n18
Torksey, John, memorial 230n18
Torrington, John Byng, 5th Viscount 138–9, 140
tourism 190–91, 237n47
Townsend, William 230n18
transepts *see* north transept; south transept

Treasury, Cathedral 191
Tresham, William 82, 83, 91, 220n13, 222n16, 234n73
triforium 28, 51, 145, 214n32, 214n48, Pl.
Tring (Hertfordshire) 86
Trinity College 223n17
   chapel 230n21
Tristram, Ernest William 179, 236n16
Tuckwell, William, farms Pl.
'tunnel', Cathedral entrance 108, 161, 177
Tykeys, John 42

U

Ulmis, John ab 81, 222n13
Underhill, John, bishop of Oxford 88, 202
Universities Tests Act (1871) 234n85
University College 127, 129, 226n28
University of Oxford, history and development:
   12th century 24, 212n43
   13th century 32–3, 215n2
   14th century 48, 54
   16th century 69, 74, 86
   17th century 124, 129
   18th century 129
   19th century 165–7, 174
   see also individual colleges
Upper Winchendon (Buckinghamshire) 6, 10
Upton, Ambrose 228n65
Urban Hall 33, 215n4
Urban V, Pope 46

Index

V

Valdès, Juan de 81
van den Heuvel, Albert 197
van Linge, Abraham and Bernard:
   Christ Church Cathedral windows
      106, 107, 117, 156, 158–9, 180,
      227n52, 231n18
   University College windows 226n28
Van Mildert, William, bishop of
   Durham 141, 231n4
Vere Bayne, Thomas 151, 152,
   233n64
verger's cottage 145, 156, 159
Vermigli, Catherine (née Dammartin)
   82–3, 222n15
   exhumation and reburial 41, 87,
      88, 91
Vermigli, Peter Martyr 81–3, 82,
   84–5, 86, 87, 221n31, 222n15,
   223n27
   Adhortatio ad coenam Domini
      mysticam 222n14
Vertue, George, engraving of Dean
   John Owen *120*
vice-chancellor's stall 114, 227n45
Victoria, Queen 157
Vikings 10, 12–14, 30
   St Brice's Day massacre 13, 14,
      212n34–5
volunteers, Cathedral 190
Vulliamy, Benjamin 172
Vyner, Frederick, Vyner window 189,
   Pl.

W

Wade, John, *Black Book* 140
Walker, Obadiah 127–8
Walker, Patrick Gordon (*later* Baron
   Gordon-Walker) 183
Walker, Richard, prior of St
   Frideswide's 56, 58, 201, 219n7
Wall, John 118, 123
Wallingford (Oxfordshire):
   Castle 49
   Priory 60
Walpole, Horace, 4th Earl of Orford 137
Walton (Oxfordshire) 17
Walton, Sir William 235n1
Ware, Thomas, prior of St Frideswide's
   56, 57, 58, 201
Warham, William, archbishop of
   Canterbury 62
Warner, S. A., *Oxford Cathedral* 191,
   230n24, 236n12
Warwick, Ela Longspée, Countess of
   236n14
   grave 179, 180, *180*
watching loft 51, *52*, Pl.
Water Eaton (Oxfordshire) 33
Watson, E. W., *The Cathedral Church of
   Christ in Oxford* 191
Watson, Sydney 208
Waynflete, William 59
Webster, William (almsman) 73
Wellington, Irene 177
Wells (Somerset) 9
   Cathedral 31
Wesley, Charles 132, 133, *133*, 138
Wesley, John 132, 133
Wesley, Samuel 133
Westbury, John, prior of St
   Frideswide's 56, 201

Westminster, diocese of 70, 73, 141, 221*n*32
Westminster Abbey (London) 31, 207, 231*n*9, 232*n*45, 236*n*11
  Eleanor of Castile's tomb 160
  Henry VII's chapel 53
Westphaling, Herbert 91
Westwell (Oxfordshire) 143
Weymouth (Dorset) 44
Wheatley (Oxfordshire), quarry 53
White, Dean Henry 179, 187, 205
Whitefriars Glassworks *see* James Powell & Sons
Whitehill (Oxfordshire) 6, 10
Whitgift, John, archbishop of Canterbury 100, 101, 224*n*40
Whittingham (Northumberland) 46
Whittingham, William 85, 223*n*25
Wilberforce, Samuel, bishop of Oxford (*later* bishop of Winchester) 160, 205
Wilkinson, Henry 117, 118, 120, 228*n*65
William III, King 128, 228*n*80
William of Gloucester, prior of St Frideswide's 33, 34, 35, 201
William of Malmesbury 212*n*34
  De gestis pontificum anglorum 4, 210*n*1
William of St Aldate's 215*n*7
Williams, Dean Alwyn T. P., bishop of Durham 181–2, 183, 187, 189, 205
Williams, Anne (wife of Roger Marbeck) 90
Williams, N. P. 236*n*24
Williams, Thomas (caterer) 73
Willis, Browne, *A Survey of the Cathedrals of Lincoln, Ely, Oxford, and Peterborough* 136, 137
Willis, John 121
Willis, Thomas 121
Winchendon (Buckinghamshire) 6, 10
Winchester (Hampshire) 44
  Cathedral 111, 231*n*9
  diocese of 73
windows, Cardinal's College 64, 221*n*41
windows, Christ Church Cathedral 28, 97, 135, 146, 148, 158–9, 180–81, 230*n*18, 231*n*18, 232*n*52, Pl.
  Burne-Jones windows 149–50, 159, 177, 180, Pl.
  Chapter House 26, 27
  Lady Chapel 159, 189, Pl.
  Latin Chapel 51, 149–50, Pl.
  Lucy Chapel 52, 180–81, 218*n*45, 221*n*20, Pl.
  muniments room 137
  St Michael window 57, 159, Pl.
  van Linge windows 106, 107, 117, 156, 158–9, 180, 227*n*52, 231*n*18
  wheel window 158–9, Pl.
windows, St Frideswide's Priory 26
  Lucy Chapel 52
  shrine chapel 38, 50
Windsor Castle (Berkshire), St George's Chapel 68–9, 89, 122, 142, 173, 236*n*11
Witney (Oxfordshire), rectory 126, 226*n*25, 229*n*88

Index

Wolsey, Cardinal Thomas:
   dissolution of monasteries and new cathedrals scheme 58–9, 68–9
   downfall and death 67, 69
   funding and construction of Cardinal College 31, 59–62, 63–6, 161, 162, 221n35

women:
   admission to Christ Church 187, 188
   ordination 187–8, 237n34

Wood, Anthony 11–12, 23, 118, 135, 210n5, 217n14

Woodstock, John 50

Woodstock (Oxfordshire) 21
   Palace 37

Woodstock Road 211n25

Woollcombe, Kenneth, bishop of Oxford 205

Worcester (Worcestershire):
   Cathedral 173, 235n99
   diocese of 73

Worcester College 69

Worcester House Declaration (1660) 121, 123

Wyatt, James 137–8

Wyche, Sir Peter 115

Wycliffe, John 48, 67

Wykes Priory (Essex) 60

Y

York Minster (Yorkshire) 31, 189

Z

Zouch, James 56–7
   tomb 56, 57

Zwingli, Huldrych 67, 81

Zurich Bible 80

The Ichnography or Platform of the Cath.

A. The Cloysters & Doors into the South Cross Isle
B. The great South Door & Doors leading to ye Canons Houses
C. The Nave of ye Church where ye University Sermons are Preacht
D. The North Cross Isle and Steeple Pillars
E. The Choir B.ps Throne & High Altar.
F. The pulpit & organ Loft Stairs
G. The Chapell for Latin Prayers
H. Two Chapells where ye Deans and Canons are interred
I. The part of the Church and Cloysters pulled down when the College was built to make room for Lodgings

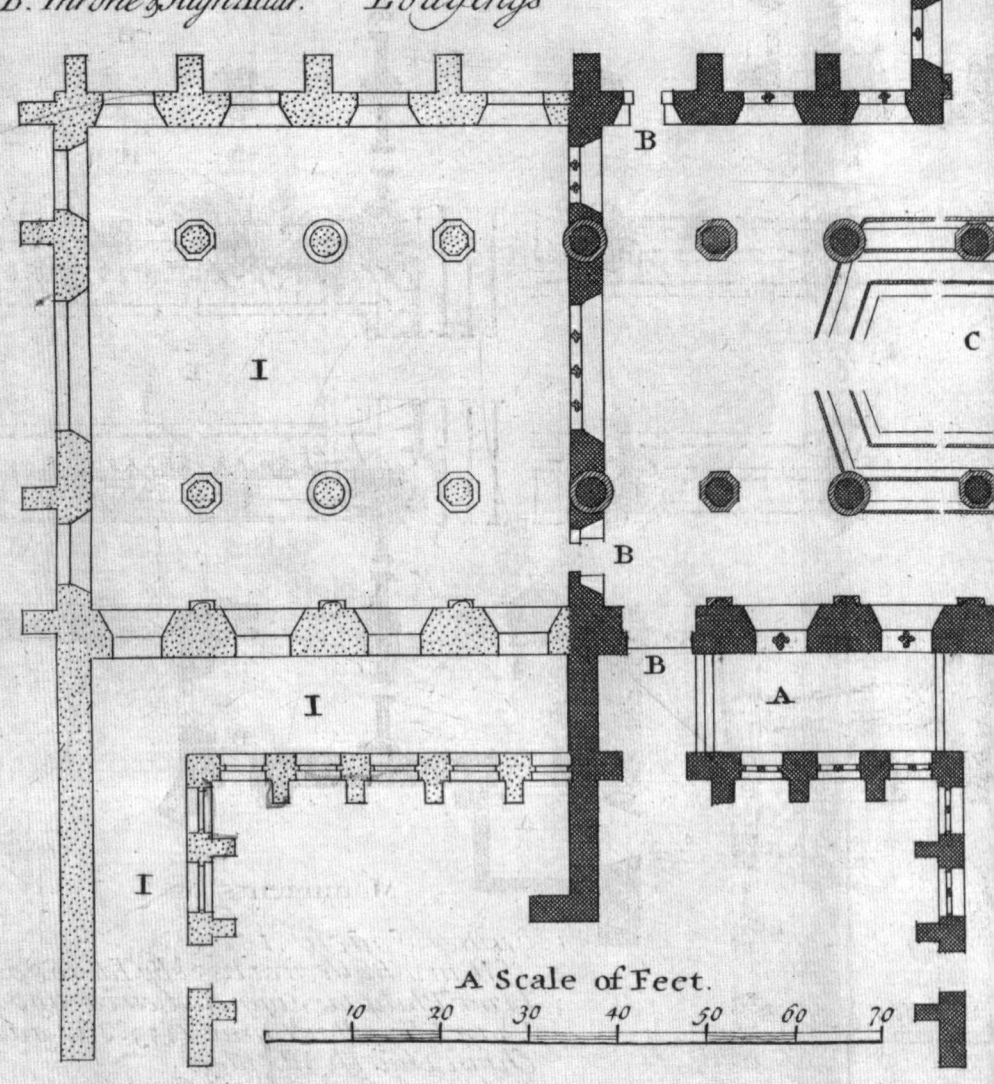

A Scale of Feet.
10 20 30 40 50 60 70